D0961429

ZEBRATOWN

THE TRUE STORY OF A BLACK EX-CON AND
A WHITE SINGLE MOTHER IN SMALL-TOWN AMERICA

GREG DONALDSON

Scribner

New York   London   Toronto   Sydney

SCRIBNER
A Division of Simon & Schuster, Inc.
1230 Avenue of the Americas
New York, NY 10020

First Scribner hardcover edition August 2010

SCRIBNER and design are registered trademarks of The Gale Group, Inc., used under license by
Simon & Schuster, Inc., the publisher of this work.

For information about special discounts for bulk purchases,
please contact Simon & Schuster Special Sales at
1-866-507-1949 or business@simonandschuster.com.

The Simon & Schuster Speakers Bureau can bring authors to your live event.
For more information or to book an event contact the Simon & Schuster Speakers Bureau at
1-866-248-3049 or visit our website at www.simonspeakers.com.

Designed by Carla Jayne Jones

Manufactured in the United States of America

1   3   5   7   9   10   8   6   4   2

Library of Congress Control Number: 2009052989

ISBN 978-1-4391-5378-9
ISBN 978-1-4391-5907-1 (ebook)

For Constance Stalberg Donaldson,
1920–2005,
and Ron "Smiley" Smith Bey
of Brownsville,
ca. 1945–2001

CONTENTS

Prologue ix

Short to the Street 1

Fresh Oaks 14

Click 23

Poison Jones 41

"So What If He's Black?" 47

In the World 51

Capone 58

Blanco 63

"You Leavin' Me?" 71

Elmira 76

"Little Girls Like Dresses" 81

Zebratown 83

The Bing 91

Cheryl 97

Third Circle of Hell 103

Dream Girl 106

Family 115

On Campus 127

Thirty Days 131

Ride 137

Felony 144

Ramsey's Place 152

"I Can't Go to Prison" 162

Temporary Insanity 171

"The Feds Don't Want This Case" 176

Judgment 187

Bedford Hills 194

Locked Out 203

Judy Clark 209

Kaydawn 214

Sister Tisa's 225

"We Gotta Talk" 232

Home 235

"Thank God" 244

Amboy 247

Strong-arm 252

Postscript 269

Acknowledgments 271

PROLOGUE

||||||||||||||||||||||||||||||||||||||||||||||||||||||||||||||||||||||||||||||||||||||||||||||||||||||||

To write this book I spent six years following a couple from the prison town of Elmira, New York: Kevin Davis, an ex-convict formerly from Brownsville, Brooklyn, and Karen Tanski, a young mother from nearby central Pennsylvania. They lived in an Elmira neighborhood known as Zebratown, where black men with white women and their mixed-race children abound.

I met Kevin Davis under most unusual circumstances. In 1993, I was finishing *The Ville*, a book about Brownsville, a proud but troubled black neighborhood, when the publisher presented me with a photograph planned for the book jacket. The image showed despair. I wanted a cover that captured the extraordinary energy and the blocked aspirations, the explosive potential of Brownsville. Searching for a better photo, I spotted a handful of youths standing under a flagpole in the Tilden Houses projects. The scene was perfect for my purposes. Though I had never seen any of these particular young men before and though none of their stories was in *The Ville*, the book was an attempt to describe their lives to a wider world.

When I walked up with the armed escort on one side and a New York *Newsday* photographer on the other and asked the men if we could take a picture, I was told that we should not photograph anyone and that my companions and I should "back up on outta here." As we retreated, a car backfired down the street. Believing the sound a gunshot, the young men under the flagpole spun toward the noise. As they did, the photographer dropped to one knee and snapped the photograph that appears on the cover of *The Ville.*

When the book was published a few months later, some New York City Housing Authority detectives took a quick look at its cover and said, "We want him." The thick-necked youth wearing a New York Yankees cap at the left of center in the photograph is Kevin Davis, then a local thug and crack dealer whom the police were looking for in connection with a particularly brutal homicide on Amboy Street in Brooklyn. Using the book as a wanted poster, detectives scoured the neighborhood. After Davis was arrested, the *New York Daily News* titled a sidebar about the capture "Book Has Neighborhood Covered." He was subsequently convicted of a weapons possession charge in connection with the homicide but not the homicide itself.

I forgot the incident but Kevin Davis never did. In fact, as he moved from Attica Correctional Facility to Elmira Correctional Facility and then Wende Correctional Facility near Buffalo and back to Elmira, in seven years of hand-to-hand battles, slashings, and solitary confinement, Davis carried the book with him.

In 2000, near the end of his prison stretch, Davis found my e-mail address and after his release his congenial messages began to appear monthly on my computer screen. Davis assured me that he harbored no bitterness, explained that his arrest had been almost certain anyway and that the book had been an asset to him in prison. Further, he believed deeply that his warrior ethic, his prison exploits, and his connection to the rap music world should be the subject of a book-length account.

Despite his frightening résumé, over the Internet Davis was articulate and bursting with a desire to explain his thoughts and deeds. As if reading my mind, he signed off one of his early e-mails, "Remember, I am a reasonable man."

I wondered. Despite the staggering rates of incarceration for black men, there is no direct connection between race and crime. I had seen firsthand how some black youth in Brownsville graduate to criminal careers as easily as middle-class youth move from high school to college. Clearly, almost all of those choices are economic and social. But what of the über-thugs, like Davis, who take to urban warfare with glee, and then, once convicted of a serious crime, appear to relish the compressed hostility of prison? Are these "reasonable men," adapted to a twisted environment? And if they are, could a man like Kevin Davis possibly emerge from his street life and incarceration mentally healthy and reasonably humane? If so, could he find a place in "the world," the term inmates use for society?

There were good reasons not to write a book about Kevin Davis. In a society where issues of race are fundamental but not simple, he sounded like a man with few doubts and no regrets, perhaps not the best subject to lead a writer to wider truths. But 650,000 state and federal prisoners are released each year in the United States. Fifty percent of them are black. Kevin Davis, I thought, might provide an unusual opportunity to write a story about that reentry into society.

In 2002, more than a year after his release from prison, I agreed to meet Davis in a Mexican restaurant near Columbus Circle in Manhattan.

Kevin Davis stepped through the crowd at the bar in the front of the restaurant and walked into the back room where I sat. Above the waist, Davis is diesel-thick, his neck as wide as a grown man's thigh. But he is short, no more than five-foot-four. He wore an oversized white football jersey and a white baseball cap pulled down so low on his head that his round face seemed to begin at his eyes. The bill of his cap, the half-moon of his face, and the thickness of his neck made him look like a cartoon character.

Davis approached with a curious shuffling gait as if he were still in leg chains and offered a handshake soft as a girl's.

"I'm late 'cause I didn't think you were coming," he said.

"If I say I'm going to do something I do it."

But Davis was used to seeing through people. Surrounded for seven years by the deceitful, the ill-tempered, and the insane, he studied me and saw something he didn't like. "If I throw this glass of water on you, you gonna start to sizzle?"

"What?"

"You heard me."

Kevin Davis was nothing like the man I thought I had come to know through the Internet, and now, sitting in the Mexican restaurant, I regretted my decision to meet him. After a moment, I understood he thought I was secretly taping our conversation.

"You think I have a wire on? You think I'm wired?"

Davis tilted his head toward a man at a table close by. He looked remarkably like me, and damn if he didn't have a wire running up from his shirt collar into a plug in his ear.

"Who's that?" Davis wanted to know.

"I don't know who that is."

Davis's eyes flicked around the restaurant. "I see things other people don't see and I always act first."

I spoke slowly, raising a pen between us. "Why would I be wired? I'm a reporter. I'm going to write down everything you say."

"I see things—"

I cut him off. "And I know things. Together I thought we could write a book."

Davis rocked back in his seat and delivered a shy smile. Though thirty-two, Davis looked no more than twenty years old.

Davis told me he was willing to talk openly about almost anything but the homicide on Amboy Street. "The person who did that particular deed is not the same person that you might meet or that you know."

I was skeptical. Davis might be difficult to work with, unreliable, and even dangerous. And what of the relevance of his ghetto and prison experiences in a country less and less conscious of color, a nation with such expanding opportunities for black women and men? After considering the matter for a few weeks, I concluded that, despite the palpable racial progress and the promise of much more, it was too soon to turn attention away from the generation of incarcerated and formerly incarcerated African-American men. I decided Kevin Davis could help me tell their story to an American society at best uninterested in their rehabilitation and at worst hostile to that possibility.

Davis wants his world comprehended, his valor and loyalty recognized, his misdeeds contextualized. I have tried to understand his truths and his deceptions, the source of his generosities and cruelties. I have also tried to capture Karen Tanski and her world and to understand why she made the biggest bet of her life on a former hoodlum one step out of a maximum-security prison.

This question is not easy to answer, in part because of the complex interplay between black and white culture over the country's history. White people have been imitating blacks and adopting aspects of their culture, from the time antebellum southerners saw how much more easily slaves could catch the feeling in church, through the 1930s when white hipsters in America and Europe struggled to mimic the detached precision of black jazz musicians. In the 1980s and '90s, the black thug became, for legions of youth worldwide, a symbol of uncompromised manhood. Japanese, French, and Eastern European young people copied the verbal inventions and clothing style they saw in gangsta rap.

In America, for black youth, the Afrocentrism of the 1960s and '70s was swept aside by the style if not the spirit of the hustler. Dashikis gathered dust while high school kids wore 'do-rags. Lessons in Swahili were forgotten as the language patterns of Memphis-born pimps tumbled across the floodplain of popular culture.

The ghetto and prison experience that Kevin Davis personifies was commodified and recommodified, exaggerated and marketed so relentlessly that by the time Davis was released from prison in late 2000 the rappers themselves had begun to embrace the cultural absurdity, choosing stage names like Ludacris as they moved toward self-parody.

To fully understand the worlds of this book—the black street and prison subcultures, often celebrated or maligned with equal degrees of ignorance, and the white Rust Belt culture, often overlooked—I made dozens of trips to Elmira. Over the course of six years, I spent weeks at a time there with Kevin Davis and Karen Tanski. I accompanied them on dates, visits to the doctor, and family outings. I sat at their dinner table, witnessed bitter arguments between them and tender connections.

I spent scores of hours on the phone with Kevin Davis's mother, traveled to Gillett with Karen's mother, Betsy. I conducted repeated interviews with judges, law enforcement officers, and friends. I functioned as an advisor and sounding board for members of the small family, seeing and hearing things that only a person who has been around for years could observe.

I have also interviewed Davis for hundreds of hours, hearing about his childhood and his youth in Brownsville, his prison years. I have watched him, moving back and forth between Elmira and New York City, walking a line between his criminal past and pursuit of a legitimate profession and stable family life, trying not to make a mistake that will send him back to jail for life.

This book is my record of Kevin Davis and Karen Tanski's lives during this period. The scenes and analysis are based on events I have either observed or have had described to me in multiple interviews, wherever possible cross-referenced with public records. I have recreated some conversations based on the recollections of the participants. Kevin Davis's name is his own. Many other names in the book, including those of Karen Tanski and her children, have been changed in the interest of privacy.

This book attempts to provide an authentic account of one recent trend of the African-American experience, the interplay of the big-city former gangster with small-town America. Finally, this book tries to reveal what it means to be Kevin Davis and Karen Tanski, together, struggling to raise a family while the economies of central New York State and the country crumble around them.

SHORT TO THE STREET

|||||||||||||||||||||||||||||||||||||||||||||||||||||||||||||||||||||||||||||||||||||||||||||||||||||

September 2000. Kevin Davis pauses in the shower area of I Block at the Elmira State Correctional Facility in central New York State. His gaze is aimed through a square of morning light out a tiny open window toward a distant hill. Davis stares through the opening for a full minute before he moves beyond the shower room back to his second-tier cell. Two hours later, a guard at the foot of the tier commences yanking levers. The sound of metal on metal approaches, a sequence of opening locks, banging louder and louder as it travels down the row. The top lock of Davis's cell pops and the gate opens a few inches. The noise fades, growing softer as locks down the line spring open in succession.

"On the chow," a guard shouts. It is noon mealtime. Davis muscles the sliding door the rest of the way open and steps out into a single file of inmates. Face directed down at the polished concrete floor now, he moves forward with short sliding steps to a flight of stairs down to the first floor, where the forty-two residents of the cell block stand to the left of a thick yellow line painted on the floor. The inmates pause and begin their ten-minute walk to the mess hall.

As they troop forward, dressed in green state-issued shirts and pants, some immaculate and sharply creased, others rumpled, these men have characters as varied as their archived fingerprints. Still, the inmates look remarkably alike. Almost all of the I Block inmates are either black or Latino. They are all young and ruggedly built. The small-boned and most of the whites have long since been harried into protective custody by extortionists. Among the company of mesomorphs, Kevin Davis stands out. He is the darkest-skinned man in the hallway and, at five-foot-four, 167 pounds, the shortest. His biceps are swollen like gorged pythons.

Like others high in the prison pecking order, Davis has little interest in the fifteen-minute mess hall meal. He has been "living good," as the inmates say, eating macaroni and tuna fish from the prison commissary in his cell. Today he is headed to the mess hall to nod hellos across the wide stainless steel tables and check for new faces. Lately, ever since he was placed temporarily in E Block and discovered that from his cell he could see through a layer of grime-coated Plexiglas to the city of Elmira and the forest beyond, Davis has been obsessed by views.

I Block faces the inside of the prison, so Davis can't see the hills from his cell anymore, but he can capture the view from the shower area and another, even better location. Later that afternoon, in the visiting room, Davis looks over his visitor's shoulder and through the tall decorative windows that open onto the steep hills that ring the prison.

A milky sky hangs above ranges of oak, red and silver maple, beech and pine trees, many shades of green in the bright autumn sun. Much closer, down the sharp slope at the front of the prison, just a hundred yards away, cars move down a street and make careful turns. The tableau is so orderly, so picturesque, that Davis is tempted to shake his head and refocus. Instead, he drinks it in. There are no people, just the occasional automobile sliding between the Norway spruces. No mounds of black garbage bags heaped on the sidewalk, no sound of whooping sirens, just a silent, soft landscape of peace.

Kevin Davis is thirty-one years old. He has been incarcerated for seven years, lurching through the upstate New York prisons system like a journey-man professional baseball player. He has been moved from one institution to another because of incidents with guards or fights with other prisoners or another flare-up in the slow-motion war between Latino and black gangs. Once, the authorities shipped Davis out of Wende Correctional Facility in Alden, New York, in the far western part of the state, because the Puerto Rican and Dominican inmates refused to step onto the exercise yard when he was outside. Here in the Elmira prison in 2000, the New York State Correctional Officers and Police Benevolent Association, in their contract negotiations with the state, used a videotape of Davis slashing an inmate named Andre Lopez and then dodging guards through the vast mess hall as proof they deserved a better deal.

Other times, Davis has been moved because he was listed as a "known enemy" of another inmate at a prison. Someone with an old beef put his name in the paperwork, perhaps because of a razor scar from a jailhouse "burner" or "gun," terms inmates use for various types of improvised knives, that Davis had wielded. Davis was never told who the complainant was or even that he had been fingered. Just, "Pack it up," and he would be on a green and blue minibus headed down a strip of highway to another maximum-security prison.

There is no shortage of penitentiaries in the forests of rural New York State. Davis has been in ten maximum-security prisons since his arrest in November 1993. In the last three years he has ridden the Department of Correctional Services buses between Wende, Green Haven, Attica, and Elmira.

In 1994 and 1995, Davis was sentenced on a number of charges, the most serious being criminal possession of a weapon in the third degree, or "aggravated weapons possession," in connection with the gruesome murder on Amboy Street in the Brownsville neighborhood of Brooklyn. On the sixth of October, 1993, at 10:27 p.m., a teenager named Dupree Bennett was shot nineteen times with an assault weapon, a Heckler & Koch HK94 auto-carbine rifle. Police officers had been advised by supervisors not to respond to calls from 10 Amboy Street unless and until there was a "callback," confirmation from the dispatcher that the call was not an attempt to lure officers to the location so they could be bombarded with heavy objects from the roof. Uniformed cops finally did answer the call reporting shots fired. When detectives arrived, they scooped up the nine-millimeter bullets where they lay flattened after blasting through the victim's body and gouging small holes in the cement sidewalk. The *Daily News* carried an account of the murder five weeks later under the headline "It's So Easy to Die for So Little in N.Y."

Brownsville is in what detectives call the "Brooklyn North Triangle," where the investigators claim witnesses, victims, and perpetrators are often known to each other and thoroughly interchangeable. Two of the dozens of people who witnessed the killing made statements identifying Kevin Davis as the shooter, but neither was willing to testify, so police couldn't prove their suspicions that Davis had committed the murder. The Kings County DA settled for his guilty plea to the weapons possession charge.

But on the streets of Brownsville and in the archipelago of the New York State prison system, Davis is known as Killa Kev or KK, not only because it was his ring name in a short professional boxing career, but because of what happened on Amboy Street.

Davis has carried the Amboy killing the way someone in the outside world would flaunt a degree from Harvard. The manner of the murder made him prison royalty at Rikers Island—or HDM, House of Deadly Men, an old name some inmates still call the New York City jail. Amboy Street placed him above the petty harassment and ritual testing most inmates undergo at Rikers.

There were more than a few killers with multiple bodies to their credit in the state system, so the Amboy murder didn't count as much when he went up north. But Davis had other advantages. In an exercise yard full of hundreds of men, he could read subtle indicators of status or hostility at a glance. If an inmate so much as squinted in his direction, flinched at the touching of hands, tensed during the ritual bear hug, Davis would make it a point to pass again very close to the potential enemy or do hundreds of push-ups or sets of thirty pull-ups in his presence. Perhaps Davis would just wink. *We both know we have something to work out,* his look would say, *and we'll do it soon.*

Such is the symbology of race in America that Kevin Davis's uncompromisingly black skin was also an advantage in prison. His complexion made him appear angry and dangerous, even in the eyes of maximum-security inmates. It seemed obvious to them that Kevin Davis was no pimp, con man, or hustler. If he had been part of a drug operation he had to have been the muscle. What they saw was a thug among thugs.

Early in his sentence, Davis quickly became close to notorious inmates, prison stars like Walter "King Tut" Johnson, the first person in New York State to be sentenced to life in prison under the 1990 three strikes law. Tut was famous for supposedly having shot Tupac Shakur five times in a midtown Manhattan robbery, starting the East Coast–West Coast rap war. "When Pac got popped I got a kite from the pens that told me Tut got knocked," 50 Cent rhymes in "Many Men," a cut on his 2003 album *Get Rich or Die Trying.* If a nobody "stepped to," or confronted, Kevin Davis in most any prison, volunteers eager to gain his approval were ready to step in and make his fight their own.

Such status has its responsibilities. In the past seven years Davis has led prison skirmishes and even started a small riot at Attica, attacking a corrections officer in retaliation for a near-fatal beating by guards of a Greek inmate, a fellow Blood. But that is all in the past. There is nothing left to prove now, to himself, to the long-termers, or even to the legions of followers and punks. Nothing left to focus his thoughts on but the real world. He is just over two months to the street. What of the future? Go back to Brooklyn and do it all again one more time, but bigger and better?

Davis has learned things about himself in prison. He has tested himself physically. But that is nothing new. He has fought with propulsive vitality since he was old enough to slip away from his mother's sixth-floor apartment on Blake Avenue in Brownsville. Kevin Davis has long known he could be ferocious. But over the past seven years he has learned just how smart he is. He read the prisoners' bible, Robert Greene's guidebook to personal ascendancy, *The 48 Laws of Power*, then studied the factors in a hundred prison formulas and every time solved the equation.

Now that it seems as if he might actually find himself back on the street, he has identified the relevant facts. Providence alone has kept him from receiving a life sentence. Amboy Street should have kept him in jail until his eyes were dim and his body rotting from some kind of cancer. But it didn't happen that way. He is going to find himself back in the world while he is still a young man.

Kevin Davis gazes out the wall of windows at the long-turning hawks above the painted perfection of Elmira and makes a simple vow not to return to Brooklyn when he is released. He knows he is a long shot to stay out of prison. Drug-dealing is not an option. With his record, Davis understands state law mandates that with one more felony conviction he can, like his friend Tut, be hit with a sentence that maxes out at life.

But going back to prison is for men with no vision and no self-control. In prison, Davis has not only learned how smart he is, he has also learned how disciplined he can be.

He isn't impressionable or impulsive or lazy, doesn't need fancy clothes and jewelry to maintain his self-esteem. Why go back to Brooklyn and the old life, with the lingering beefs, the constant emergence of young guns? Why dodge bullets, duel with razor blades, and box with braggarts, lunatics, and fools? When and if he gets out of prison—nothing is certain—he will stay away from Brownsville, move to the very street he can see from his prison window, walk quietly and confidently in a new world with brand-new challenges. He will relocate to Elmira and not only sample the good life but master it. He is so proud of what he has overcome in prison, precarious confrontations like that beef he had with King Allah in 2000, situations he had controlled and survived, that he might just wear his state-issue greens on the streets of Elmira.

I can never forget the thing with King Allah at Elmira Prison, 'cause the way I reacted at that particular time tells me who I really am. It was the last incident before I went home in 2000. I was in general population at that particular time.

We was out in the yard, me and a couple of dudes, when all of a sudden, boom, a big commotion goes on by the exercise area. A couple of dudes scrambling. Goin' at it. Dude named Badass comes runnin' toward me—Yo! I seen him bend over an' stuff somethin' in the grass. Yo, I realize I had a beef with Badass in Rikers. But after that we got tight. After that he was my homie. Now, I knew the dude Badass cut was a Five Percenter. In prison they call themselves Godbodies, and they are militant, very retaliatory-oriented. The leader of the Godbodies in the whole state system is named Allah and he was in my house. Looked like war to me.

Now I was in a bad position and a powerful position at the same time. I'm short to the street. Just two months. Eight weeks to click. If I back Badass, we start scramblin' in the yard and I get a charge, I can get years for that. Then I got to stand up again, which is more likely than not. Then I'll be like Allah. Maybe I'll never go home.

But I don't allow myself to think like that. That kind of thought makes you weak and vulnerable. I'm about consistency. If standin' up for Badass is the right thing to do when you got ten years, it's the right thing to do when you got ten days.

So that was not a good situation for me. I was just placed in it, as the case may be. But that's how life is. You get placed in a situation and you deal with it according to who you are. You just got to know who you are.

On the other side of the situation is the simple fact that I got so many people on my side that I can't even count them. The next day when they break us out for recreation I told my dudes to stay on the other side of the yard where the basketball court was at. There was fifty to sixty on my side. The Godbodies had only twenty-five to thirty people. So the leaders of the Five Percenters, Allah and Nation, came out. It was around Thanksgiving. I had my war gear on. I had the state Carhartt jacket, green wool war hat pulled down, green pants. State boots. I always fight in boots. I also had newspapers rolled up under the jacket and stuffed around my chest and my upper back like a vest, a jailhouse bullet-proof vest. That's how we do. I'm standing with my people.

Allah makes like a time-out sign and he makes a motion with his hand like he wants to holler at me. So just him and me walk to the middle of the yard.

He's tall and light-skinned and I'm short and black. He had real gray hair, almost white, and these nice spec glasses. He looked to me like a college teacher, a father figure. But I didn't even think of him like that 'cause he was so light-skinned and my father was supposedly real black, like me. He got murdered in Brooklyn when I was fourteen years old.

Allah starts talking. "Yo, Kev, I respect you. I know what you're about. I know what you're capable of doin'. And check this out, my respect don't have nothin' to do with the fact that you have the upper hand here in terms of num-bers. It has to do with you showin' me your loyalty to your man and you are willin' to lose your freedom behind this."

Right away I'm alert, 'cause I'm not gonna let my release date have any effect on allowin' him to influence me in any way.

"That's right," I told him straight up. "That's what I want you to see. If it means me losin' my freedom, we gonna still stand up."

Now Allah starts talkin' very direct like he was a fuckin' father or some shit. "Kev, I want you to hear somethin' straight up from my heart. I don't got a chance to go home but you do. I need you out. I don't need you in here."

I didn't know exactly what he meant about needin' me on the outside, 'cause we was never close like that. Later on, I came to the conclusion that he meant he needed the feelin' of seein' somebody he respected go back to the world. It wasn't political. It was personal, meaning that he was forgotten by the world but he

wanted somebody who he felt in his heart was like him to go back and not be
forgotten. It was like him gettin' a little piece of his life back. I admit that my
heart was touched but I was still on point.

"No doubt," I told him. "It's love."

We shook hands and hugged and I walked over to my people on the back
side of the yard.

"Be easy," I told them. "It's a wrap," and walked away. Still I was ready.
Anything could happen. It was still unpredictable. People still lie.

With his shirt off Kevin Davis looks as if he is wearing black armor. His
muscles are not for show, sport, or to impress the opposite sex. They are for
safety, like a Kevlar vest of human tissue. In a street fight, Davis notes the
length of the knife in his opponent's hand. Using prison slang for a short
knife, he explains, "I walk right through a three-finger joint."

Davis's face is pleasantly symmetrical except for a permanently swollen
left cheekbone, the destination of too many right hooks in the boxing ring.
His stump of a neck is set on broad sloping shoulders, but his hands are small
and surprisingly delicate. The fact that he could have won so many hand-to-
hand battles on the streets and in prison with such childlike hands tells of
assaults quick, brutal, and perfectly aimed.

Davis's body carries no gang insignias, no tributes to lost comrades or
family members. His only tattoo is a bluish tear below his left eye, barely
discernible against his dark skin. The best clues to Davis's identity are the
scars. A round ragged discoloration the size of a fifty-cent piece on the front
of his right thigh comes from an assassination attempt when he was seven-
teen. Davis caught the bullet as he walked near the corner of Mother Gaston
Boulevard and Blake Avenue in Brownsville, half a block from the top-floor
apartment where he grew up with his mother and younger sister, Tonya.

Those were the days when he was a principal in the territorial warfare
stemming from the project drug trade and the neighborhood jousting for status, the days when his own mother was so frightened of being shot by bullets
aimed at her son that she ordered him never to call her "Mommy" in public
and crossed the street when she saw him approaching.

On the afternoon of the attack Kevin Davis heard the rustle of startled
birds and a holler from a window above, turned and saw a four-man team,

a full backfield of assassins in black ski masks, crouched and moving in formation behind him. He ducked, twisted, and ran, so close to the ground he could touch the pavement with his palms. As he sprinted, he yanked his nine-millimeter Taurus from his belt with his right hand and fired two shots across his body. A return shot kicked up a puff of concrete dust to his right. He whipped around and glued himself to the quarter panel of a maroon Lincoln Town Car. The escape was almost perfect, especially when a Good Samaritan, a female corrections officer, threw the door of her moving car open and sped away with Davis beside her. But as he darted away from the Lincoln, laying his gun on the ground as he moved, a final barrage of nine-millimeter bullets blasted a bystander in the buttocks and caught Kevin's trailing leg, one bullet exiting through his hamstring.

Both Kevin and the wounded bystander were taken to Brookdale Hospital. The unfortunate woman, stretched on a bed in the same room as Davis, on the other side of a dingy scrim, wasn't talking. Kevin Davis thought it was because she was a nice person. Detective Bobby Desmond of the Housing Police thought it was on account of fear.

"I promise you one thing," the lawman said from Davis's bedside. "We won't go looking for the one who kills you."

There are more scars. A two-inch welt rides high on his left cheekbone. In 1995 when he was twenty-four years old Davis had come down to Rikers Island jail from upstate to fight his last remaining and most significant charge, the Amboy homicide.

There was a Muslim inmate from Bed-Stuy in Brooklyn in his housing unit, C-95, and he was chasing an acquaintance of Davis's armed with a shank stripped from a locker. Davis was on what he called "accelerate." If there was any altercation with the slightest connection to him he was going to engage. The Muslim inmate ran right past Davis to the gate and Kevin jumped on his back and swung at him with a razor. Hopping and bucking, the inmate reached back across his own left shoulder and with a wild lucky swing sliced open Davis's cheek.

A dangerous piercing under his right pectoral and the twisted skin on his left trapezius are from a battle with Puerto Ricans in the yard at Orleans in 1997.

Despite the ruined patches of skin, as his release date nears, the thirty-one-year-old Kevin Davis looks like a much younger man. When he was a free man he rarely drank alcohol, never smoked cigarettes or marijuana or took hard drugs.

"I'm not thinkin' about goin' back to no jail," Davis says aloud to no one as he steps into his cell and pulls the gate closed for the evening count. The electric lock slams shut with a metallic clap. He shuffles back a step and squats on his cot, flexes and unflexes his fingers, and rolls his shoulders.

Somewhere below, a prisoner is chanting the lyrics to a popular rap by Ice Cube. "It's the American Way / cos I'm the G-A-N-G-S-T-A." Davis chuckles. Here he is locked up, while rappers, mostly soft dudes, are making millions rhyming off his story line. Kids all over the country, the world, are wearing the baggy clothes he and his boys in Brownsville wore to conceal guns they called "ninas," "biscuits," and "three-pound-sevens." Smart people selling his clothes and his words, the story of his life, to get rich.

Davis knows that if he tries to live up to that zero-tolerance standard the rappers crow about, that outlandish hype, he will end up dead or back here locked in a cage forever. He also believes that in this country a black man with brainpower can turn that gangster image to his advantage, the same thing he had done with Amboy Street.

It is hard to say what really happened on that October night behind 10 Amboy. Davis himself spins the killing many ways.

I got a call from Francesca, my girlfriend who later became my wife. She told me that she had a fight with this dude who had been beatin' up a little kid, her nephew, kicked him down the stairs and was beatin' on him in the lobby of 10 Amboy where she lived. She was hysterical so I went over to the location. As it turns out, the dude who was beatin' the kid got shot nineteen times and everybody was of the mind that I did the shooting. Boom! The police was lookin' for me everywhere. Basically, for a couple of months I was on the run. I was in Manhattan mixing in with the crowds when I got a call. "Yo, Kev, you on the cover of a fuckin' book!" It was a picture, most definitely unauthorized, just a shot a photographer took of me and some of my friends standing in the Tilden projects.

I jumped into a bookstore and found the book, and shit, there I was. Right on the cover wearin' the same jacket and the same Yankee hat that I had on at that moment. I pulled the hat off and turned the jacket inside out. Jesus Christ, I felt like I was on America's Most Wanted.

I was with my cousin Reggie in Brownsville when I finally got snatched. But they didn't know who I was. They thought I was Keith Williams, that's how my prints always come up. So I was in the police van on my way out the lockup at the Housing Police precinct on Sutter when Desmond, the detective who sleeps in his car and knows every fuckin' thing, spots me. He's like, "Where you takin' him?" The cop drivin' the van is like, "This is Keith Williams and we takin' him to Gold Street for burglary." An' that sloppy-ass Desmond is like, "No, that's Kevin Davis and we want him for the Amboy homicide in October. Take him back inside." The detectives in the squad room had a copy of the book and Reggie signed it for them, "Killa Kev." Why not?

Not that many people that I associate with read books. So, even though I don't appear in the actual book, people saw my picture on the cover and assumed that the book was about me, and that always worked to my advantage.

I have never assaulted good people. I tend to locate the bully in a group, the intimidator. Then I bully him and intimidate him. So the fact that the dude on Amboy was beatin' up a kid and had a fight with Francesca would have been more than enough reason for me to get involved.

People talk about the nineteen shots and my man Bang even had the autopsy picture of the victim. I don't know where he got it but they had it in prison. What do you think of a person who would shoot someone so many times? You think maybe that person has mental problems. Ever since Amboy that's the way people have looked at me. That's some ill shit, they think, an' the person who did it must be an animal, some kind of a beast. Where I come from, bein' known as an animal is a good thing. Case closed.

If nothing goes wrong at Elmira Correctional Facility, Davis will be released in a matter of months. He has received no meaningful vocational training while in prison. Most of those programs were done away with in the 1970s and '80s as the prison population grew darker. Legislation passed across the nation in the late nineties augmenting a system of collateral, or "invisible," punishment will make it more difficult for him to build a life when he is released. In most states he will be denied the right to vote if he is on parole. In ten states he will be disenfranchised permanently. While Kevin

Davis has been shuttling between upstate prisons, Congress passed legislation allowing the exclusion from federally supported housing of individuals
convicted of drug crimes or violent acts. Davis has been convicted of both.
His record will also disqualify him from receiving a student loan or adopting
a child.

As the lights in Davis's cell flicker and go off, as he lays his head on his pillow and listens to distant shouts and the same voice chanting the same lyric,
"It's the American Way / cos I'm the G-A-N-G-S-T-A." Another inmate bellows, *"Shut the fuck up. Don't make me kill again!"* The rapper squeezes out a
couple more lines."Cos I'm scarin' ya / Wanted by America," and pipes down.
In the silence, Kevin whispers, "Elmira."

Kevin Davis knows nothing of the Rust Belt economy of central New
York State, the factory closings and the rampant unemployment that have
forced over 40 percent of young adults to quit the Elmira region in the last
decade. He cannot visualize the city's hard-bitten east side, where young
mothers look forward to public assistance checks while their boyfriends hustle cash by peddling crack to people with jobs who ride in from Pennsylvania
or nearby Corning. Instead, Kevin is sure he can feel the steady, unhurried
pulse of a gentle town through those walls. That is enough for him.

Just as Davis's vision of Elmira is cobbled together from bits of movies,
television shows, and the deceptive view from his prison windows, his evalua-
tion of himself is based largely on myth. He has concerned himself little with
the welfare of others. Even his good deeds have been, in some measure, about
personal glory. He has only a vague notion of how a healthy family works or
how a father and a husband should behave. No matter how sharp his mind
or how strong his willpower, Davis has no idea how difficult it will be to earn
a living legally, adapt himself to life among everyday people, and retrofit a
nervous system designed for urban war. He will also have to learn to live in
anonymity.

In Brownsville and in prison, Kevin Davis has always been a star. Like
other young toughs in Brooklyn, Davis has taken great risks to ascend the
ladder of status in his neighborhood. But like them, he had a broader stage in
mind when he stalked the streets with a gun.

Race and economics have pushed these young men to the outskirts of
the city and, if not for their criminal ferocity, to the edges of the national

consciousness. They have watched the American drama unfold with its high production values and glitzy props. Instead of accepting the role of outsiders, shuffling extras in the blockbuster movie *America*, they grabbed a major role. Maybe they were not cut out to play the square-jawed hero, but, like the "Nigga" in Ice Cube's rhyme, they sure knew how to play a bad guy. Black rappers like Noreaga and Capone name themselves after every public enemy they can think of but Hitler. With no real ideology beyond the wish for stardom, Kevin Davis has accepted the casting, complete with his own ominous stage name. He has never been the good guy, but at least he has always been a featured character. The hardest thing now will be to accept the role of bit player.

Fresh Oaks

||||||||||||||||||||||||||||||||||||||||||||||||||||||||||||||||||||||||||||||||||||||||||||||||||||||||||

It is early spring 1999. Karen Tanski is standing on the second floor of the shopping mall in Big Flats, a few miles outside of Elmira. Twenty-one years old, blond, and shapely, she ignores whispered suggestions from passing teenage boys. Behind her is a Burger King franchise. From fifty feet to her left comes the calliope of a video game room. Julia, Karen's three-year-old toddler, is rooted to the floor, mesmerized by the popping, gurgling sounds of the arcade, the flash of lights, and the screams of the older children. No measure of Karen's urging has succeeded in getting the child to come along.

It has been a tedious afternoon for Karen. She searched for a new car seat for Julia with no success and rummaged for sales on children's clothes. Empty-handed, she was headed for the escalator and the parking lot when the girl fell under the spell of the game room. When Karen picked her up the child kicked and slapped and clawed the air.

As Karen waits for the tantrum to subside and for the pull of the arcade to weaken, she thinks back to her own childhood. There had been no place for tantrums then.

Karen Tanski grew up in Gillett, Pennsylvania, ten miles outside of Elmira down a two-lane country road where, just over a twenty-foot-wide creek and at the base of a hill, lay the Fresh Oaks trailer park. Two hundred feet from the ungated entrance to the encampment of aluminum-sided mobile homes sat the green and white Carnival model where Karen lived with her mother, Betsy Hahn.

Betsy was a struggling single mother, just as Karen is now, but life was much harder then. On winter mornings back in 1983, Betsy and five-year-old Karen would be up before dawn. Betsy would study her face in the bedroom mirror, combing her champagne-blond hair while Karen brushed her teeth in the tiny bathroom. Betsy would look at her own huge green eyes and bangs and announce, "Your mommy's looking good." At five years old, the precocious Karen, pulling on her mittens and hat, already behaved and sounded more like a miniature mother than a child. "You got your gloves, Mommy?" Holding each other's hand, the two would step down out of the trailer and onto the frozen ground.

It would still be dark, Karen remembers. Betsy was due at work at six forty-five and there was a short drive and then a quarter-mile trek up a steep dirt road to her sister Grace's house, where Karen would stay until Betsy picked her up in the evening. There were no headlights behind or ahead as Betsy guided the old Dodge down the two-lane road, picking her way carefully around patches of black ice, to an unmarked turnoff where she aimed the car toward the woods. At Grace's mailbox, mother and daughter climbed from the car. Karen was already used to playing in the snow wearing only a sweater, and the freezing darkness didn't bother either of them.

After all, Betsy Hahn was from real, full-blooded American pioneer stock, the kind that pushed west into the wilderness when the country was new.

Everybody in Gillett knew Betsy had problems, that she had a history of outbursts, tantrums that just wouldn't stop. After she met Frank Tanski, a Polish boy whose parents had come to Reading, Pennsylvania, from Kraków, Poland, the explosions just got worse.

Frank had his own problems. His parents had spent years in Germany and were deeply prejudiced people, able to voice their hatred of Jews in German, Polish, and broken English. In a reversal of historical accounts of the Polish pogroms and the infamous Kristallnacht, when the windows of Jewish homes and businesses were shattered during attacks, the Tanskis told the local Pennsylvanians how their home in Poland had been surrounded at night by Jews and how their windows had been shattered by rocks hurled by snarling kikes.

But there weren't many Jews to be found in the woods of eastern Pennsylvania. So when the Tanskis' son Frank was beaten and robbed in Reading by a group of blacks, the family venom turned to people of color. "Be careful, the monkeys are coming," the Tanskis warned.

Betsy's new husband, Frank, had more pressing difficulties. Even as a young man he would drink himself stupid and fall down in the street. After he moved in with Betsy Hahn, he rarely came home after work. Instead, he spent his evenings chugging beer in a one-room strip club while passing folded dollar tips to the dancers. When his money ran out he stumbled outside. Once, Betsy arrived just as the cops were about to sweep her husband off the street.

Maybe Betsy should have left Frank just where he lay instead of hoisting him up, helping him home, and putting him in bed. When he woke, Frank Tanski staggered from bed and threw roundhouse punches at Betsy's chest and face as their two-year-old daughter, Karen, stood in the corner.

But Frank Tanski should have known better, should have stayed his hand. He knew the mother of his child would rave about nothing, launch into a two-hour monologue about him not coming home at night and spending his time with naked dancers. After he slapped Betsy, the real firestorm began. As it turned out, Frank Tanski's violent temper was no match for Betsy Hahn's fury. No measure of stumbling, drunken pushing and slapping or manhandling could match the energy and devastation of Betsy's verbal attack, the pitch of her howling indignation.

Betsy finally threw her sodden boyfriend out of their small apartment, stopped shrieking just long enough to get a lawyer and sue Frank for support. He didn't even fight the case. All Frank Tanski did was work and drink. He worked for twenty years as a machinist. Somewhere along the line he tore up his hands badly and suffered a broken pelvis, so that he had to limit his activities to drinking and falling down in the street. But he was always able to pay the $15 a month the judge ordered in '83 and then the $65 a week that was mandated a few years later.

Karen remembers seeing her father for only a few hours on one day a weekend. And even those visits trickled to a stop before she was nine or ten. Frank wouldn't show up at the appointed time, and when he did he would have a scowling girlfriend with him. Karen would sit in the backseat of his car and listen to the two of them trade hard words back and forth faster and faster until Frank would carry Karen over to his mother's house and leave her there in the living room to watch television. Then he would drive off somewhere with his lady friend. Finally, Frank Tanski stayed away from his daughter altogether. He always paid the money, though.

More than a few of Betsy's mother's people had been institutionalized over the years for mental illness. Since she was a teenager, Betsy had been aware of her fragile purchase on reality. When the voices came and she had seen how people looked at her when she talked back to them, she simply stopped talking back, just listened.

After she stopped working, Betsy began to get an SSI disability check for $989 a month. She never did get Medicare. The voices in her head went away for a while, and the occasional visits by Fidel Castro in his underwear and later Saddam Hussein sadly subsided after she started the antipsychotic medicines, the Risperdal and the Cogentin.

Karen had done reasonably well in elementary school, despite the troubles at home. The breakup of her parents was a blur, but her mother's descents into paranoid schizophrenia were deeply disturbing. When Karen was in second grade her mother started to "flip out" again. Betsy would stalk into the little girl's room and demand, "Tell me. Tell me. Tell me." As her mother yelled in her face, Karen would just wait for the tumult to pass. The next morning Karen would arrive at school on time but would soon lay her head on her desk and fall asleep.

At fifteen, Karen began working at Wendy's. Soon after that, she was suspended from high school for poor attendance. It wasn't that she minded the classwork or even the social life. There were the skateboarders, the farmers, and the "wiggers," white kids who acted like they were black. Karen floated between the cliques. She even managed the volleyball team for a season. What she couldn't stand was the forty-five-minute bus ride with all the chattering kids going up and down these rolling hills over and over again. It was like a roller-coaster ride and it made her nauseous.

Gillett is at the northern tip of the Appalachian Plateau, which runs from Mississippi and Alabama in the South all the way up to Chemung County and Elmira. The people in the Appalachian swath have never been rich, but until the last few decades those in the northern sector had jobs—mining in

Pennsylvania, agriculture and manufacturing across the border in New York State. Not anymore. The people there are almost all white, poorer than ever, and less educated than the rest of America. In Gillett the crime rate is low and flat; there is almost nothing to steal.

There are a few attractions. The nearby Susquehanna River has its own Grand Canyon. The camping is good for visitors, the fall foliage sublime. But there is also very little for locals to do but drink and smoke. The largest store in Gillett sells tobacco in bulk, rolling papers, and various devices to put the two together.

As she grew into a woman, Karen slid into the rhythms of Gillett, smoking and drinking to pass the hours. She and her friends would aim their trucks up the dirt roads into the high hills and chug beer, raise hell, throw beer cans, and take their clothes off. Then they would drink some more and weave back down the hill.

Once, Karen chugged Mad Dog, a fortified wine, till she couldn't see straight. On the ride home, she pushed open the passenger-side door and watched the white line on the road stream by at fifty miles an hour while she threw up. When Betsy found her sprawled on the step of the trailer, Karen moaned, "I'll never do it again." At sixteen, Karen gave up on school and started working full-time.

By 1998, Karen Tanski was a sturdy woman with hazel eyes. The nose she inherited from her Polish father jutted over a softly clefted chin. She hadn't been far out of Gillett, or nearby Chemung County, or achieved anything big, but she was confident all the same. Almost swaggering. She had raised herself, hadn't she? Held a job for two years and even joined an after-work program that gave her a high school diploma. She had outtalked and outthought all those country boys in Tioga County, Pennsylvania, and those fake hustlers from Elmira. In New York or Los Angeles, she would have been lounging on a beach or sneaking into nightclubs. Here on the central New York State–Pennsylvania border, she had to settle for slipping away from the Fresh Oaks Trailer Park, riding with her friends into Elmira, cruising up and down the streets, over the bridges. It beat the dirt roads up in the hills.

The city of Elmira is set at the western edge of a flat plain that stretches forty miles long and five miles wide between ranges of ridges and hills to the north and south. The city is sliced by the broad-channeled Chemung River, sometimes almost dry in the summer but capable of flooding Elmira, as it has done ten times in the last 150 years. In 1972 a storm washed out all four of the bridges connecting the north and south sides. The center of the city boasts the standard complement of office buildings, banks, and courthouses. But Karen Tanski, driving downtown, drawn to the activity and the stately buildings, fails to notice that the windows of many of the downtown storefronts are smudged, plastered with outdated flyers. Many formerly bustling retail outlets are now gloomy thrift shops with tables of jumbled used clothing.

Ibzard's, the four-story department store that once ruled the corner of Main and Water Streets, has been closed for more than fifteen years. The building on that corner now has two floors of offices. The rest is vacant. Next door is a tattoo parlor. Kresge's is gone. So is Newberry's 5 and 10 next door. Karen drives past bars and realty offices with three times the space they need and a men's clothing store, H. Strauss. There used to be seven men's stores in town. H. Strauss is the only one left.

And she doesn't note that there are no crowds on the street at lunch hour in the business district. The only throngs congregate outside the First Arena when there is a concert or the Jackals, a minor-league hockey team, are playing a home game.

On Lake Street, Lovell's ice cream parlor, which made the best chocolate-covered caramels, is gone. Farther north, away from the center of Elmira, where strip malls once stood are moldering lots. The rest of the street is lined with weary three-story homes, wood-framed High Victorians with freshly painted gingerbread details, just bright and cheerful enough to distract from their age and swaybacked roofs.

One evening at the Joycrest Skating Rink way out on Lake Street, near the Mark Twain Motor Inn, Karen stumbles into Bill Utley. She is eighteen and the boy who grins in her direction each time he wobbles past on his skates, she finds out quickly, is a year older. Utley is an auto mechanic, he tells her in the parking lot, who doesn't get a paycheck but is paid money under the table.

I shoulda known, I guess. Everything about him was under the table. But this is when he was blond and good-looking, before he got a crater face and his

teeth was all gone to hell from smoking weed constantly. To tell you the truth,
I didn't realize his hygiene was so bad till later on. Yeah, he was blond and
funny. I would say charming and sweet. At least that's the way it seemed to
me at the time. I didn't know nothin'. I guess it was my time to be swept off
my feet.

Mutually smitten, the teenage couple moved into Bill's grandparents' basement for a while. Then they drifted to an apartment with two roommates, who came in handy to step between them when the fights started. Bill would raise his fist and, in a sequel to the Frank Tanski and Betsy Hahn battles sixteen years earlier, Karen would counterpunch with a fury. Karen wasn't crazy like Betsy, but she was young and strong and she was raised on hand-to-hand combat. As the fights escalated, so did Karen's disgust with Bill. He was receiving SSI disability checks, and his interests seemed confined to watching NASCAR races on television and smoking marijuana.

The battling couple soon got their own efficiency apartment in Elmira. Karen found a better job. She worked at Elmira Stamping, making enough to buy a car, while Bill put his name on the lease and managed the rent. Three months after they got the efficiency, Karen started feeling queasy and went to the clinic for a checkup. One rainy evening after coming home from work, she parked in the street in front of the apartment and remained in the driver's seat of her car. That morning the couple had had another fight. They weren't just tussling anymore. They were gouging, scratching, and punching, trying to hurt each other. Karen hadn't seen much of life, a small hill town and a trailer camp, a high school in the woods, but she was smart and very pretty now, with blond hair to her shoulders and those eyes, a mix of green, brown, and gold, morning sun on a woodland river.

She turned the car off and sat watching the raindrops drain down the windshield. Maybe it was far-fetched to think she would travel the world and live the life of a millionaire, but there had to be something better than a disability check and a smoker's cough, exactly what Betsy had. Why did she have to settle for a stoned-out loser with teeth rotting out of his head who liked to slap her around? She had some things going for her. Like her mother, Karen didn't mind hard work, and now she even had some money in her pocket from the job at Elmira Stamping.

Karen worked for $5.50 an hour pushing buttons on a machine that punched holes in a stationary plate. She was taking home $175 a week, enough to pay for the car and a small apartment. That was it, she decided. She would get rid of Bill and get a place of her own. No roommates. She'd had enough of that.

Karen stepped briskly through the rain into her apartment. Thank God, Bill wasn't home. He was the last person she wanted to see when she got home from work. Soon, she hoped, she wouldn't have to worry about his empty eyes and his temper.

The answering machine held a message from the clinic to call. As she waited for the receptionist at the clinic to pick up the phone, she glanced again into her future. Get rid of Bill, go back to school, and what could stop her?

The cheery voice on the other end of the line solved the mystery of her recent health concerns. No doubt about it. Karen Tanski was pregnant.

There was no escaping now. The fights continued for another year. At the end the couple battled with the baby just a yard away. Finally, the police were called for the last time and Karen quit the apartment with her baby. The officers wouldn't let her take her things, though. Karen was working forty and fifty hours a week at the Elmira Stamping job, and with the help of a girlfriend she got her own apartment. But all her clothes, her personal effects, were still locked up in the efficiency. Bill was keeping them out of spite and because he wanted her back.

Karen laid the groundwork of her plan to recover her belongings. She recruited a few of their mutual friends to accompany Bill to his uncle's house for a Saturday afternoon session in front of the big-screen television watching NASCAR and drinking beer. Bill took the bait and Karen slipped into the apartment.

"I took everything I could from that son of a bitch. I took the phone cord, the toilet paper, and the towels. I took every goddamn thing I could and laughed about it."

Karen had been reunited with her possessions but there was trouble at Elmira Stamping. The coolant, designed to keep the machines from over-heating, would spray out over Karen and the other operators. Karen broke out in a rash up and down one arm. Then the coolant started soaking through her pants and the rash spread to her legs.

She and a female coworker went to OHC, the Occupational Health Clinic, where a technician examined their rashes and pronounced that both girls had scabies, a contagious skin disease, though they lived in different homes and had no contact with each other outside the workplace. The other girl launched a lawsuit. Meanwhile, another worker had taken a sample of the coolant and had it analyzed. It was found to be transmission fluid. What Karen had received were simply chemical burns. Karen needed the money, so she hung on to the job for several more months before she left. Later a small welfare check was just about enough to get by, so she enrolled in school, the Elmira Business Institute, to pick up the clerical skills she needed to get a better job.

Those were good years, with her own apartment and her own car. She named the blond baby girl with the arched eyebrows Julia and called her Jewel. Betsy would watch the baby whenever Karen wanted to go out, or Karen would drop Julia off at day care and go straight to school. Karen was smiling all the time, singing to herself. Her baby was gorgeous and she was all but rid of Bill. She had just undone the first big mistake of her life. And it didn't look like she was going to be stuck in some dirty dangerous factory for the rest of her life either. She was going places.

A year and a half later Karen graduated from the Elmira Business Institute. With her straight hair parted in the middle, she posed for a photo wearing a blue and pink floral print dress, balancing a dozen white and red roses in a plastic bundle in the crook of her left elbow and gripping her diploma in her right hand. A few feet away six-year-old Julia stood, hands to her mouth, swimming in her mother's graduation robe and cap. After she snapped the photo, Betsy leaned to her daughter's ear and whispered, "I saw a shooting star last night. Does that mean someone is going to die?"

CLICK

||||||||||||||||||||||||||||||||||||||||||||||||||||||||||||||||||||||||||||||||||||||||||||||||||||||||||||||||||||||||

It is three weeks before Christmas, 2000. Kevin Davis is sitting straight-backed on his bed reading a letter from an inmate in another New York State prison.

The corrections officer is moving down the gallery with a clipboard asking who will be going to exercise and later who will be headed to the evening meal. This morning Kevin is scheduled to be at a Parole Board hearing. But he has taken to ignoring such appointments. What is the use of going to parole? The events at Amboy Street cut both ways. No matter how peaceful and cooperative he is, he knows he is not going to get paroled. Even though he was not convicted of the murder, the Parole Board is privy to the circumstances surrounding the weapons possession charge and has reacted as if he were the killer everyone believes him to be. "We cannot overlook the type of weapon used in your IO [instant offense]," the board had written in an earlier denial of parole. "We cannot in good faith approve you at this time."

Every two years they hit me. This counselor lady tells me, "You look pretty sharp." Then she says something about the gun possession. She is talking about Amboy Street. So I come right back: "Nobody has the right to kick and punch a little kid." She makes it known that the board thinks I'm not sympathetic enough about the situation. That I am in a state of denial. They refuse me so

I start refusin' them. I start to deny them. I tell 'em I don't want to go home.
Fuck parole. Watchin' you all the time. In the house at eight. Bust in your crib.
Fuck that.

There is some question about Kevin's paperwork, some mix-up on his
release date. He has written again and again for a recomputation of his time,
a confirmation of the conditional release date. There are inconsistencies in
the numbers that are driving him crazy. He pores over the details of his
sentences. There is the three-and-a-half-to-seven-year sentence for Amboy
to run concurrently with the three-to-six for a previous gun possession
charge connected to an arrest for which he was also charged with criminal possession of a controlled substance in the third degree. There are prior
credit months, and even a so-called "Grace Day." He reads and rereads the
letter from the Department of Correctional Services: "Pursuant to Section
7.0.30(1a) of the Penal Law, the maximum terms merge in and are satisfied
by discharge of the term which has the longest unexpired time to run." Still,
the numbers don't seem to add up and there is nothing he can do about it
but write another letter.

The guard with the clipboard faces Kevin's cell. "Pack up. And get rid of
that stuff." The CO waves his free arm toward the stacks of foodstuffs and
personal care items at the rear of Kevin's cell. "You can't take that where you're
going."

"Where am I goin'?"

The guard checks his clipboard. "You're Keith Williams, right?"

"Right?" Kevin chuckles at the idea that after fifteen years dealing with the
state many of his official documents still use his alias.

"You're on pack-up."

"Where'm I goin'?"

Along the second-floor tier, voices drift from the cells.

"Kev, what's goin' on? They got you on pack-up?"

"Yeah, but I don't know where the fuck I'm goin'. I'm gettin' ready to go
home. What the fuck they gonna send me to another jail for?"

After his miraculous avoidance of a lengthy sentence for what happened
on Amboy Street and after all the jailhouse fights and stabbings, the Blood
affiliation and what happened at Attica, Kevin is on the lookout for a con-

spiracy. Maybe the system is going to send him someplace where they can take one last shot at him.

He has been through the drill many times before, ten at least. Fold up his clothes and pile them, pants and shoes and sneakers on the bottom and whites, T-shirts on the top. Letters and pictures in another plastic bag. Toiletries last, wrapped in more plastic and squeezed in beside the letters, which are all tied in a soft knot so it won't be too difficult to untie.

"Williams? You packed up?"

"Yeah, I asked you where I'm goin'."

"They got you goin' to Queens work-release."

Now Kevin is sure that he is being mocked. He is ready to max out. There are to be no conditions to his release, no interim stops. That is the way he wanted it. No bullshit parole, fake freedom where the cops could "trail him, nail him, and jail him." Kevin has decided he would do a year if he has to, two years, before he will take three years' supervised parole. But he doesn't even have to think about that now. He is three weeks to the street by his numbers, six weeks to click even by the state's math. Not to work-release.

"Stop bullshittin' me. I'm not goin' to no work-release program."

"Yeah, you are. They been sending inmates who max out to the work-release program close to New York. Then you go home in another three weeks."

The guard checks a paper in his hand. "Yeah, Keith Williams. Queens work-release."

"For real?"

The rapture begins in his chest and flows upward and down till it engulfs him. So many years he had kept his feelings to himself, staring hard at inmates and guards alike, taking beatings without a yelp, and mastering situations without a gloating smile.

Sure, he wetted up a few pillows when that bitch Francesca started fucking somebody on the outside. Sure, he asked to see the psych that one time when he thought he was losing it. But he kept all that out of the public eye. Now he is about to wild out, scream and dance like a lunatic right there in front of the guards and within earshot of his public.

"For real?" he says again, a smile forcing itself on his wide face, pulling his top lip upward. He presses down hard with his diaphragm, fighting the explosion.

"It's real."

As the stress of prison life drains out of him like dirty oil, it is replaced by the clearest elixir of pleasure, flowing through his veins and filling his lungs. It is the finest, cleanest sense of joy Kevin Davis has experienced or thinks he ever will.

If a dying man sees his past flash before his eyes, Kevin sees his future. Sees it and touches it. He is wrapping his arms around old buddies in front of the candy store on Rockaway Avenue in Brownsville. He hears his friends laugh and smells his mother's hair and tastes the salt of a woman's sweat. He whiffs sizzling beef at a backyard barbecue. He sees people, not prisoners in green with dark thoughts but people with dreams and smiles.

Kevin is still in his cell as inmates arriving from the yard pour through the gate. There are others standing up, faces to the bars of their cells. Word flashes up and down the corridor. The chattering, hooting inmates are struck quiet by the news.

"Yo, Kev," someone yells down the line. "Serious? You outta here, son?" Kevin doesn't trust himself to answer. He nods ahead and to the side as confirmation spreads up and down the line and to the gate where a group of inmates waits to enter.

A gap-toothed inmate from the cluster by the gate bellows the joy that Kevin Davis feels. And then he bellows again, "Son, go home!"

The words ignite the cell block. The screaming and yelling mounts and spreads. Grown men are stomping on the cement floor and yelling in celebration.

"Yeah, get pussy."

"Go home, nigger, get pussy!" The inmates howl. They advise and they plead. Their exhortations have but one theme. They don't tell Kevin to go out and enjoy a steak dinner or a walk in the park, see a first-run movie or get drunk at a club. They simply beg him to "get all that pussy!"

Then the requests start flowing in from inmates who aren't going anywhere for a long time. Those who aren't going to get any pussy for years or decades or ever, begin to think of what they can get for themselves. The send-off is over and their requests center on their own quality of life. "Yo, son, let me get the sheets."

"Kev, let me get your deodorant."

"What about your soap?"

The guard repeats, "You can't take those things with you. Rules are you take a pair of state greens, your personal letters and pictures and toothpaste. Hold on a second. We gonna crack you out so you can give your things away."

It is nearly Christmas and Kevin walks the gallery with a pile of gifts like Santa Claus. Then he steps back in his cell and repacks for home.

The next day in a damp and sallow dawn he steps out through a door into the razor-wire-enclosed sally port, the spot where vehicles enter and exit the prison. There are four inmates in a blue and green minivan. The bus stops at Auburn Correctional Facility to pick up others who are being sent down to work-release in Queens. All on board are just weeks from freedom.

Kevin sits in the back near the window and watches the hills. This time there is no smudged Plexiglas, no wire screen to block his view. Tendrils of mist rise above the trees. A wide river flows beside the highway, lunges away from the road, and reappears.

Kevin studies the new cars and readies himself for New York. A thought chills him for a moment: It's so easy to die for so little in New York. The old headline passes from his mind and he is happy again as the minivan powers down the New York State Thruway.

"I'm gonna fuck my bitch. I'm gonna fuck my bitch. I'm gonna fuck my bitch," an inmate with dreadlocks chants, rocking back and forth in his seat. Another inmate, three rows in front of Kevin, testifies to a different intent. "I'm gonna kill my bitch. I'm gonna kill my bitch." Another large man down the row raises his handcuffed wrists to his face, wipes his tears. "I miss my moms. I'm goin' to her grave."

Other men, like Kevin Davis, are just happy. Ready to go out there and be happy. Be easy.

When the tip of the Empire State Building appears and then the distant ramparts of Manhattan, somebody hollers the chorus of a hit song of a few years earlier. "Whoomp! There it is." Instantly, the giggling band of erstwhile stickup men, thieves, and dope dealers sings together in perfect pitch. "Whoomp! There it is. Whoomp! There it is."

As the bus rolls over the George Washington Bridge down the Cross Bronx Expressway and through the streets of western Queens, the smells of New York, even in December, seep through the slightly open windows. For seven years, Kevin had been used to the pine-scented breezes of rural New York State, the crisp clean winds off the ridges outside the prison walls. Inside, there was the sharp sting of disinfectant and the smell of cheap boiled meat from the mess hall, the dull musk of dry cheese. There were body odor and farts, sure. But this is so much stronger. Now there is the stench of wet pavement, rotting garbage, and the exhaust fumes of a million cars and trucks. Kevin watches and listens as jackhammers blast, construction cranes pirouette, and crowds race across the streets like some kind of a land rush.

The mixture of the smells and the swarming people turns Kevin's stomach, and for a moment he thinks he might throw up. It is the strangest combination of nausea and elation. Kevin Davis thinks he might be the only person who ever tried to laugh and throw up at the same time. The light turns green and no vehicles move, nobody expects to move. It takes forty-five minutes for the bus to travel ten blocks. But Kevin doesn't mind at all. He wouldn't mind sitting in this traffic jam all day.

As the van inches through the pitted streets of Queens, it passes a community college. And there they are, all shapes and sizes of girls and women. It doesn't seem as if there is a man in sight. Kevin studies the women carefully. They have changed. When he went to jail in 1993, the young girls were copying the boys, wearing baggy work pants, oversized T-shirts, and billowing hoodies.

But now out the windows of the bus it seems that the tight jeans are part of a scheme to drive fifteen men in a minivan insane. Through the locked windows and the bars, the prisoners scream and beg for attention from the girls.

"Yo, yo, yo, brownskin."

At the work-release center Kevin has his picture taken, sees his familiar prison ID thrown into a box for disposal. He wants to ask if he can hold on to the ID for memories. He isn't one of those who wants to put prison behind him, wash seven years out of his system, and move on. Prison will always be a part of him.

Improbably, even as Kevin Davis walks to his room with his bags and his armful of clean sheets and towels, even as he fingers his temporary work-release ID, he is committing a crime for which he could receive a sentence of one to three more years in prison. In his rectum, slightly rusty, despite being wrapped in toilet tissue and sealed in a plastic sandwich bag, is a razor blade. He will dispose of the weapon only later when he is out of the state corrections system.

On his first day in work-release at the Queensboro Correctional Facility on Van Dam Street in Queens, Kevin Davis is told he won't be allowed to drink alcohol or ride in a taxicab. These are minor restrictions, things he probably wouldn't do anyway, but they remind him of why he was never very disappointed those times he was denied parole. Who wants the state looking into your business, watching who you associate with, and all that nonsense? During the first days in work-release he wanders the streets looking for a job, amazed at the rocketing Yellow cabs and the way people stroll onto the street when the blinking DON'T WALK signs tell them not to.

On the Number 2 subway, Kevin sits beside a middle-aged white woman who wears a gray business suit and a pearl necklace that looks real, as if it cost thousands of dollars. Kevin glances over at the story the woman is reading and without looking at him she moves the paper closer so he can have a better look. Kevin smiles and she nods, her lips parting slightly.

What if this woman knew who I am? he thinks. Knew exactly who she is smiling at? What if she knew about Amboy? I bet you she wouldn't be smiling then. She'd probably scream and get up and run off the train.

The thought both pleases and disturbs Kevin. He luxuriates for a moment in the power of being underestimated. He could do anything he wanted to with these clueless people. He imagines himself taking the woman to a hotel or, better yet, to her apartment. Wouldn't that be something, walking past the doorman? Maybe he would wink at the dude as he passed, going to the elevator. The woman almost smiles again. She probably has a thing for black men, he surmises, and he makes a mental note never to get so comfortable in life that he will let his guard down like these white people do. On the other hand, he wonders what it would be like to be easy like that.

Kevin Davis certainly has never wished that he were white. But he does have to admit that white people have some things figured out just right. They are the people who bought Manhattan Island from the Indians for a bunch of beads and in his view they are still selling shiny things to people of color for way more than they are worth. He both admires and identifies with the understated way the white man carries his power.

Black people are always publicizing, giving their game up. When I get my hands on a couple of bucks I might even get myself a Volvo. That's right, drive back onto Blake Avenue wearing my state greens drivin' a Volvo.

At night, back in the facility, Kevin minds his own business and waits for the three weeks to end. The next afternoon on a landing between the first and second floors, he spots a man with a slim nose, a tilting Afro, and a big furry beard like some kind of black Moses. Kevin is still on point, studying all those around him, watching for signs of trouble, looking for old enemies in the mix. It is just as easy to die here as it is behind prison walls. All it takes is one lapse and he can have his throat cut as quickly here as on the yard at Attica.

Kevin Davis still believes it is too good to be true that he is getting out of prison. There has to be at least one more obstacle. Just as he is looking out for that last assault, he passes the bearded man again. Must be some kind of a religious thing, he surmises, or a disguise. The next day the bearded man passes him on the stairs again. Kevin looks closer and his head snaps back involuntarily. The man behind the beard is World, an acquaintance from the Clinton prison, famous in the system both for the seven bodies he supposedly has in Brooklyn and the fact he is rap superstar Lil' Kim's boyfriend. Later, World will become even more notorious when federal agents detain him on his way back from a mysterious visit to Iraq. His explanation for his prewar sojourn to the Middle East will be that he is the Savior Jesus Christ Himself.

Kevin puts on his symbolic state greens. It is December 18, 2000. Release day. He carries a bagful of mail and his bundle of belongings into the bare release room where he is given $40 and a bagful of street clothes. Kevin ceremoniously returns the flimsy shirt and pants. He has planned this for a long time. He'll step into the world wearing his black leather Marc Buchanan jacket his mother has sent him over his state greens and his all-black Timberland chukka boots. He stands for a moment in front of a glass door while he is uncuffed. Through the thick glass he can see the figures of his friend Beans and Francesca, the woman he had married early in his prison stretch, in the outer room. Francesca, pacing, looks more nervous than he is.

As Kevin Davis steps through the last door to freedom, Francesca strides forward with her arms outstretched. Kevin holds still for a moment before he moves into her embrace.

A coffee-skinned Puerto Rican an inch taller than Kevin, with sturdy bones, a prominent forehead, and long shiny black hair, Francesca stands stiff-legged as she wraps Kevin gingerly in her arms. She pulls back quickly and studies his face.

There is no doubt that Francesca has been the love of Kevin Davis's life. There had been plenty of other girls, including the one from the Langston Hughes projects, enemy territory, where Kevin had braved death from Born Son and his people to make love on a rooftop. A half hour under the stars on the tarpaper roof and nine months later he was the father of Pamela, a baby girl who is already getting ready to go into high school. Then there was the Italian girl he had met at the beach at Riis Park and talked with on the phone for months before daring to show up at her house in the all-white Howard Beach neighborhood. Her parents had surely assumed that the polite "Kevin" on the phone was a white boy. When he pulled up in the backseat of a cab, the entire family, except the father, was seated outside on the porch. "You're Kevin?" the mother croaked. When Kevin confirmed his identity, the woman shouted over her shoulder to her husband, "Charlie, you better come out here. You're not gonna believe this."

And there was that crazy ride with Shorty Dip, the legendary Brownsville booster and pickpocket, with the quarter-inch-wide scar on her face and the apartment full of hot jewelry and rack of stolen fur coats.

But there had never been anything like Francesca Milan. The first time he saw her pass his building on Blake Avenue, he swallowed hard and looked to the heavens. Kevin soon found Francesca had a voice as deep as most men's, was quick-witted, flighty, ghetto-volatile, and possessed of limitless passion. When they were together, in the early nineties, the years just before Kevin went to prison, their love had been incendiary.

When I was an adolescent she could provoke a lot of things in me. The thing about Francesca was that I never got tired of making love to her. We would go for hours and hours, locking fingers and toes, and we would only stop when we was too tired to move. And then when we rested a little we was right back at it. And that's the way we would go. Anytime, anyplace, for as long as we could keep moving. And I never stopped feelin' that for her. No doubt we used to drive each other crazy. I never experienced that kind of heat before or after Francesca. But then she cheated on me when I was in prison and broke that bond of trust. And she did it with a young dude from the neighborhood. So it was violation two ways.

So, boom, I get out and she got her arms around me and I'm thinkin' about what she did to me. And I am thinkin' about 10 Amboy too.

Francesca knows what I'm thinkin'. No doubt she's glad to see me and, though she is not a fearful-type person, she has to be thinkin' about what I might do at some point in time, because she knows I am not the kind of a person to forget. Nevertheless, she is there and at that point in time I am feelin' happy to be free and be with my people.

On the ride home, Kevin marvels at the skill with which his buddy Beans handles the automobile, the way he is programmed to avoid other cars, react without thinking.

Francesca, relieved of her initial concern about a punch in the face, is reporting in her pit-bull voice about Brownsville rivalries. "It's all about Marcus Garvey and Brownsville now. G'd up. MG is Folk and Brownsville ABG, Anybody Gets It," she says, supplying names of the new gangs in the neighborhood. "Li'l motherfuckers! Crazy shoot-outs." As Kevin listens and watches his friend drive, all he can think of is that Francesca is still lost. Her face looks puffy and her arms are loose. She hasn't been taking care of herself. While he was doing "G's," a thousand push-ups a day, she was watching Spanish soap operas. She has turned into a middle-aged woman while he was gone.

Beans guides the car toward Brownsville. Kevin can spy the tips of the tallest projects. He has no longing to return to Blake Avenue and the Brownsville Houses, not just yet anyway. Francesca slips her hand over from the backseat and lays it on his shoulder. Then she traces the scar on his cheek with her index finger. Suddenly she sits up straight, withdrawing her arm.

"Where we goin'?"

"Amboy? I'm takin' you home," Beans says, looking to Kevin for confirmation. Kevin nods without turning. They will drop Francesca off first. Francesca and Kevin's mother haven't been on speaking terms for years, ever since the murder, really. The rift was widened when Francesca was said to be cheating on Kevin. There is no way Kevin is going to bring Francesca into his mother's house. Not today.

It isn't that he is angry at this moment. Kevin Davis has so many other things on his mind. He spots Main on the corner of Sutter and Rockaway, one of the little boys who used to run behind him, do errands. The boy is almost six feet tall now. Looks like a grown man, almost. The car glides to a stop at the corner of East New York Avenue and Amboy. Then Beans makes the turn and stops again in front of the building, two hundred feet from where Dupree Bennett lay splashed with blood just seven years before. His first hour out of jail and here he is.

It is winter, and sheaves of icy rain blow by the car. There is nobody standing in front of the building, no one on the benches. No relatives or friends of Dupree who swore to make Kevin Davis pay for what happened here. Kevin tilts his head back, remembering, surprised as his heartbeat quickens.

"Ain't this a bitch," Francesca says, climbing out of the car, "after seven years?" Francesca can read Kevin. It's more than the problem with Kevin's mother. So be it, she thinks. At least he isn't out for blood. She kisses Kevin on the cheek and steps off.

"Later."

Unlike so many inmates, Kevin Davis has the good fortune to have a room waiting for him. His mother has managed to move out of the ghetto, has left Brownsville behind and bought a small house in Mill Basin, so far out in Brooklyn that it edges on the marshes of the Gateway National Recreation Area.

Margaret Davis appears in the doorway with her arms outstretched. "My baby's home." As they embrace, Margaret and Kevin Davis offer a startling contrast. Even with his face lit into a smile, Kevin's rugged features are dark, sub-Saharan black. His wide, unbroken nose sits perfectly in the center of his broad face. The mother is short and powerfully built like her son. But her face echoes the tale of some interracial South Carolina coupling. She is ashen-skinned, thin-lipped, with a narrower nose than Kevin's. Beside her son, Margaret Davis's pallor is luminous.

Margaret Davis loves her son dearly and has always tried to protect him when he was in school and even when he was in prison, sending letters and making phone calls whenever Kevin asked her to. Margaret knows how to stand up for her son and is proud of him. But there is not a glimmer of doubt in her mind that, for her, the genetic roulette wheel stopped at just the right spot, that her pale skin and European features are more desirable than Kevin's dark skin and that African nose.

Margaret's nine siblings are varying shades of brown, and her father, Elijah, at ninety-two is as slim and healthy a black man as you ever could see. Elijah and his wife raised their children in Orangeburg, South Carolina, in the fifties. The children grew up picking cotton, five a.m. to six p.m., stooping low between the rows, plucking puffs of fiber from the shell, working with both arms, filling two sacks at a time. They worked till they couldn't see well enough to pick, till the white man would gather them up and carry them home in his pickup truck.

Elijah was a minister and a pastor who slept with a double-barreled shotgun beneath his bed and raised his children the hard way, with a wide horse strap for beating the boys and a slim belt for whipping the girls. His punishments were so painful that, to this day, Margaret swears they bordered on child abuse. But as terrible as the beatings were, Margaret Davis, next-to-last-born and the youngest girl, never flinched from the lash. She took her punishment so calmly, repeating her whipping offenses so consistently, that Elijah gave up beating her altogether. He insisted his pale daughter got her fearless streak from her grandmother on his wife's side, a full-blooded Indian who "didn't take nothin' from nobody." People in Orangeburg marveled and told each other there wasn't a thing on or beyond this earth that could scare that ghost-faced Davis girl.

Elijah Davis himself was not going anywhere, but he was smart enough to see that picking cotton was a thing of the past. One day in 1955, the patriarch instructed his children to pack their things in cardboard suitcases and line up for a ride on a Greyhound bus to New York City, where they would stay with relatives.

The Davis children joined the throng of black faces in Brooklyn looking for education and jobs. Soon after they arrived in Bedford-Stuyvesant, the white people and the jobs went missing.

When Margaret Davis was sixteen, grown enough to bat her eyelashes, she chose a five-foot-five jet-black man for a boyfriend. Sure, Margaret favored light skin when it came to beauty, but when it came to sexual attraction, a light-skinned man couldn't do anything but show her where to find a black man.

When he was eighteen years old Margaret's boyfriend, Little Joe Davis, had moved from Summerton, South Carolina, just a half-hour drive through the cotton and okra fields from Orangeburg. He loved nothing better than light-skinned women and big shiny automobiles. Had to have more than one of each. It didn't matter a bit if the cars were a few years old; the bigger and shinier the ride, the better. One morning, he cruised up beside Margaret as she toted her books down Pennsylvania Avenue on her way to Thomas Jefferson High School. Rolling up ever so slowly in his purple boat of a Buick Regal with the white leather seats, he offered the Caucasian-looking country girl a gift of transportation.

"Why you wanna walk when you can ride?" he said, his voice rumbling.

"Why you wanna stop when you can go?" Margaret replied.

She turned the ride down as if Elijah Davis himself were watching, but gave Little Joe Davis her phone number and later bore him a son who looked just like him and already had his last name.

Margaret had always looked forward to light-skinned children, but it had been just fine that Kevin was black. That was right for the street, and before she found the church, before she was saved, Margaret was close to the street. Joe was hardworking and hilarious. He would talk to anybody. Every few weeks he would stop by and take his son for rides in his Buick with power windows, electric seats, and Dynaflow transmission. But Joe cared more about his romantic conquests and his cars than he did Margaret. He didn't propose marriage, didn't even come by often. After a while, unless you spotted his car in the morning tucked in the very back of the parking lot of some project building where a pretty girl made her home, it was downright rare to see him. So Margaret cut him off.

She sent her baby son down to Summerton to stay with Joe's jolly round-faced mother. For almost four years, Kevin scampered through the red dirt fields, watching out for the wild pigs that sometimes poked their heads from the forest. He was so quick and alert Grandma Davis would send him over to deliver items to her mother, who lived a quarter of a mile down Bill Davis Road. Kevin was so fast-moving he would return in what seemed like a minute. "I was worried the cars might not spot the little boy, so I made him wear a big straw hat so they could see him. All you could see was a big hat zipping down the street," Grandma Davis says.

When Margaret traveled down to South Carolina to collect her son, Grandma Davis broke into tears. The boy looked so much like Joe that it was as if she were losing her son a second time. As Margaret paused on the steps of the railroad car, Kevin waved his tiny arm. "C'mon, Grandma." When the woman stayed on the platform, Kevin himself began to sob. Margaret says the boy cried all the way to Virginia.

After Joe, Margaret chose a boyfriend named Rawhide, who fathered Kevin's younger half-sister, Tonya. He was a leader of a Brooklyn gang called the Tomahawks. One day some boys stole a pair of Margaret's jeans off her fire escape and when the thieves heard who her boyfriend was they brought the pants back.

True to form, Margaret Davis holds her cards close now as she guides her returning son into the house. Doesn't utter a word of her concerns about how he will live and what his influence on Travis, her peaceful teenage son, will be. "My baby. My baby. My baby," is all she says.

Kevin sets his bag down and reaches for his mother again, holding his scarred cheek against her face and looking with narrowed eyes at the living room furniture.

With its miniature rooms, the house in some ways isn't as livable as the spacious project rooms in which Kevin grew up, but he is used to even smaller living spaces than this. Besides, the house in Mill Basin is far out of the line of fire.

The adage that you can take the boy out of the ghetto but you can't take the ghetto out of the boy has some truth. But there is a related truth about leaving the ghetto. It is, of course, a triumph for Margaret Davis to have left Blake Avenue behind. She has done so by saving her money carefully, by marrying a pastor who had a little savings of his own, and by taking advantage of a low-down-payment, low-interest mortgage that was available in the late nineties. Hers is no small feat of planning. She has seen the effect of the neighborhood not only on her first son but on her daughter,

Tonya, who by this time has done prison time for credit card fraud. Margaret doesn't want the same thing to happen to Travis, eighteen years younger than Kevin.

It has not been easy for Margaret Davis to get out of Brownsville, but in another important way it might not be quite so difficult for Kevin Davis to leave the ghetto life behind. Unlike members of the Mafia or other organized branches of the criminal underworld, ghetto thugs like Kevin Davis have little fear of being followed out of the neighborhood by old enemies. The beefs carry over into the prison system, but rarely will a Brownsville tough guy go looking for an enemy, even a snitch, outside the neighborhood.

Kevin studies the wide ungated front window. No, there will be no armed strangers showing up here. No drive-bys. Amazingly, the kind of people Kevin associated with before he went to prison and the men he had met in jail have never heard of Mill Basin, though it is just a few miles from Brownsville. Even the crowd at 10 Amboy won't know how to get here.

"You got your own room, Kevin," Margaret says proudly as she cocks her head to the stairway. Kevin hesitates, studying a row of family pictures on the wall along the stairs. There is a framed photo of Kevin as a round-eyed, smiling five-year-old.

When he was that age, after watching a karate movie on television Kevin would bolt from the front door of his apartment building and assemble with his tiny playmates. Leaping and spinning in the air, they would practice the moves they had just witnessed on television, high kicks, spins, and sharp jabs. Boy screams bounced off the brick walls.

By the time he was nine years old, the neighborhood rivalries had already become heated. He started sneaking out of the apartment to run with his friends across the street to fight neighborhood rivals. Then he would rush back to be in the house, watching television, when his mother got home.

I was a little guy but I always did man things. My moms wasn't exactly strict but she was watchful. She stayed in the window watching every fucking thing that we did. I was limited as far as a lot of things that were going on because of my stagnation in front of the building. Sometimes, my boys would go over to Langston Hughes projects to play a game and they would win and the Langston

Hughes guys couldn't accept the loss so they would beat them up and chase them back to our building. I was not a ballplayer. I was just into fighting.

One time there was this guy Roger, he was kind of built like me, and he was a bully. One time he caught two of my friends on the back of the bus and beat them up and he chased them back to my building and I happened to be playing stickball outside in front of my house. These guys went swish right past me and I said to Roger, "What the fuck is you doin' over here?"

I threw the stick down and just went over and started punchin' him up. So we was fightin' for like maybe five or ten minutes. So I wound up takin' a knife out, little pocketknife that I used to carry in my sock, 'cause I used to play in the dirt a lot with my knife and stuff like that. Boom, I poked him right in the nose and when I did that he was bleedin' and everything and he just took off. My friends that was outside that he chased was like, "What the fuck is you doin'? He's gonna bring the whole fuckin' L.H. over here." I tell them shut the fuck up. These guys leave me outside. They run in the house and they start lookin' out the window. They're fuckin' scared. So I stayed outside. And before you know it nobody came. I waited outside. I had my stickball bat and my bottles. I had my knife. I was waitin'.

Most people got their fear to keep them safe. Since I was young I had to rely on my intelligence 'cause I can honestly say that I did not feel fear. I was oblivious to a lot of things. I actually wanted to find out if I could get my ass kicked and get the shit kicked out of me 'cause it never happened and I was curious. That was my attitude. I probably would have liked it if I had got my ass knocked out. I would have been like, Yeah, okay, all right, now this can happen. I would probably feel different. So I never got the shit beat out of me to the degree that my attitude would change. So my attitude never changed. It's still the same.

As a boy, the only person Kevin Davis feared was his explosive mother. To this day, he does not raise his voice or curse in Margaret Davis's presence. Standing at the bottom of the stairs, demure in her prim clothes, with her church hat on a chair near the door, Margaret Davis might fool a lot of people, but not her son.

He is too familiar with the fault line between her flaming temper and her cool conviction in the justice of the Almighty. In the projects, he had seen her erupt at the slightest provocation, descend from the sixth floor and scrap in the street over nothing but words. He watched her and he learned that anger could be a good thing.

My moms was on television one time 'cause she hit my art teacher. I didn't like that teacher. She had called me stupid in front of the class. We had an art project and I messed it up and she came right out and said, "You are so stupid." A white woman. I went home and told my mother. I was like in the second grade. My mom stood outside the school and waited for the teacher to come out. My mom said, "Is that her?" I said, "Yeah," and my mom punched her right in the face. And the woman didn't even fight back. She just cried. They had a parent meeting and my mom didn't get arrested. She had to participate in some type of counseling for two or three years.

As his mother looks on, Kevin moves gingerly up the staircase, the opening just wide enough to receive his shoulders. At the top of the stairs, Travis steps forward and the brothers embrace. It is strange to see Travis now, already several inches taller than Kevin, willowy and handsome, draped in a voluminous T-shirt and a pair of denim trousers so oversized they look like they belong on a circus clown.

"You look like Lil' Bow Wow. That hip-hop look ain't the way to go."

Travis ignores the criticism. "It's good to have you home, Kev. We been waitin' for you." The kid sounds so sweet and sincere that for a second Kevin thinks he might be gay.

Kevin shakes his head to clear the thought and speaks gruffly to fracture the intimacy. "You think *you* been waitin'."

In the tiny upstairs bedroom, Kevin takes off his leather jacket, sits on the bed, and unlaces his Timberland chukkas. He notices a floral fragrance rising off the bed and breathes deeply as his hand slides to touch the pillow. Like a person who has had a near-death experience Kevin savors the smallest sensations, feels a trill of excitement as he bounces gently on the mattress. Then he stands, walks three short steps, and deposits his plastic bag full of photographs, documents, and letters on the floor of the closet. He lays his white socks and underwear into the dresser. Holding his state greens up to the window, he brushes them free of lint, snaps them in the air, and smooths out the creases before hanging the uniform on the hook on the back of the door.

He looks at the green shirt and pants hanging separately, takes them down, brushes them again, holds them up to get a look at the stenciled number, 94A5049, and hangs them back up again. If he had been another color, or the same color from another neighborhood, he might have been a graduate looking at his worn college sweatshirts instead of a prison uniform. The green pants and shirt hanging on the back of the door mean much more to Kevin Davis than nostalgia. The outfit is like a military dress uniform representing discipline, focus, and bravery. He contemplates putting it on. It might help him think, plan strategically. Kevin walks to the door and gauges the silence; somewhere in a back room he can hear the sound of a video game. He turns to face the room and stands still, gathering himself. He had wanted to leave prison behind but now he doesn't want things to move too fast. He wants to slow things down, to note and understand everything that is happening to him. He doesn't want to tumble headlong into the world, get caught up in all the hype, go back on the promises he has made himself.

Kevin considers dropping to the carpeted floor and knocking out sets of push-ups when he spots a small gold statue on a cracked ivory-colored plastic base sitting on the dresser. It is a trophy he had been given when he was fourteen years old. MOST IMPROVED BOXER.

Poison Jones

‖‖‖

When he was thirteen years old Kevin noticed that one of his play-mates about his age, Bernard Peterkin from the Brownsville Houses in the next block and across the street, seemed to disappear a lot. Because there was so little privacy in places like Brownsville, Kevin had always been fascinated by the effect of simple absence. As a boy, he daydreamed about disappearing from the block, making people wonder about where he was and what in the world he might be doing. Kevin stopped Peterkin on a Saturday morning.

"I'm on a boxing team," Peterkin announced.

Peterkin took Kevin to a gym in the basement of the YMCA on Atlantic Avenue, a few blocks down from Thomas Jefferson High School. The place was rank with the smell of feet and sweat.

The stink of the basement and the grunts and the sound of blows exhila-rated Kevin, made him feel he was in a kind of devil's workshop. Kevin liked Ray, the mailman who acted as boxing coach, and listened to the man as he had never listened to a male adult. Kevin learned quickly to work the heavy bag and punish the speed bag, to make it cry. For the first time, at the age of thirteen, Kevin Davis became a student of something.

In the noisy dungeon on Atlantic Avenue, Kevin was learning to control his anger. He also noticed that other boxers were wary of him.

A middle-aged boxer pounding on the heavy bag stepped back when he saw Kevin walk into the gym one day. "I thought I was black. Son, you must be the original black man."

These were the days when another son of Brownsville, another bad boy, Mike Tyson, was mugging opponents in the ring, crushing their faces and their hearts. Kevin could have taken the comment as an insult.

But Kevin did not consider his blackness any kind of a deficiency. When he answered the old boxer, "Mike Tyson's white compared to me," Kevin was talking about more than skin color.

"Good for you, son," the pug answered, "'cause black don't bruise."

Soon Kevin was getting more and more serious about boxing, running in Betsy Head Memorial Park in Brownsville every morning with a pack of stray dogs trotting silently at his heels. Kevin loved the image. He even thought of making a video of him and his dogs.

Ray put Kevin in the ring with Junior "Poison" Jones, at the time a twitchy five-foot-five, 110-pound two-time Golden Gloves champion. At eleven and twelve years old, Jones had won state and national championships. He would go on to become a five-time professional world champion as a bantamweight. Sinew and bone, Jones looked like a Doberman pinscher.

As Kevin approached the long-armed junior champion, the sparring session looked like an awful mismatch in Kevin's favor. But Junior Jones was a rare prodigy who was already a seasoned boxer. Jones's first body blow delivered a spike of pain. Kevin had to bend over to collect himself as the spindly Jones shuffled back and waited. Kevin inched forward, hunched, protecting the spot below his ribs where he had been hit. Somehow, with his next punch Jones hit the exact same spot and then he hit it again. Jones floated forward, following the usually hard-charging Kevin Davis around the ring, hitting the Brownsville tough guy where he wanted and as many times as he wanted.

Junior kept jabbing. Pop, pop, pop. Kevin's nose was numb. "That's enough," Ray said finally, but Kevin was infuriated and the aggression had not been beaten out of him. "Get the fuck out of the ring," Ray ordered. Kevin climbed out of the ring, but he planned to wait near the doorway and snuff Junior Jones, sneak-punch him in the face after he got dressed.

After a few minutes, Bernard Peterkin, who knew Kevin well enough to read his thoughts, stepped close to him and explained, "Once, I wanted to kill a motherfucker. But sometimes you got to accept it to learn the trade."

Davis got back into the ring with Jones a week later and went a full two rounds. He had now survived six minutes with the champion, but it was still trial by ordeal. Nonetheless, he felt himself becoming calmer as he practiced his combinations, left hook, right uppercut. Then, as he continued to spar with Junior Jones, to pace himself through the punishment, he discovered that Junior Jones didn't hit as hard in the third round as he did in the first. At the beginning it was just a theory. Then, as he ran around Betsy Head Park with his convoy of bony dogs, it became a plan.

The next time they sparred, Kevin Davis took his usual three rounds of punishment. This time, as the third round ended and Jones walked back to his corner ready to have his gloves removed, Kevin hollered, "One more!" Jones hesitated. "Let's go one more round, Ray!" Kevin yelled again.

"Kevin, get out of the ring," Ray ordered.

"I ain't gonna get out the ring till he get me out. Let's do three more rounds. Look at him, he's scared. I got him." Finally, the future world champion heard the murmurs around the gym.

Jones nodded to the coach and the fourth round began. Kevin was moving quickly enough now to block some of Jones's body shots. Then he fired a left hook–right uppercut combination, and then another, and just like that he started stalking the stalker. Kevin howled with glee. "You ain't got nothing!"

When Jones moved forward and clinched, Davis threw him to the mat. There was plenty of Brownsville left in him. The regulars stopped skipping rope, hitting the bags, and watched. Damn if Jones wasn't holding on and backing up.

Jones's nose started to trickle blood. There was nothing likable about Kevin Davis. He was a sneering, thick-necked thug from the Brownsville projects, but the gym rats couldn't help but smile and nod their heads as he pounded away at Junior "Poison" Jones. After the fourth round, Davis grinned as he hugged Jones. When he stepped out of the ring Ray threw a towel in his face. "Motherfucker, you think you're really bad."

It wasn't such a momentous victory. After all, Kevin Davis outweighed Junior Jones by thirty pounds. But it was an important moment in Kevin Davis's life. The turnaround had been so impressive that other boxers in the gym started working harder. Started telling Ray, "I want to go five and six rounds." Kevin learned that he could adapt, learned that he wouldn't prevail on flash and speed but on heart and endurance. Years later, in a prison near the Canadian border, when the guards beat him and threw him battered, naked, and shivering into a cell with a barred but open window, he had laughed out loud. The grunting corrections officers who'd beaten him didn't know it but they were in his world. He was raised on pain, built to receive and dispense it.

After Junior Jones, Kevin knew he was a survivor. And there was something else. He was not just a creature of instinct. He had figured out a way to beat a champion, and in the same way he would figure out a way to make his mark in the world.

Now, on his first night of freedom, Kevin simply cannot sleep. He lies still and listens for sounds from his brother's room down the hall. He's used to a routine that put him to sleep in prison. First, the lights would dim, and then the cells would slam open, operated by individual levers at the guard station. Then the inmates would step inside and slam their own cells shut, many with a vengeance, trying to break the mechanism. Then the guard would come by, checking each cell to make sure it was shut. After the guard's pass, the inmates would pull their curtains. Anything that would obstruct vision into an inmate's cell was forbidden at other times, but after the cell check at night they were allowed to hang a curtain as they used their toilets. At the sound of the next cell check, a guard jangling his oversized keys as he stepped down the walkway in front of the cells, the curtains had to be removed.

Here in his mother's home there is no familiar pattern to lull Kevin to sleep. Four o'clock in the morning and he is wide awake, lights on, eyes jammed open, staring at his prison greens hung on the back of the door. He rises and adjusts the shirt so he can see the inmate number 94A5049 again. That number means more than his Social Security number or even his professional boxing won-and-lost record. That number is who he is. Kevin stoops to the floor and reaches into the clear plastic bag with his letters and cards. Even when he was assigned to a cell in a prison for what should be a matter of years, Kevin kept his personal effects in bags so that nothing would be lost in a quick move. He reaches in and pulls out a letter he received at the work-release center just a few days after his release. The letter is from a Marcus Robinson of Queens, who made sure to thank Kevin for passing him a shank on the day Kevin was released. "Good looking on the arm," he wrote, using a prison term for a weapon. The penmanship, the capital letters, the furious energy of the words, draw Kevin back inside and he relaxes as he reads.

YO KILLA I'M FEELIN THAT BRO. DON'T BELIEVE THE HYPE THOSE DUDES IS TALKING ABOUT ME. BROTHERS HAVEN'T BEEN THRU ANYTHING SO THEY DON'T UNDERSTAND HOW SITUATIONS CAN HAPPEN SO FAST THERE'S NOTH-ING YOU CAN DO. MURDOCK CAME OUT OF THE BLEU AND JUST HIT SON. I DIDN'T EVEN SEE THE FIRST HIT. I HEARD IT CAUSE I HAD MY BACK TO BLACK'S DIRECTION. BY THE TIME I JUMPED UP AND TURNED AROUND LOMAX WAS SPEEDING OUT THE CLASS. BLACK COULDN'T EVEN HELP HISSELF. SON WAS PLAYING NO GAMES AND HE ROCKED BLACK LIKE A CRADLE. BUT BLACK ASKED FOR IT. INSTEAD OF STEPPING 2 HIS BUSINESS WHEN HE DISSED SON. HE SQUASHED IT AND GOT HURT. HE SHOULDN'T TALK IF HE WASN'T READY TO BANG. THIS IS REAL LIFE. I KNOW THIS AND YOU KNOW THIS BUT A LOT OF DUDES DON'T. THEY THINK THIS IS A SOAP OPERA. AND BROTHERS SWITCH LIKE THE WIND. THEY BLOW A DIFFERENT DIRECTION EVERYDAY. I CAN'T DEAL WITH THAT. IF IT AIN'T REAL IT AIN'T RIGHT. I GOT A HORSE ON MY BACK. DUDES GOIN' HOME LEAVING ME WITH THERE BEEF. I KNOW YOU TIRED OF BANGING FOR DUDES WHO WON'T BANG FOR THEM-SELVES AND CAN'T THINK PAST GO. I GOT STABBED 3 DIF-FERENT TIMES ONCE FROM BEHIND AND TWICE GOING GUN TO GUN. AND NONE OF THE BEEF WAS BECAUSE OF ME OR WORTH SHIT. SO I DECIDED TO TAKE MY BEEF AND STEP. REAL NIGGERS LIKE YOU AND MY OTHER COMRADES WHO HAVE PURPOSE AND STAND FOR SOMETHING AND DON'T GO FOR ANYTHING GOING TO ALWAYS BE COMRADES. BUT THESE OTHER CLOWNS CAN EAT A DICK. I CAN SAY THAT CAUSE I'M GONNA GET BUSY FOR MINES. I PROMISE YOU IF

JAHARD OR J.B OR IZ GET INTO ANYTHING I'M GOING TO HOLD THEM DOWN TO THE FULLEST ALSO B.REALS. MAKE IT HAPPEN OUT THERE I'M TRYIN' TO BE THERE SOON. 2 LOVES. GOOD LOOKING ON THE ARM. WHEN I USE IT I'LL THINK OF YOU. LAUGH.

Kevin folds up the two sheets of white lined paper, places the letter carefully back in the plastic bag, lays his head on the soft white pillow, and falls asleep.

"So What If He's Black?"

||||||||||||||||||||||||||||||||||||||||||||||||||||||||||||||||||||||||||||||||||||||||||||||||||||||||

It is late morning on a Saturday in the fall of 2000. Karen Tanski is awake but her eyes are glazed with sleep. She is trying to remember something about her new boyfriend, something . . . She conjures his face, wide and handsome, blue-black hair, and television teeth.

Her cell phone is on the table by the bed set to vibrate. But there are no calls. Mark was supposed to call when he got back from hanging with his friends. He was supposed to call but didn't. Just like the time two weeks before when he had left her waiting all afternoon.

Mark is a square-shouldered former Marine, an eye-catching body builder who takes the best care of himself. He smells so good, a clean biting scent that fills Karen's nostrils when he is near. She's slept with him a couple of times. Why not? That was nice too. Then she allowed herself to look into the future.

Maybe he would be good for Julia, and Karen and Mark could have a couple of kids on their own. They sure would be beautiful children with her eyes and her skin. Everything else could be Mark's. Yes, a boy or two to go with her daughter, a picture-perfect family.

Mark had contacts in the area and could make something of himself. He was smart and he certainly had the look. Maybe, he told her, he would go back to school and get a business degree. Or become a salesman.

It seemed that at precisely the moment Karen began to peer into the future the ex-soldier started not showing up, not calling, lying to her face and then smiling.

Karen steps out of bed and stretches, tossing her head back and yawning. Julia is at Grace's house in Gillett for the weekend and there is absolutely nothing she has to do. But her pleasure is cut by a shard of anger. Last week Mark's roommate had tried to fuck her.

She had gone looking for Mark, knocked on his door. His roommate answered and they kicked it for a while, listening to music and waiting for Mark to come back. When the roommate went to the kitchen and returned with a couple of beers, he sat on the couch instead of the chair and then he touched her shoulder as he reached over for matches. Then he brushed a wisp of hair from her forehead, leaned over, and tried to kiss her. Karen was almost high enough from the weed and the beer, almost angry enough at Mark to part her lips and accept the kiss, but she hadn't. She'd had enough of horny assholes. Karen didn't say anything to Mark about it, until he'd brought it up a couple nights ago on the phone.

"What's up with you and my man?" he had asked with a trembling note in his voice.

"Nothin' at all."

"Not what he says."

"Oh, an' what does he say?"

"Umm."

"Don't play no fucking games, Mark."

Mark had terminated the conversation with a giggle, told Karen he would call when he finished hanging with some Marine buddies he said were in town. But he hadn't called last night. Just like he hadn't called and hadn't shown up last week. But it was the sound of his voice that strikes Karen now as she stands naked in her bedroom looking at the mirror into her own eyes. That laugh. Mark was not only ignoring her. He was laughing at her. He knew about his friend on the couch because his friend had told him, and his friend had told him because Mark had given him permission to take such liberties, had designated her common property. Mark probably had her on speakerphone with his roommate at his side when he'd called up giggling. Nothing that lazy, smelly Bill had ever done, not the lies or even the punches, had been as bad as this low-down disrespect. Karen wants to spit in his Marine face. But she has a better idea.

She reaches for her phone. There is a guy, a young smiling black fellow from Rochester she had met at a club a few weeks before. Her friends told her that he is some kind of a drug dealer, that he comes from a family of drug dealers in Rochester. So what? she thinks. He is funny and sweet and he can buy drinks all night long. This is Elmira, Karen thinks, I won't have to go to Rochester and get involved in any of that drug gang mess.

Elmira is a city that has always been friendly to hardworking, upstanding blacks. Heisman Trophy winner Ernie Davis, "The Elmira Flash," who had died in 1963 at the age of twenty-three, is the city's favorite son. The recreation center on the east side is named for him. But it is more than that for Karen and many of the young white girls in Elmira. They like the swagger and the slickness and the way the young black men take care of their clothes. Some white girls Karen knows have corresponded with black inmates from the Elmira prison and it is not uncommon for white Elmira women of any age to visit black inmates at the prison up on the hill. Karen winces when she overhears racial slurs, can't understand the hostility she hears from some older whites. Though she hadn't grown up with any blacks, Karen always knew that they were regular people. Many of them had grown up hard in broken homes just like she had. And it's not as if she is attracted to just any young black man. Some of them are cool and some of them are not. Beyond that, for the life of her, Karen can't understand what all the fuss is about.

Karen goes out with the Rochester guy a couple of times. He even moves some of his clothes in so he can stay an entire weekend, taking Karen out to clubs and restaurants without driving almost two hours back to Rochester. He's all right. So what if he is black? Doesn't mean a thing to Karen.

But it means something to Mark, whose interest had been rekindled by not hearing from Karen. He thought he had the girl just where he wanted her, had her nose open just wide enough that he could hang with his friends, date other women, and come back whenever he felt like it. But then Karen stopped answering his calls. Mark waited for her to crack and come knocking, even bet his roommate that she wouldn't hold out a week. But two weeks have passed, so he drives by her house. Takes a ride down Brand Street to catch a glimpse.

What he sees is a wiry black man with a broad forehead striding out Karen's front door with a flash of blond hair right behind. Mark whips his head straight and guns his engine.

Mark just can't control himself. He passes Karen's house again and again in the next week until he spots her by herself getting out of her car.

"What's going on?"

"There is nothing going on, Mark. How are you?"

"Not so good after I seen you got a nigger boyfriend."

"That's your problem."

"How's that?"

"Besides bein' a conceited asshole, you're prejudiced."

"You got no respect for yourself."

"I got too much respect for myself to mess with you. Just not prejudiced like you."

Karen is smiling as she carries groceries in both arms up the walkway to her front door. She twists her body to reach the doorknob and dips her shoulder to hold the door open as she steps inside. Almost laughs out loud as she hears the squealing tires.

IN THE WORLD

Travis had visited his older brother in prison and was surprised how calm and upbeat Kevin had always been. Now, at breakfast and when he is home for dinner, he notes how quiet and serious Kevin has become. He also notices that though Kevin had always talked about coming home, now that he is free he rarely spends time at the house.

First, Kevin visits the Wildcat Service Corporation on Battery Place in Manhattan, where he is handed a fistful of subway tokens and a list of employers who give jobs to ex-cons.

The first job he gets is at Visual Graphic Systems at Tenth Avenue and Thirty-seventh Street in Manhattan. Kevin's assignment is to receive packages containing parts of large commercial signs like those for restaurant chains such as Boston Market. The packages arrive with enough parts for twenty or thirty signs at a time. Kevin reads the instructions and uses a hand drill and a screwdriver to assemble the aluminum and plastic signboards. Each job takes him about fifteen minutes to complete.

In 2001, $8.25 an hour is not laughably low and the job is satisfying. Even if the pay was a joke it wouldn't matter much to Kevin. He considers working a regular job like working out in the gym, a test of his ability to overcome tedium, to concentrate and persevere. It isn't about the money. How much money can they pay you an hour? Even if he makes twenty, thirty dollars an hour it won't be enough. No, it is better that the money is an afterthought to the activity. He eats meals at his mom's house, takes enough for subway fare, and just stacks the checks up or puts them in the bank. He looks at the paychecks like gold stars. The company permits employees to wear their own clothing and Kevin takes the opportunity to show up one day in his state greens.

As he works in the fabrication area at Visual Graphic, Kevin dreams about his boxing career. His professional boxing debut had taken place on June 25, 1992, at the Marriott Hotel in midtown Manhattan. His opponent had won his previous two fights by knockout. But a pounding, hooking Davis knocked him down in the first round and he spent the rest of the bout running. The decision for Davis was unanimous. His purse was $800, half of which went to his manager and his promoter. Kevin was glad to get the $400.

A detached retina caused by a stickball accident when he was a kid shortened his boxing career after six fights. Now glory in the ring is a memory, a fantasy that crops up every once in a while. When things are bad he talks about making a comeback. Long after he stopped fighting professionally or even working out in the gym, boxing remains an identity, a dream, and even an excuse. Boxing was many things to Kevin but it is not a plan.

Like many others, Kevin Davis is impressed with the idea of making money out of being himself. To him, that is the real American Dream. There is the hip-hop world. Gangsta rappers are making millions rhyming about the very life that Kevin Davis had led and is leading. They sang about surviving on the street, going to prison, and coming out. Nas, the rapper from the Queensbridge Houses at the foot of the Fifty-ninth Street Bridge, even has a song about trying to live a peaceful life after prison. Two former street warriors with old beefs pass each other in the street and their eyes meet. A simple message is communicated. "All my just-comin-homies, parolees! Get money / leave the beef alone slowly." Nas pleads for reason. We know what we are capable of but what is the sense? What is the sense?

Kevin loves that rap because it catches his frame of mind perfectly. There was the time when he was in overdrive, every provocation a trumpet call. As proud as he is of that period in his life, he has moved on. Still, he wonders what will happen the first time someone out here pushes him.

Kevin has listened long and hard to the rappers, even considered telling his story in rhyme, but ultimately the thought repulsed him. But couldn't he find a place in the business? He does have a half-brother named Joe on his father's side who is a hype man with a small music studio in Queens.

In prison, Kevin mulled over the subject for untold hours. He continues to wrestle with the idea as he wields his screwdriver and stacks the finished signs. There must be a way to get into the business. If not as a rapper, then as a business manager, bodyguard—some way to make a living and a mark in the world.

As much as the black gangsters or would-be gangsters talk about "getting paid," talk about "dollar dollar bill," it is not really about the money. It is about rising above the tide of humanity. Men from Kevin Davis's background don't often take their cash and retire to an island or a mountain retreat. They rarely go anywhere they aren't known. He will break that mold, Kevin tells himself. To hell with the public life. He will take his money and move right out of New York City, straight back up to Elmira and the peaceful street with the slow-moving cars. Kevin Davis has not forgotten that window at the Elmira prison or the vow he made to return to that city. Kevin loads yet another finished sign on the work rack and sits down to lunch.

A girl sits down across from him and begins unwrapping a Whopper, separating the paper from the hamburger with spidery fingers. "Wa gwan?"—What's going on?—the Jamaican girl says with a giggle, raising her eyebrows so her eyes appear larger, richer, and more vulnerable. The girl who introduces herself as Felicia definitely is attracted to him. Maybe it is his shoulders exposed by his strap T-shirt, swollen and gleaming in the heat of the work area.

It isn't surprising to Davis that this attractive young woman is flirting with him. Despite his short stature, women had always been drawn to him, his impossibly thick arms, his fluid charm.

"Ya from Brownsville?" Felicia chooses her next words carefully. "Ya know somebody name Ben, from Brownsville? Him stay in Queens?"

"That's my cousin," Kevin says, brightening.

Felicia's hand flies to her throat. "Him try an' kill me."

Felicia is Ben's estranged wife. More importantly, she is the object of his obsession. Kevin had heard in prison that Ben is wanted for at least one body, that he is on the run from Queens detectives with a gun in his belt.

Felicia doesn't take another look at her hamburger. What had been a pleasant flirtation has become a threat to her life. Her eyes suddenly red,

Felicia begs Kevin not to divulge her whereabouts to the madman who had tried to choke her to death. Kevin is reassuring. He hasn't seen Ben in years and most certainly would never bring her name up.

But two months later, when Ben visits Kevin's mother's house in Mill Basin and borrows Kevin's cell phone to make a call, he spots his wife's name in the memory and goes berserk, demanding to know where Felicia is and what Kevin is doing with her number. But Kevin is rock-solid.

"No, I told you, dammit. I don't remember nothin' about that girl. I meet lots a shorties," Kevin says, using the street term for young women.

Ben isn't having any of it. What is worse, he suspects that Kevin is having an affair with Felicia. The only thing that sticks in his craw more than the cursed woman who had left him, the only thing that tortures him more than the loss of Felicia, is the thought of her having sex with another man. Kevin studies the television as Ben's rage mounts.

"I know what you doin'. You can't fool me, KK. You fuckin' her. You fuckin' her." Ben stomps around the tiny living room. Then he sinks into the chair across from Kevin and rests his face in his hands. Suddenly he leaps to his feet and reaches for his gun. "You my cousin but I'll kill you."

Kevin looks up at his raving relative. His eyes never shift to the pistol. Neither does he make a move to rise from the couch or explain. Kevin is, in the face of Ben's threats, about as concerned as a certified public accountant might be upon receiving word that he is being audited by the IRS; the very real threat is mitigated by knowledge of exactly what course of action to take.

Kevin looks back at the video on the television screen, thinking, *Just my luck. Three months out of jail and I run into this mad motherfucker. Now I'm gonna fuck around and kill him and end up in jail.*

Ben rails on. "Aha. I know what to do about this shit. This is how the shit ends. This is how it ends." Ben bolts from the house trailing threats. "This is how it all ends!"

To make matters worse, life is becoming downright uncomfortable in Margaret's house. After work, Kevin is going to the 2 OG Odyssey, a music studio on 108th Street in Queens, hanging around, hoping his half-brother Joe's connection there will help him find a place in the rap business. There has to be a job for him here. But his time spent at the studio in Queens means he is coming home to Mill Basin very late at night and Margaret Davis does not like that at all.

Margaret is at her best in a crisis. In February 2000, when Kevin was mysteriously returned to Attica, where he had started a small riot in 1996, he suspected a setup. When there is an incident where a guard or guards are injured, the offending inmate is taken out of the facility permanently. The possibility of reprisal on the inmate by staff is just too great. But there he was, back at Attica, brought into the facility in the middle of the night and housed away from the population in a cell in the deserted medical wing of the prison. Alarmed, Kevin wrote his mother immediately and pleaded with her to call the Director of Special Housing, Donald Selsky, to have him moved away from the very real danger of retribution from the guards. Margaret had responded quickly and effectively.

But these days Kevin is outside her door at two o'clock in the morning, knocking, asking to be let in the house. It isn't just Margaret's irascibility and her impatience, it is her recollection of gunshots at night, of the stamp of running feet on the grass and the cement walkways outside her window, of the police sirens. It is all that and something else.

When I got home from prison, me and my mother was strangers to each other. I wasn't the same person that my mother knew from before I went in. I wasn't even the same person from the letters that I sent. I was an alien to her. And she was different too. She acted all Goody Two-shoes like she was just about the church, but I didn't buy it. Fact is, we didn't really trust each other no more.

Of course, it would be simple to give her firstborn a key to the house but Margaret Davis isn't going to do that. She is afraid that he will slip easily back into his old life. It isn't that she doesn't want her son to stay in her house. She feels twinges of guilt over the way Kevin turned to the streets. Though she has never spoken the words, she knows she spent too much time thinking of her own social life. Besides, she has read his prison letters over the years and she knows he has things to teach Travis.

Still, she watches for a sign that Kevin is headed back to his old ways. Margaret waits till the next morning to say her piece at the breakfast table. Travis picks at his cereal and listens. He is feeling guilty too. The boy had tried to stay up late again and let his brother in the front door, but he had fallen asleep.

"You keep bangin' on that door late at night, I am not gonna let you in. If you can't come in a decent hour, you gonna have to find yourself somewhere else to live."

Kevin stays silent, thinking this is like being on parole. Travis glances down at his bowl of flakes, then up from his breakfast across at his big brother, and he is sure that Kevin won't be staying home much longer.

The studio in Queens is where things are happening. The rapper Ice-T comes through, as does Styles P from Jadakiss and G. Dep. To Kevin, standing in the background, doing whatever job comes up, it is heady stuff. There are leather couches to sleep on and a bathroom to wash up in. There is no shower but the freedom still trumps living at home with his increasingly annoyed mother. Soon Kevin starts staying full-time at the studio.

Kevin is amazed how fast the days and weeks pass out here in the world. Kevin is making pocket money at Visual Graphic Systems during the day and watching the parade go by at the studio at night, searching for a place in the music business. Three times a week he finds homicidal ravings on his cell phone messages. One night in May, Kevin decides to put an end to Ben's threats. He boards a bus to the building in Bushwick where Ben is now hiding out from the police and rings the buzzer in the lobby. "It's KK. Come on down. We got to deal with this shit."

The moment Ben hears Kevin's voice on the intercom, his breath comes quick and dry. "Hold tight, I'm comin' down," he shrieks into the wall unit. Ben's mad song has equal measures of fear and anger, resolve and regret. "Hold tight. I got somethin' for ya. Oooh, I got somethin' for ya."

Kevin waits at the mouth of the elevator for Ben to come out shooting but when the silver door slides open only two plump teenage girls appear.

Kevin rings again. "Where you?"

"Don' worry. I'm comin' now. Right now. I'm on my way, motherfucker, you just wait."

But Ben never does come downstairs. Kevin's cousin's fear has gotten the better of his rage. Kevin has seen this many times in jail. Somehow he always knew that Ben was not going to shoot him. He reached the correct conclusion, as he had so often before.

But the problems with Ben are not quite over. A few weeks after his visit to Ben's building, Kevin is putting yet another sign together when he receives a frantic call from Felicia on the first floor of Visual Graphic Systems. "Why ya tell Ben where me at? Ya promised."

"I didn't tell him shit."

Ben had followed Kevin to work, lurking in the following car as Kevin rode the train from Mill Basin to Thirty-fourth Street. He followed behind, ducking into the doorways of auto repair shops and small businesses as Kevin walked west to Tenth Avenue and the job site. The next day Ben arrived at Visual Graphic early in the morning, before Kevin got there. He stood at the loading dock haranguing the workers, demanding to see Felicia and threatening to shoot people. The police were summoned. Felicia was told of the uproar when she showed up for work at 9:30 and called Kevin immediately.

The next day, in the office of Visual Graphic, the manager, an ex–dope addict and street-smart operator, doesn't beat around the bush when he talks to Felicia and Kevin. "I don't care who's right and who's wrong. Y'all two can't be here no more." Sitting across the table, Kevin does not say a word or look to his left at the weeping Felicia. He plucks his Yankees cap off his knee, rises, and walks out the door.

When Kevin quickly picks up another job from Wildcat Service Corporation, this time cleaning an old folks home in Queens, he calls Francesca to ask her to work there with him.

"Fuck that con game you steady tryin' to make money at. That three-card monte bullshit. You young and strong. Stop smoking those fuckin' cigarettes. Maybe you could walk up some stairs. Do some fuckin' work for once in a blue. Least it'll make you tired and you be able to sleep better."

Then Kevin gets a break. His prison exploits have made him a hero on the streets, a decorated veteran. He has established a reputation for reliability around the Queens studio. That and his war medals are just the thing to lend a bit of credibility to a promising white rapper named Johnny Blanco, or Whiteboy. Just like that, Kevin is made a member of the road team for the rapper from Corona, Queens. It is a good fit. Kevin has always gotten along with white people. It is a side of him that has surprised and impressed his black friends.

Although Kevin gets the Johnny Blanco job through his half-brother, he has other connections in the rap game. In fact, he holds a priceless IOU.

CAPONE

||||||||||||||||||||||||||||||||||||||||||||||||||||||||||||||||||||||||||||||||||||||||||||||||||||||||||||

Joe Davis Jr., Kevin's half-brother, had worked on an album by a South Jamaica, Queens, rapper named Capone. His first album, *Stick You* (as in "stick you up"), was performed in collaboration with another gangsta rapper and Queens superstar, Noreaga. The album was a big hit and later Capone continued to team with Noreaga to produce more million-selling albums and hit singles. But Capone also ran afoul of the law and was sent to prison in 1997 on a gun charge. That was where the millionaire rapper met Kevin Davis.

Capone was in Collins in '97 when I came through. Regular population. CNN was Capone's label and he had worked with my brother Joe. But I didn't know that at the time. I just knew him as a rapper and a celebrity of some type.

So it's the summer and Capone is in there. I'm just coming in and I get a letter from my brother. The letter says, "I did the album with Capone and he's at Collins so look out for him." So I wrote a letter back, talkin' about how I'm tryin' to stay out of shit 'cause I'm ready to go home and besides, it's too late for me to intervene 'cause there are some dudes from Brooklyn who already have him. I write to my brother that Capone put himself in that predicament and I can't do nothin' about it. They already established that. It's out of my hands.

A couple of days go by. So I goes to the yard. I'm workin' out every day. Same routine. Capone goes to the basketball court and he passes me. "Yo, Kev. You Killa Kev? Somebody told me you was here." I'm like, Oh, shit. 'Cause I know exactly what's comin'. I try to separate myself from him, just nod and walk away. But he comes after me. "Your brother did my joint Stick You."

"Yeah, no doubt. No doubt." My conversation was brief. It was really just a momentary talk. I'm thinkin', I gotta go home. I gotta go home. I was tryin' to stay in mellow. Nothin' except for a direct challenge was gonna get me outta my cave.

But my brother writes again. Usually it's all happiness when you see a letter. You actually got to control yourself to keep from smilin'. But when I saw that the envelope was from my brother I had no good feelin' at all. I was shakin' my head. "Yo," my brother writes, in words that was reachin' me, even though I was still resisting, "if you could just try to make things a little better for Capone." Then the letter goes on to describe how these dudes was takin' Capone's commissary, his cookies, and his cigarettes. They was takin' his mail. Bitches was writin' him from all over the world and these dudes was takin' the letters and answerin' back theyselves. Then my brother writes somethin' about, "I understand if you can't do anything."

Now, I did feel sorry for Capone. My heart did hurt for him. He just in there tryin' to survive an' get back to the good life and these grimy dudes makin' his life a torture thing. But the truth is it was the part of the letter about "can't do anything" that got to me. Made me tight.

I called the dudes to the yard. "Let the dude alone. I'm not orderin', but you gotta be smarter about this shit." I fucked with they brains. "Think about this shit. This dude got all the money in the world when he goes to New York. Be chill with homie an' he'll look out for you when you go home. Think long-term." They was talkin' about takin' his army jacket. I'm sayin', "Why you extortin' a jacket an' some cookies when the dude got millions?" "Yeah," they was like, "yeah, you right."

After that, I thought these dudes was on the same page I was on.

That evenin' I'm up in my house sittin' up lookin' out this open window out onto the yard. I look out an' I see it's Capone and the dudes from his house goin' down the road comin' back from commissary. They marchin' along. Then I see this guy Bigger. He's fat an' he got a limp like Biggie Smalls. I'm watchin' him. He creeps up behind Capone and throws him in a yoke. Another dude runs up quick and snatches Capone's cigarettes.

The dude who snatches the cigarettes yells somethin' like, "Handle that."

I'm watchin' this shit unfold and I am tight 'cause these dudes violated me. My mind-set changed right away to a war mentality. Not some stupid anger action but real war strategy that I was good at an' known for. Within an hour, I had went to my Spanish man, Leo, a dude I know from Bushwick. Leo and his people didn't like Bigger an' them. They didn't like blacks anyway.

In jail, the whites and the Spanish stick together much more closer than blacks do. You could look at it a lot of ways. Some say we blacks don't stay loyal to each other and united 'cause from slavery times we always was at each other's throats. I tend more to think we got minds of our own. I knew that I could use the lack of organization among the blacks who was the Bloods to my advantage. You might think that was a grimy thing to do on my part. I didn't feel bad goin' to Leo and his Spanish people for a couple of reasons. I don't take color into account when I'm addin' up right and wrong. Maybe that's 'cause I been around so many black people all my life that color was never an issue. An', hey, Bigger and them was exploitin' one of their own by rippin' Capone off anyway.

So I speaks to Leo. He like, "I been wantin' to get at these dudes." I tell him, "Hit Bigger. Get the fat one up outta here." He knows I'm short to the street and he tells me to stay out of the shit. "I don't want you in the yard or nothing," he tells me.

So they do it. All the Puerto Ricans move together on the yard the next day. Two of them shot Bigger up. Stabbed him twice.

I'm lookin' out. It was chaos on the yard. Spanish and blacks yellin', fightin' all over the place. Chaos. But while all this is goin' on I'm upstairs in my Fila slippers an' my sweat suit. I'm fixin' a tuna fish sandwich. So the bell rings and they lock the jail down. We didn't have cells, we had cubes like in a dormitory. Spanish dudes passin' my cube on their way back to their bunks, givin' me nods. The blacks pass by lookin' at me confused. They could see by the fact that I was in my cube instead of the yard and by what I was wearin', like all leisure shit, that I had something to do with this attack, that I was in the chain of command. They lookin' at me like, You a snake.

The police come in and invade the yard and escort the rest of the inmates to they cubes. We get locked now. Now all these dudes have access to me but I wasn't worried for two reasons. One, they didn't really know what my role was. They just knew somethin' was wrong. And number two, I was holdin' this reputation that if a dude just looked at me too long he would start to worry. So I had a comfort zone an' I was feelin' that.

After that, the sergeant ordered everybody to sit on their bunks. The cubes are six feet high, so if you sit, you can't see what's goin' on. So, I sits on my bunk. Then I hear a bunch of slave chains draggin' on the floor. Everybody knows that noise means they takin' somebody up outta here.

At first, I had the thought that they were comin' for one of the perpetrators of the fight and my comfort level remained high. But then the sound of those dragging chains just got closer and closer and I start to think, Oh, shit, somebody snitched on me. The chains are gettin' closer and the footsteps are getting closer till I hear them just outside my cube. I just stands up, throws my tuna fish sandwich in the basket.

"Davis, on your feet now!"

"What I do?"

They don't even wait for me to react. They rush me. Chain me up. Shackle me up. Chain around my waist and shackle me from the back. Just like some slave-ship movie. They escort me to a private van.

"Where's my clothes? I need my stuff."

"It'll meet you in ten days."

Police take me to Lakeview an hour and a half away an' put me in admin seg [prison terminology for solitary confinement].

Later on they send me to Green Haven, but I have to pass through Collins to get inmates who were going with me 'cause it was a long ride to the hub. Prisons in New York State are organized into circuits called hubs, a max like Attica and a medium like Orleans are on the same hub. I'm sittin' on the minibus and three inmates get on the bus shackled. I gots my hat pulled down all the way so you can't see my face.

It's two of the dudes that was exploitin' Capone. They comes to the back. I pull my hat up slowly, glasses down.

"What's up? What's poppin'?"

They didn't answer. So I kept up. "Which one of you-all cut Capone?"

They was quiet for a couple of seconds. Then one bitch-ass punk speaks up. "I got at him 'cause he started mad shit between peoples."

I tells him, "I can't get to you now, but down the line. Down the road, homie. 'Cause niggers violatin' hard."

He comes back, "This nigger start mad shit. An' you comin' at me? We peoples."

"We ain't peoples. It's how you play the game. You can play it dirty. Well, then . . ."

Numbers is not strength. A man is strength. If I start some shit with this dude it will never end. When you start some shit with me, that's KK. Fuck you, you stupid. But that shit with Capone was fucked up. These niggers tryin' to get me killed I'm tryin' to go home.

BLANCO

||||||||||||||||||||||||||||||||||||||||||||||||||||||||||||||||||||||||||||||||||||||||||||||||||||||||||||||||||||||||||||||

Johnny Blanco and the managers at 2 OG Odyssey have heard from Kevin's brother and from the star Capone himself about the incident at Collins and are delighted to enlist Kevin Davis. It is like a group of actors cast to play Eskimos presented with a real Inuit to study.

At first Blanco and the crew treat Kevin Davis as a mascot of sorts. He is, above all, sociable and they find it hard to put his friendly manner together with his reputation. But then, theirs is a business that purposely blends violent fantasy and reality in a confusing but profitable mix.

Kevin's sober demeanor, the respect he commands from his peers, and his palpable intelligence soon lead to increasing responsibilities and finally promotion to the position of road manager for Blanco.

In 2001, John Ellsworth, who called himself Johnny Blanco or Whiteboy, was another of the thousands of young men trying to strike it rich in the rap game. The gimmick, already exploited by Detroit native Eminem, was that he was white. The story goes that Blanco got his big break in a Queens supermarket where he cornered producer Kool G Rap and shot him a mouthful of rhymes he had polished in case just such a moment presented itself.

"My flames is matches, my kerosene catches and detaches skin from bones and turns flesh to ashes. And I don't give a fuck about no case. That shit flyin' out my waist 'bout to spit in your face." Kool G Rap nodded and Whiteboy pressed on, rhyming about "niggaz and weed," ending with a poetic warning to skeptics, something about slamming "a Louisville Slugger right in your jugular."

Kool G Rap studied Blanco, an average-looking kid in a baseball cap and oversized white T-shirt. He was not heavily muscled, nor particularly menacing in any way. But the verses did have an undeniable power.

Ten or twenty years earlier, a white man mouthing such language in a black man's presence would have ignited a blaze. But hip-hop had led to a pop culture where color lines had been blurred, where poor youth and those playing at being poor united behind the rhythms and vocabulary of some African-Americans. Suddenly middle-class youth were talking about "hos" and idealizing gangsters.

In an increasingly integrated society that promised financial rewards if people of color would only "go along to get along," there arose a widespread regret over "selling out." That was when the criminal underworld of bandanna-wearing gangsters, pimps, and whores was marketed to the mainstream. A young black man might have to wear a button-down shirt and awkward cordovan shoes to his job at a bank, but in his hours off he could tie on a bandanna, listen to gangsta rap, and affect the style and language of the outsiders he had come to admire. It was a short step for white youth to develop a fascination with the thug life.

It mattered little to Kool G Rap that the most dangerous thing that the broad-faced, blue-eyed Queens rhymesmith Whiteboy had ever done was chain-smoke. Neither the message nor the racial epithets bothered the producer, who wanted to sign Blanco. The deal he offered was not a good one, so Blanco pushed forward on his own, working with Joe Davis Jr., cutting a CD, and lining up a tour. Johnny Blanco was the opening act for Ludacris in 2002 for a tour that included concerts in Norwalk, Connecticut, and Atlanta.

Kevin's responsibilities as road manager are to make hotel reservations, supervise the road crew, and disburse the per diem for the roadies, the three bodyguards, and Johnny Blanco himself. He also checks the microphone before each show and drives the black Chevy suburban with twenty-six-inch rims and Johnny Blanco's picture painted on the side. Lastly, Kevin is in charge of conducting the fame-crazed groupies to Blanco's room.

It is now January 2002 and Blanco and his crew are headed to a concert in

Norwalk. Kevin has never driven an oversized SUV like the Suburban, yet he handles the vehicle with ease through the traffic in Jamaica, Queens, and onto the Van Wyck Expressway to the Whitestone Bridge. Kevin loves his new job and he takes it seriously. During a bathroom stop he goes through a checklist of his responsibilities. Straight from jail to show business, he thinks. It isn't that much different. Just watch what is going on around you, keep on top of the details. Back on the road, Kevin glances in the rearview mirror at Blanco and the roadies. No one is watching him drive, just like no one questioned him when he gave instructions or handed out the money. Kevin soaks up the confidence he feels from the other members of the team. As he turns onto I-95, the New England Thruway, and heads the fifty miles to Norwalk, his mind drifts to a few months before, when he was on tour with Blanco.

It had been about eleven p.m. outside of Cleveland. As Blanco and his group checked into their hotel, Kevin spied two carloads of men he believed were talking together on cell phones in the parking lot. Definitely scheming, Kevin decided as he unloaded the truck. As he walked into the lobby, he looked over his shoulder and thought he saw the men in both cars watching.

Kevin prided himself on a sixth sense for danger. Always, he had moved just when he had to move, ducked just before the bullets flew. By habit, he took the initiative when trouble presented itself. Kevin was ninety percent sure that the two carloads of men were up to no good. It made a certain sense. Rappers are often targets for local thugs and robbers. There is the matter of jealousy and then there are economics and an unusual aspect of the hip-hop culture that makes performers sitting ducks.

The mantra of the rap world is the admonition to "keep it real," which means not to stray far from your roots. At the mere hint that a rapper has crossed over, lost his or her ghetto attitude, the street credibility that helps make one rapper's rhymes resonate more than another's evaporates. Hip-hop fans demand that rappers wear expensive jewelry and spend at least some time in the ghetto. The formula can be deadly.

Even in Cleveland, the hard-luck locals knew that a group of out-of-town rap performers were sure to be carrying cash and wearing at least some precious stones. An added incentive to potential thieves is that the rappers may not even report an incident to police if they are robbed, fearing damage to their gangster persona.

As they waited for the elevator, one of the roadies had his headset turned up so loud Kevin could hear the words to a rap. "Go hard or go home, no bullshit permitted, / Fuckin with the kid get a clip in ya fitted."

Blanco's words about protecting his turf in a ghetto building were just that, words, pure fantasy. He was a young poet and businessman who knew little about selling dope or shooting people. But the man standing beside Blanco, Kevin Davis, was a different type. Many times on the street and in jail he had prepared the ground for battle, and he would do so now.

"Chill with wifey," Kevin told Blanco, who stood with his girlfriend. "Just go ahead to the room. Somethin's goin' down." As the group waited for the elevator, a tall man, who looked like one of the men in the cars in the parking lot, emerged from a side door. He was dressed in black from head to toe and wearing sunglasses.

The man stood behind Blanco's group as the elevator door opened. Kevin gestured for him to step inside first. As their eyes met, Kevin, his hand in his pocket, as if on the handle of a gun, winked. The man smiled.

Kevin noted the floor when the man got off, held the elevator door, and leaned out to see what room he entered. Kevin saw Blanco and the rest to their rooms, pausing in the doorway of one room. One of the members of the crew carried an illegal .380 and Kevin considered borrowing the weapon for a few moments. He didn't need the gun for confidence; he already possessed a surplus of that. Moreover, he knew all too well the ways a gun could produce unwanted outcomes, changing cold confidence into reckless swagger and frightening the opposition into a first strike. He left the .380 behind and, congratulating himself on both his powers of observation and his ability to seize the initiative, headed straight to the room where the man in black was staying. Kevin knocked and when another man opened up asked, "Yo, can I borrow some soap?"

"Soap?"

"Yeah, soap," Kevin said, pushing his foot in the doorjamb. The man noted Kevin's hand in his pocket, his foot in the door. "I'll be right back," he said, then retreated into the hotel room and emerged with a plastic bag full of small bars of soap. Kevin smiled and backed out of the doorway.

There had been no proof that these were stickup men, no visible guns. There had just been Kevin's instincts. And that was enough for him. Kevin's fears might well have been pure fantasy, a wisp of paranoia. But as far as he was concerned, he had just foiled a robbery and maybe even prevented a killing.

"That was a stickup. You fail to realize what's goin' on and you get murdered," Kevin lectured the Blanco team waiting in their rooms. Those who believed that Kevin had been buggin' out, paranoid, held their tongues. Those who believed he had foiled a robbery called Dan Ramirez, one of the owners of 2 OG Odyssey, giddy with relief and bursting with news of Kevin's heroics. It was one thing to talk or rap about the street, another to watch Kevin Davis under pressure. Even the local men Davis had sought to intimidate were impressed. The next day they stopped Kevin in the lobby.

"Y'all from New York?"

The Norwalk concert goes without a hitch. Over the first few dates in the concert tour, Kevin begins to feel comfortable as road manager. But then Dan Ramirez hires a friend, an awkward-looking straight arrow and gives him the title of label rep. That is fine with Kevin until he realizes the new hire is looking after the per diem money that Kevin had been responsible for. It is as if Dan Ramirez doesn't trust him to dispense the per diem cash and handle the incidental expenses anymore. Kevin has no idea what he might have done wrong. Still, Kevin is determined to do his best to work with the new guy, whom he calls "Belvedere," a reference to a straitlaced character he had seen in some movie or on television.

The next concert is in Norfolk, Virginia. The morning after the performance the Blanco group's caravan of four cars begins its trek back to Queens. The members of the team and Blanco start talking about breakfast. The custom with the group is not only to dip into the petty cash to eat whenever and wherever they want, but also Kevin has taken it upon himself to split the unspent road money among the group. Now, even though Kevin does not know of any complaint or directive from Dan Ramirez not to do so, Belvedere is on hand to curtail such loose behavior.

"Yo, we gonna eat at the IHOP," Kevin tells Belvedere. "Break off some money, son."

The label rep hesitates.

As Belvedere stutters through a phone message to Dan Ramirez, Kevin calls the owner himself on another cell phone number and gets permission to take the team to breakfast. As they stand in the parking lot of the motel, Belvedere admonishes Kevin, "You're not supposed to call Dan yourself. That's my job." Kevin Davis knows when he is being dismissed, belittled. In the past he had attacked individuals on the mere suspicion that they were capable of such disrespect.

It has been Kevin's contention, from the first arrival of the new man, that he doesn't belong, that he is wrong for the job, a man from a different world, "a brother from another planet," as Kevin calls him. The new man's casual dismissal of Kevin Davis, whose street name, Killa Kev, alone should give him pause, proves that Belvedere is indeed out of his element.

In another fundamental way, though, Kevin Davis is out of his element as well. Kevin is philosophically opposed to participating in one of the most basic aspects of work life. He is not about to discuss the matter, to hear and be heard, to negotiate an arrangement of some kind. It is Kevin's credo that women argue; men fight.

Kevin delivers a left jab–right cross combination that sends the road manager to his knees in the parking lot. What happened was entirely predictable. Verbalizations of respect are so critical in a street world, where there is no written law, community, or corporate culture, where interchanges are sometimes so courtly as to be comical. Belvedere might have gotten away with something like, *I got love for you, Kev, and I respect the position that you hold and the way you deal with things, but I got instructions I got to follow.*

In the professional mostly white world, the legal field, finance, or politics, it is common for bosses to yell, curse, and demean their employees, even their peers. Such behavior is often accepted as a sign of passion or commitment to the shared task of making money. The exchange of insults in black street culture is much more nuanced. Insults in certain contexts can be a friendly challenge, a form of entertainment, but they are not easily tolerated as an expression of status in a social or a business situation. Belvedere had been simply oblivious to the language of the people he was dealing with. Stunned and injured, he is about to learn another lesson.

In the street world, observers don't often intervene to stop a beating. In fact, a display of weakness, one man being dominated by another, often inspires the opposite reaction. As Belvedere kneels on the asphalt clutching his face with both hands, the rest of the team, roadies, bodyguards and, not to be outdone, Blanco himself, sprint over from their cars and kick him down to the pavement. Then a member of the group reaches in Belvedere's pocket and yanks out the fifteen hundred dollars at issue.

Even Kevin Davis is surprised. What the Blanco team, led by "Killa Kev" Davis, has just done has been to beat down and rob their own label rep.

A meeting is held the following Saturday at the studio to decide what will result from the bizarre incident. Joe Davis Jr., who also serves as a senior assistant to Dan Ramirez, is not present. But the bruised Belvedere and Kevin are both on hand, as are Ramirez and a handful of producers.

"Yo," Ramirez begins with studied understatement, "I think that what happened was unprofessional. What Kevin did was wrong and could have been prevented by him being smarter. Therefore, I don't want him on the road anymore."

The team is up in arms. It is not so much that they like Kevin Davis, or that he might have saved them from being robbed in Cleveland. Secretly, they aren't sure whether or not the whole robbery threat had been real. No, it is that Kevin has come to represent the street credibility of the group, of Whiteboy, and in a way of the entire studio. Without Killa Kevin, it simply will not be 2 OG anymore. Dan Ramirez is sweating. He doesn't really know what to do. He has $100,000 invested in the building and another $150,000 invested in Johnny Blanco. He knows that the pleasant-looking white kid from Queens who rhymes "My flames is matches my kerosene catches" can use some publicity. The worse, the better. Say, an item in *The Source* magazine about how Blanco stomped his label rep and robbed the petty cash. In the end, though, Ramirez decides he can't allow his staff to mug his label rep. He stands his ground and upholds Kevin's ban.

"That's all right, I'll go on the road in my own car," Kevin announces, even though he owns no vehicle. Dan Ramirez says nothing as the road team murmurs approval. Kevin Davis never ventures back on the road with the Johnny Blanco team.

Kevin's dilemma is one that he shares with many young black men from his background. It is the same characteristic that makes it more difficult for them to start at the bottom in any job, any career, or even in college, where they do much less well than their middle-class counterparts and even less well than low-income black females. They are less likely to tolerate disrespect. Americans are fond of pointing to men who have worked themselves up from the mailroom to the boardroom, but men like Kevin Davis are reluctant to accept the indignities that come with that journey. Perhaps they know that journey is much harder for a black man and next to impossible for a former felon like Kevin Davis.

"You Leavin' Me?"

IIIIIIIIIIIIIIIIIIIIIIIIIIIIIIIIIIIIIIIIIIIIIIIIIIIIIIIIIIIIIIIIIIIIIIIIIIIIIIIIIIIIIIIIIIIIIIIIIIIIIIIIIIIIIIIIIIIIIII

Now that the road manager job is gone, Kevin spends his days working full-time at a long-term care facility in Queens, trundling a cleaning cart. At the end of the second-floor hallway, an old woman is shrieking, "All the wrong decisions! All the wrong decisions!" Other patients sit slack-jawed.

Kevin doesn't mind the noise and the smell, the shit even. The nasty conditions are invigorating, even purifying somehow, like prison had been. But the cleaning fluid is irritating his nasal passages something awful. His eyes are red, the skin around them puffy, and his nose is stuffed. There has to be a way, Kevin thinks, of making a living at being himself. If that is not possible, he will adjust. He is smart enough to know he has to do that, and strong enough, he figures, to pull it off.

Meanwhile, Kevin is having trouble with Francesca. She took the job with him at the long-term care facility but has been fussing and complaining from day one. One afternoon they are working the same shift. Francesca is standing at a landing at the top of a flight of stairs, wheezing, with her right hand on the cleaning cart for support, when she decides to let Kevin know what is on her mind.

"Damn, I'm gettin' tired of pushin' this bitch-ass cart up and down these hallways. An' you got to bump that shit down these three stairs."

"The fuck is wrong with you?" Kevin snaps. "You smoke so many cigarettes you can't breathe. You damn thirty-two years old an' you act like you fifty. You a damn middle-aged woman. They got old people can do this pussy-ass job."

"Fuck you. Cleanin' up people's shit. That's a job?"

"You makin' nine dollars an hour."

"You out you fuckin' mind."

Kevin has started sleeping with Francesca again and the fact that the sex has been as good as ever heightens his annoyance. "Only time you don't get tired is when you fuckin'. How come you don't get tired behind that sex shit? Do me a favor and tell me why you can fuck hard but you can't work hard."

"Kiss my gold Puerto Rican ass."

"Fuck you."

"That's all you can do. Is fuck."

Kevin has no heart anymore for the banter. All the two of them have in common now is that inexhaustible torrent of passion.

Kevin had married Francesca as he waited in prison to be tried for the Amboy shooting, mostly in the belief that it would allow her to legally refuse to testify. But there was another reason for the marriage: conjugal visits. His memory of their sex life was so intoxicating that when he was at Attica in '96, Kevin actually toed the line for months, transformed himself into a model prisoner, just to get a taste of Francesca. He chose a work detail that had him on a gang loading bags of garbage all day to keep out of trouble. On the yard and in the cafeteria he kept his head low, doing his best imitation of a little punk. All to get a shot at something called the Family Reunion Program they had instituted at Attica a few years before. Outside the old stone housing unit were four trailers, mobile homes, reserved for the coveted conjugal visits.

"Yo, son. Eat your heart out. I got trailers!" Kevin bellowed. The trailers were small mobile homes fashioned with amenities like carpeting and a color television with a VCR. Each trailer had a tiny kitchen with a stove, but no knives or forks. Once, an inmate had used a knife from the trailer kitchen to kill a wife he believed was cheating on him. The trailer program was such a valuable incentive that Attica and other prisons kept it despite the killing. The kitchen doubled as a living and dining area and led to a bedroom with a double bed. Inside the miniature bathroom was an honest-to-goodness private shower.

Within three months, Kevin had qualified for a trailer visit. At Attica, the trailers were just beyond the looming brick walls of the maximum-security prison and yards from the entrance to Wyoming, a medium-security facility next door.

It was a Friday afternoon and Kevin was led outside to the mobile unit. He mounted the steps, and the door was closed behind him. In prison, Kevin had conditioned himself to take the initiative and as he sat and waited, he became more and more agitated.

He was waiting for the arrival of his wife, a thoroughly enjoyable prospect. Still, it was a posture that made him uneasy. In all the years he had been in prison he had never paced his cell. But now he stood and paced the trailer and stared at the door for a few more minutes. As he studied a water stain on the ceiling he was seized by an idea. Carefully, he removed his clothing, placed his pants and shirt neatly under the bed, and sat naked on the toilet, waiting.

When Francesca stepped through the door, Kevin leapt naked from the bathroom sporting a prodigious erection. In midleap he knew that his joke had been a bad idea. Instead of amusement and titillation, Francesca was understandably startled as she saw the short muscular man bounding from the bathroom in her direction. She drew back against the far wall of the trailer.

The long bus trip north had been grueling, the outer wall of Attica exceedingly grim. The place looked like one of those scary castles she had seen in Frankenstein movies when she was a kid. Even though she couldn't quite place it, there was something insulting about the way she was handled by the guards; no outright sneers, or words of disrespect, just the unspoken rhythm from people who could tell her to turn around and go home on a whim.

She had been searched and escorted inside the gates. As she stepped through the door, the trailer had seemed surprisingly pleasant, almost cozy. Still, she was in no mood for stupid games as she saw Kevin fly out of the bathroom. "The fuck you think you are, Batman?"

Kevin embraced Francesca, waltzing her toward the bedroom. "Give me some."

"Calm down. What's wrong with you?"

"Boo Boo, you know what's wrong with me. Let's take care of it."

"Hell, no. The fuck you think I am? I don't want it like that."

Kevin dressed quickly and stared at Francesca as she placed on the table

the bags of groceries she'd brought and began to unpack. He slid his chair
closer and held her hand so she couldn't continue her task. She tugged to get
away and then gave up and sat on his lap as he pulled her toward him. In ten
minutes they were lying naked in the small bedroom, touching each other.
Then the payoff: roaring, growling, heaving sex.

If Kevin was to spend years locked in a cage, at least he could holler. "Shut
the fuck up, you crazy little bastard," Francesca hollered back. "Just shut up."
But Kevin roared again and she matched his volume with a howl that folded
into a moan as he entered her again.

Laughing and fucking and yelling, this was no tender, faltering, honeymoon coupling. Wrapped in Kevin's arms, her fingers splayed across his back,
Francesca couldn't have been happier or more fulfilled. Nobody, but nobody,
had it better than she did at this moment and Francesca felt like roaring too.
Instead, she just wailed. "You crazy little motherfucker. Just shut up and fuck
me."

The trailer visit was delicious but maddening. Even as he reveled in Francesca's flesh, Kevin understood that the visits would not continue. He rankled
under the pressure of having to obey every rule. Seven trailer visits and that
was it.

A month after the trailer visits stopped, it dawned on Kevin that Francesca had another man. Kevin guessed the truth even before an old-timer put
it into words. In prison he had learned to focus with superhuman intensity
on whatever he saw fit. He learned to feel Francesca without her presence
and he believed that he came to understand the woman far better than she
understood herself. He could tell when she was desperate or confused by the
spacing of her words on the telephone, and when he read her letters he could
taste her longing and see the spinning colors of her fantasies, feel the thud of
her boredom.

*Then one weekend Francesca promised to come up for a visit and didn't. Then
she writes a letter with a lame excuse and a few lines later she says somethin'
about how I once cheated on her with another girl, some bitch in the past, and
then she writes that she loves me, and then she comes out with I hate you, and
she was all over the place, gettin' all emotional. Boom, it all came to me. She was
gettin' laid. That's when it all started to spin for me.*

In prison, the balance of control and despair is so delicate that a significant abandonment can throw a man's universe into chaos. Images and impulses rocket and collide. There is no one to turn to, no safe place to mourn. Only the path to madness and surrender is lit.

The solution was to get Francesca out of his system, forget her. But it wasn't easy at the time. Even now that he was on the outside and he had grown far beyond her snappy ghetto ways, her limited scope, he still wanted her body as badly as he ever did, still needed to grapple and hold her and feel her pounding heart and have her again and again.

In the long-term care facility in Queens, Francesca takes a long look at her husband Kevin looking at her and yanks her hand off the cleaning cart. All of a sudden, she isn't tired.

"I can't believe you thinkin' about leavin' me. Just 'cause I don't want a fuckin' stupid job. Well, suck on this. I quit."

"Good for you," Kevin says.

"Lemme get this straight. You leavin' me? You piece of shit. I'm suppose to leave you, you little fuckin' black dot."

"Fuck that. I went to jail 'cause I was protectin' you. And now you gonna get tight at me after that bullshit you did when I was in jail? Fuckin' some dude."

"A job cleanin' fuckin' bathrooms. Cleanin' up old people's shit. That's your plan for the future? Fuck that. Fuck you."

"No, fuck the dude you was fuckin' when I was in jail. Fuck him. That's what you did when I was locked up. I couldn't do nothin' about it. I ought to whip you ass. When I was defenseless and you out there fuckin' somebody."

"Don't cover this shit up, you little monkey. I don't know why I ever fucked with you in the first place."

Kevin shrugs off the slur. "In the first and the second place and the last place 'cause you loved every second of fuckin' this little monkey. I can never trust you. That's part of the reason I'm movin' up to Elmira."

Kevin moves out of the music studio where his angry and lovesick wife can no longer bother him and he soon loses the job at the long-term care facility. He'd been hired by a substitute manager who was desperate enough for help that he had gone to Wildcat. In January 2002, when the regular manager returns from his leave of absence, background checks are performed and soon Kevin is without a job. He is now also without a reason to stay in New York City.

ELMIRA

||||||||||||||||||||||||||||||||||||||||||||||||||||||||||||||||||||||||||||||||||||||||||||||||||||||||||||||||||

After the Blanco thing it seemed like all my options had ran out, so I decide to look at the scenario in Elmira.

I got in touch with Beans from the Brownsville Houses. The thing is that Beans is extremely interested in girls, so I tell him all about Elmira, about how the white girls visit the black guys in prison. I inform him that there is a very good chance that he will meet some girls in Elmira. So he jumps right on it.

I went so far as to make an appointment with this white girl, Wanda, who I had been writin' letters to since I got out of prison. I arranged with her for me to come up to Elmira on a certain date. Beans and his brother get these cars from the Queens repossession auction. The back passenger door didn't open up. Two of the windows couldn't roll down. He had to open up the hood to start the car. No fuckin' heat and its like January or February.

We left out two in the morning. I had a plastic bag with a change of clothes. Beans's original plan, he said, was he was gonna drop me off and come back. But I knew he was hopin' for some pussy. Ya heard? I had maybe three or four hundred an' I promised to pay his gas and feed him. As we were goin' to the gas station before we got started I could feel the cold air comin' out of the vent. I said, "You got cold air."

"Yeah, you right about that," he told me, "This shit here don't have no heat."

I'm talking about, "You think we can really make it?" It wasn't that cold in New York City, so he was confident and he says, "Yeah. It's good. We can make it." But the thing is that he didn't understand that we was headed north. I had spent years up there and that shit ain't no fuckin' New York City. That shit is Canada. You know what I'm sayin'? And sure enough, as we start movin' out of New York City it starts gettin' fuckin' cold. I was numb. The snot that was comin out of my nose was turnin' to ice. I was huggin' myself to stay warm, curled up on the seat like a cheese doodle. And I was so pissed at him I told him turn back when we was comin' up on Binghamton, an hour away. Almost there and I tell him to turn back. That's how cold I was. I was tight.

"You're unfuckin' believable," I told him. "We could die up here, you stupid fuck."

"I didn't know it was that cold. It wasn't that cold in New York, Kev."

"Don't 'Kev' me. We goin' almost to Canada. We ain't goin' to the beach."

The car was goin' through mountains and shit. I kept sayin', "We could die out here. We could die out here."

We pull into town in the middle of the night an' I call the girl. We was on Lake Street. She gave me directions to get to her house.

We eventually get there. By now it was startin' to get light out. Me and him both get out. I kicked the car door closed. There's the house right there and I'm tryin' to walk but I couldn't even move, I was so twisted. I am tellin' you, I didn't feel normal. My body wouldn't move like it was supposed to move. I wanted to kill the dude. We both walked up to the door and knocked. We waited two minutes. Knocked again.

Boom! That's when she opened the door. She opens the door, looks at me. "You Wanda? I'm KK."

"Come in." She turns around, walks away from me. I goes behind her. I look at my friend and he walks behind me. We both lookin' like we got concern on our faces. We almost died from the cold and now here is this fuckin' fat meatball with glasses. I almost died again from the shock of seein' her ass. Don't get me wrong, I knew she was fat before I came up there. But I had never actually seen her and she covered up the worst of it in the picture. I couldn't blame her for that. Hey, in jail we used to send some fake-ass pictures too. The trickery worked both ways. But along with the shiverin' and her pink pajamas movin' up the stairs, this situation was bad. I looked at my man again. That's when she continues on upstairs without sayin' nothin', and we sit on the couch. We there for like fuckin' five minutes.

We rubbin' our hands tryin' to get warmed up and come back around to our senses. Like fifteen minutes go by, no lie. We sittin' there and we don't hear shit. I go up the stairs and look in one room and see some boys' bunk beds. Turns out her son was at her mom's. I get to her bedroom and don't you know this bitch is lying in her bed and she is snoring. She got two strangers downstairs and she got the stupidity to go upstairs an' go to sleep. This bitch is fuckin' nuts. Let two strangers in your house. Never seen her before and she just layin' there, 'sleep.

I stood over her and woke her up. Yo. So, boom, I tell her, "What kind of hospitality is that? Yo, you don't even know me. I could've killed you."

"I ain't thinking about that," she said, just like that. That's when I knew something was wrong with that town. Elmira town is so fuckin' loose.

It was so loose that I thought maybe I was bein' set up. I thought, I'm black and she's white. Maybe her father is a police or maybe she is a police or somethin'. I swear to God, I thought I was bein' set up.

Either I'm bein' set up or this is the strangest shit I have ever seen in my life. She goes in the bathroom to take a shower. I come downstairs and tell Beans, "This bitch was upstairs fuckin' asleep."

"What she had on?"

"I don't give a fuck what she had on. This bitch is fuckin' stupid." I wasn't thinkin' like Beans. My attention turned to something different. I saw carelessness. He saw freaky shit.

Beans came out like, "Yo, it's just you and her here. I'm about to break out, Kev."

I wasn't gonna be left alone with her, so I'm like, "You ain't goin nowhere."

So Beans is like, "Where her friends at?" So Wanda comes downstairs and makes a phone call. Then Marlene shows up. We thought Wanda was bad. Marlene's like six feet one and two hundred and eighty pounds, with a big fuckin' lump on her back, lookin' like Big Bird. We ain't been in this house no more than half an hour.

This motherfucker Beans took one look at Marlene, one fuckin' look, and says, "I'm goin home." He stayed a little while longer, just long enough to get warm. He made sure I had my money. I was thinkin' about goin' with him. But I refused to get in that fuckin' car. There was no way I was gonna die twice in one day. I told him, "I'm fuckin' takin' a bus home."

After Beans left, Marlene stayed askin' questions. "Why don't you bring a real dude for me? I need a dude."

We sat around and I was tellin' stories of Brooklyn. They wanted to hear anything about New York. Finally, I asked them, "What's this area about? What's goin' on here?" They could tell that I was askin' about the black-white thing, 'cause these girls seemed so comfortable with black dudes.

And Marlene was like surprised that I didn't know what was goin' on. She was like, "Yeah, I got a black man now. My baby's mixed. There's a lot of black and white shit goin' on around here. This is Zebratown."

"Zebratown?"

"Yeah, the whole east side, black and white, Zebratown."

I told them, "I don't really know nothing about this. I'm from Brooklyn." They was like makin' little smart remarks and playin' a Dr. Jekyll and Mr. Hyde. "You never had a threesome?" they ask me.

"What the hell I look like, havin' two bitches I only got one cock?"

They was like straight-up sluts. Ya heard? They expected me to just strip and start fuckin', but I was more aware of the situation.

Marlene leaves. Me and Wanda wind up stayin' an' we talked. I'm askin' questions like where do you work, are you a nurse or a teacher? She tells me, "I work at Burger King an' I got one kid." The house was pretty clean. Everything was spic-and-span. Beds was done, no dirt and no dishes in the sink. I was kind of surprised. It smelled good.

That night we ate at her mom's house. Libby cook like a black fuckin' woman. We got crispy fried chicken, rice, yams and collard greens and cornbread. Her husband Lennie was black. All these bitches got black men. I couldn't believe it. He was from Mississippi. And I'm like havin' trouble understandin' this place where black and white people are together as couples, so to speak. I'm havin' trouble acceptin' what I'm seein' and hearin' in Zebratown.

The next morning I got up, took a shower, and put on the change of clothes that I had. There was a bus leavin' at nine-thirty, which I missed, but they had *a bus at twelve-thirty. Her mother and her badass black son, they drove me to the twelve-thirty bus and I came home.*

Now then, when I get home I get a change of thoughts. Finally, I decide to play that Elmira card every other weekend. Peace. Quietness, peacefulness. That's mainly what I was lookin' for.

"LITTLE GIRLS LIKE DRESSES"

IIIIIIIIIIIIIIIIIIIIIIIIIIIIIIIIIIIIIIIIIIIIIIIIIIIIIIIIIIIIIIIIIIIIIIIIIIIIIIIIIIIIIIIIIIIIIIIIIIIIIIIIIIIIIIIIIIIIIIIIIIIII

It is January 2002. Karen Tanski is in Elmira Family Court on William Street, seated on the hard wooden pew with her squirming six-year-old daughter on one side and her mother on the other. There was no problem in getting full custody of the child from Bill Utley. But because of his disability he was exempt from child support in New York State. The unemployed mechanic is now fighting for visitation privileges. The application for visitation is a joke on many levels but Karen isn't laughing. Time and time again Bill has arrived late or failed to show up at all.

"She 'sleep?"

"You are nothing but a liar, Bill."

"I was workin' with my uncle."

"I could really use your help when I work overtime but I can't trust you."

"You could trust me. I was workin' at my uncle's."

"By the way, did you move to Ithaca? I heard you moved to Ithaca. I'm askin' you a question."

Bill has moved to Ithaca without informing Karen. What's more, he has been arrested on a crack charge and some girl has gone to the police and charged him with unlawful imprisonment. While those charges are pending, the court has mandated that Bill take domestic violence classes to keep his visitation. Once, while in Bill's car, Karen comes across papers that indicate Bill is not attending the program. When he does show up to see Julia, he has the child out till all hours, driving aimlessly back and forth over the bridges spanning the Chemung River.

Finally, Bill steps into the courtroom and sits to the left of Karen, her daughter, and her mother. He is pale and his teeth are dark and cracked. The report in front of the judge looks just as bad.

Judge Peter Buckley peers out over his glasses and measures the young father. He looks at the trio to his right, the frowning mother, Betsy, and the beaming child.

"Bill Utley?"

"Yes, Your Honor."

"I am not going to go into your legal difficulties at this point. They seem to be serious and ongoing. But that is not for now." The judge straightens his back and his baritone quavers. There are about twenty people in the court-room and it is as if he is speaking to all the men on hand, all the balky fathers. So what if the factories have fled south or slammed shut, so what if the good jobs are gone? There are still ways to make a living. There are still ways to be a man.

"Before you step into my court, before you make any requests whatsoever, you get a job! Do you hear me? Get a job, Bill. I have news for you: Little girls like things. They like shoes. They like dresses. Do you understand me? Get a job!"

After Judge Peter Buckley's order, Bill Utley does get a job, in a gas station doing car repairs. He keeps it for a few months but when he sees his pay-checks he is almost nauseous. All those hours and all those days underneath oil-dripping cars and most of the money is going to taxes.

By January 2003 Karen hasn't seen or heard from him in a year.

ZEBRATOWN

||||||||||||||||||||||||||||||||||||||||||||||||||||||||||||||||||||||||||||||||||||||||||||||||||||||||||||||||||||||||||||||||||||||||||

It is April 2002. Kevin is headed back up to Elmira on one of his biweekly reconnaissance missions. He keeps his eyes glued to the window of the bus. There is a thin crust of gray snow over the grass on both sides of the road. Ahead and behind, the wind-scoured highway stretches black. In all those prison buses for all those years he had never been so interested in the landscape. It is still winter and the soaring hills of the Southern Tier of central New York are umber, stands of white birch edging the highway. In the distance, steep rises are threaded by swaths of dirt where tractors have leveled trees to place towers for electrical power lines. A late afternoon shaft of sun pierces the clouds for a moment, turning the hills the palest pink.

Kevin had no idea such a beautiful place existed. He feels at peace already, as if things are falling in place, as if the world he had built in his mind has magically appeared. He notes a sign on the side of the road announcing CHE-MUNG COUNTY.

In 1771 this region was the eastern end of what was known to the Indians as the Forbidden Trail. The name Chemung means "place of the horn" in the Delaware dialect of the Algonquin language, named after the discovery of a mammoth tusk in the riverbed.

The path Kevin is traveling as the Trailways bus hums along Route 17, close to the Susquehanna River, leads to a spot near Elmira where there was a fork in the old Indian path. One branch led to the lake region and the other, the so-called "warrior's path," to the Genesee and Allegheny country.

In those days, these forests had been the domain of the Seneca, with scatterings of refugee coastal tribes from the south and east.

In 1779 at the Battle of Newtown, the original name of Elmira, the Revolutionary army drove those Indians and their Tory allies out of the Chemung Valley for good. The victory opened the fertile farming country of the upstate New York region to settlement by the Dutch, English, and French settlers who poured in. In 1811, a local judge was so smitten by the beauteous daughter of an innkeeper he managed to get a legislative act passed naming the city Elmira, after the girl.

In 1833 the Chemung Canal connected the Chemung River in Elmira to Lake Seneca. And in 1849, the Erie Railroad was finished as far as Elmira. Two years later it had reached the shore of Lake Erie and Elmira flourished, an agricultural and industrial success story—rich farmland just thirty miles from the coalfields of Tioga County, Pennsylvania. The "Queen City," as it became known after the establishment of the Elmira Female College in 1855, became famous for its tobacco. In the Big Flats area north of town, tobacco warehouses dotted the landscape.

Because of the canal and confluence of railroads, Elmira was a natural hub, a depot. But the city's fortuitous location also led to a grim episode. A Civil War prison camp, opened north of the city in July 1864, became infamous for neglect, cruelty, and death. During the only year of its operation, nearly three thousand southern prisoners of war perished of disease, starvation, and exposure, almost 25 percent of the prison population. The death rate was the highest of any prison camp in the North and gave it the name "Hellmira."

In 1876 a prison of entirely different purpose and character was constructed on the western edge of Elmira. The New York State Reformatory, dedicated to the "task of human salvage," stood upon sixteen acres on a knoll with a grand view of the city. Thirty prisoners were transferred in from the Auburn prison in July of that year. By August there were fifty men in the Elmira reformatory. Touted as the first reformatory in the world, the institution was designed for first-time offenders and dedicated to rehabilitation through education and vocational training. It was also the first institution to accept prisoners with indefinite sentences. Good behavior, as judged solely by prison officials, brought quick release. According to the first warden, Zebulon P. Brockway, bad behavior was "admonished with certitude and celerity."

By the beginning of the twentieth century, "The Hill," as the reformatory was known locally, had become a familiar presence and Elmira was viewed by residents and outsiders generally as an admirable mixture of industrial factories and fertile farmland. A brochure describes the city then as a "thrifty and thriving community" with a "most enterprising class of citizens . . . financially of the staunchest character."

As the big bus spins into the bus terminal on Church Street, Kevin spots Wanda standing beside her car at the end of the parking lot. Beside her is the hulking figure of Marlene. What a welcoming committee, Kevin thinks. Then he dismisses the thought. Shit, if making this kind of move was easy, everybody would do it. Kevin schools himself to follow the plan, be cool, and stay in the background. He reminds himself not to make commitments or connections, just the way he did each time he moved to a new prison.

As he rides downtown, even in the icy weather, Kevin takes note of an unusual sight. Mixed-race couples and their children abound. The interracial families stand together bundled up on the porches of the shambling Victorian homes and in clusters on the street corners. "I never seen so many half-breed motherfucking kids in my life. Fucking Zebratown," he says to Wanda and Marlene.

In the front seat, the women burst out laughing. "Now you got it."

Kevin knows that there are some ex-inmates with white girlfriends in the area and he has heard that some family members of prisoners have found the city inviting and have relocated here, but this is unbelievable.

The idea of race in New York City was simple. The so-called melting pot of the country was really about separation. The majority of the black people lived in the famous ghettos of Harlem and Bedford-Stuyvesant and other poor neighborhoods throughout the city. Black professionals and well-to-do white people lived in a few mixed neighborhoods throughout the city but predominately in Manhattan. The artists and young professionals of all races gravitated toward hip neighborhoods in Brooklyn like Park Slope and Williamsburg.

White people were infiltrating the historically black neighborhoods, and light-haired couples dragged laundry carts up the steps on Bedford-Stuyvesant brownstones where twenty years before a white person who wasn't a cop or landlord or social worker was as rare as a bluebird. But Kevin had been in jail during these new developments. And when he returned to Brownsville, with its wall-to-wall projects, there was no hint of the gentrification that was going on a few blocks away and certainly no race blending. This Elmira mixture is simply baffling.

The interracial phenomenon both pleases and challenges him. He loves white girls, always has. It isn't that Kevin has anything against *being* black. He is about as comfortable as a black man can be in his skin in this country in this day and age. Part of the reason for his comfort is that there is no ambiguity about his identity and his position.

Over the years, he has even used his skin color to his advantage, especially in Brownsville and in prison, where for many dark skin is a sign of toughness. It makes some kind of twisted sense. The blacker you are, the lower you are; the lower you are on the totem pole, the less you have to lose. In prison, having nothing to lose is one of the only valuable cards an inmate can hold.

Kevin is good with all that. But there is something else. It has just been clear to him from an early age that long soft hair and blue eyes, which he associates with a sweet attitude, are to be desired in a woman.

He has listened to his light-skinned mother and just about everybody else in Brownsville extol narrow noses and straight hair. Despite his apparent pride in his own heritage and appearance, this reflexive appreciation for Caucasian features has quietly but surely lodged in Kevin's psyche.

As he rolls through the northeast side of town, Kevin studies the neighborhood. Most black families live here, as they have for 150 years, in a neighborhood once known as Slabtown, after the wide plank lumber used in home construction.

Kevin knows none of this but he does know that something is different. There seems to be a prevailing attitude toward race that he can't fathom. As he rides through, looking at the inhabitants of Zebratown, Kevin is suddenly comforted by a familiar sight. There are several areas of attached one-story homes with no porches, fences, or trees. The areas in front of the structures where grass should be are beaten bare. A twisted tricycle lies on its side near the front door of one building. Some windows are curtainless. Parking lots at the rear of the houses hold several rusty cars. One sits on its rims. It all spells "housing project." As unlikely as it seems, Kevin is buoyed by the thought that he will have somewhere to hang, to grab a taste of home.

He rides by another housing development, this one boarded up, closed tight. The sign is long gone but this place is the Jones Court project, built in 1963 and closed in 1988, named for John W. Jones, a former slave who became a leading citizen in Elmira after the Civil War. Jones was born into bondage in Loudon County, Virginia, in 1817. The young man fled Virginia with five other slaves in 1844. The story goes that the group reached South Creek in Bradford County, Pennsylvania, a few miles south of Elmira, and Jones and his companions crawled into a haystack at a farm owned by a white man named Nathaniel Smith. Smith and his wife fed the fugitives for a week.

The group arrived in Elmira on July 5, 1844. John W. Jones had $1.46 in his pocket and reportedly earned fifty cents that day chopping wood. In Elmira, Jones learned to read and write and was eventually appointed sexton of the first Baptist church and assistant sexton of the Baptist church cemetery and the Second Street cemetery. When the three thousand southern prisoners of war died of systematic starvation and wanton neglect in the Elmira death camp in 1864, it was the dutiful John Jones who transported the bodies from the camp, methodically recorded their identities, and laid the wasted cadavers in neat pine boxes to rest in plots along the river.

Jones, paid $2.50 for each burial, was able to purchase a spacious yellow house that he used in his capacity as an agent in the Underground Railroad. During the nine years of Jones's active operation, some eight hundred fugitive slaves passed through Jones's house in Elmira and none was ever captured.

Most escaping slaves moving from Philadelphia northwest followed the Susquehanna River up from the Chesapeake Bay to Williamsport and then, moving under the cover of night, through the hills and down the valley along South Creek and into Elmira. There, the parties of six or seven would seek out John W. Jones. During one period there were as many as thirty former slaves concealed in the yellow house on one night. Most often, the slaves were without funds of any kind when they arrived and money had to be raised. The numbers of brown-skinned people moving through the town and the

efforts to solicit funds made Jones's activities obvious. But though many suspected his role in helping the escaped slaves, Jones was not interfered with in
any way.

Passengers on the Underground Railroad were sent from Elmira either
north to Ithaca or west to Bath along Honeoye Lake's West Lake Road,
up through Lima and Brighton to Rochester. Then to the shores of Lake
Ontario and on to Canada.

Some of the escaped slaves decided to remain in Elmira. By the time of
the Civil War there were sixty "Negro" households in the city. Five of the local
former slaves walked all the way to Boston to join the Fifty-fourth Massachu-
setts volunteer infantry, the first regiment of blacks authorized by the War
Department. By 1868, there were 179 black households in Elmira. They were
masons and teamsters and dominated the barbering trade.

Still, this was no racial utopia. In 1925, the Ku Klux Klan held their
annual state convention at the Chemung County Fairgrounds in Elmira,
calling themselves "militant protestant forces of the State of New York." Two
thousand to three thousand Klansmen strutted in billowing white robes in
downtown Elmira.

Kevin spots another mixed couple, a thin black man and his plump white
woman trailed by a child. They are walking somewhere. It looks as if they
don't have a car. These are poor people, Kevin decides. Wanda waves, pulls
over, and introduces Kevin, who reaches out from the car and touches the
child. As they pull away, Kevin thinks back to the times he stood looking
out of the prison window over the city of Elmira, envisioning his release and
relocation, planning to be a pioneer. So what if when he arrived he found that
other black men had gotten here first? He may not be the pioneer but he sure
as hell is cut out for this town and it certainly seems as if it is made for him.

Trailing Wanda and Marlene, Kevin steps inside the Manos Diner on
College Avenue. Inside the front door is a small lobby with a counter covered
with free newspapers for the patrons. The people at the counter and in the
booths could easily be from Tennessee or Texas. The men wear jeans and
oversized western belt buckles. Some even have on cowboy boots. The wait-
resses are clad in baby blue.

"This place looks like Mayberry," Kevin tells Wanda as they find their way to a booth. Kevin takes note of the waitress, a short girl with a snub nose whom he had seen earlier with a black man and a mixed kid. With an almost infallible memory for faces and names, Kevin believes he recognizes the guy from a short visit to Binghamton.

"Ready to order?"

"Ain't I seen you with a dude named Petey, from BK?"

"Yeah."

"That your baby with him, I seen you with?"

"He's a asshole. Stone-ignorant asshole."

Kevin snickers as he reads through the menu.

"I don't mean my kid. Petey, not the kid."

"I know. What he do?"

"Nothin' at all. He's just a big asshole. An' I really don't want to talk about him. Can I get you something?"

"Yeah, pancakes. No sausage or bacon. Just the pancakes. Sorry to hear."

"About what?"

"Oh, put the eggs fried over easy on the top of the pancakes. About him bein' an asshole."

"Yeah, what you drinkin'?"

"What's your name?"

"Emily."

Then Kevin spots a man with a neck as thick as a fire hydrant at the cash register and stands immediately. The bruisers make eye contact and move toward each other with arms outstretched. They hug long and hard.

The two men look so much alike—short, thick-limbed—that they could be brothers. They are also dressed similarly, in fantastically oversized white T-shirts and baseball caps. But they aren't long-lost siblings or fraternity members or teammates from some championship football squad from another decade or even soldiers who have gone through basic training and walked through minefields together.

They have gone to battle side by side, shed blood together, but they have done it in the green uniforms of the New York State Department of Correctional Services.

"Yo, Kev. I thought it was you. The fuck you doin' here? I din' know you was on the street, son."

"I thought you was in too. It's all good."

Each man knows that the specifics of his release are too complicated and sensitive to be dealt with in passing. All that is important is that they are both out in the world and that neither has a stain on his reputation resulting from cooperation with the state. Neither has bought his freedom. They are both thugs in good standing. The reunion is heartfelt. With scant patriotism, no religion to speak of, no civil rights movement to dedicate themselves to, nothing to believe in but fame and money, these men have a commanding urge to believe in each other. Kevin's double, holding a handful of bills as his change, steps back and studies Kevin for a long moment.

"Attica, son, '96."

"No doubt."

"Killa Kev. You was wildin', come on the yard talkin' about, 'Man up. I'm takin' the guard.'"

"I'll never forget that shit. Or them pussy-ass motherfuckers who backed down."

The man edges toward the door but never takes his eyes off Kevin Davis. The two men glow with the memory of a job well done.

THE BING

||||||||||||||||||||||||||||||||||||||||||||||||||||||||||||||||||||||||||||||||||||||||||||||||||||||||||

May 2002. Kevin Davis is still trying to gain a foothold in Elmira, taking the Trailways bus from the Port Authority in Manhattan four hours north and west. At times, the bus cruises alongside Department of Correctional Services buses and Kevin strains to see inside, to see if he recognizes anyone. Other times he chats with the passengers.

On one trip he meets a stripper from Binghamton on her way to New York. She confirms what he had heard about a contingent of Brooklyn natives, she thinks maybe even from Brownsville, living in "Bing," Binghamton, just an hour east of Elmira. So on his next trip Kevin hops off the bus in Binghamton and looks up his friend Randolph.

After several stints in prison and a couple of bouts with drugs, Randolph, who had learned to cut hair in jail, managed to relocate to Binghamton and open his own barbershop serving the substantial black community there. Delighted to find Randolph in his place of business, scissors in hand, Kevin is all smiles and hugs as he enters. The same social skills that made Kevin popular in Brownsville and powerful in prison are evident now. He remembers names, makes rapid-fire connections of who is related to whom and in what way, and is quick to laugh.

As he greets Randolph's friends and relatives, Kevin fingers a roll of hundred-dollar bills in his pocket. In 2001, six months after his release, a prison friend had contacted Kevin, asking him to pick up and hold a package. When Kevin received the large manila envelope, he hefted it in his hand and guessed that it contained money. Loyal to his trust, Kevin secreted the package in various locations, in attics, behind bookcases, and wedged behind broken plasterboard. He watched and checked and fretted over the package compulsively until the man who gave it to him was released from prison in summer 2002. Kevin handed the well-worn envelope over to an intermediary. Two days later, a man he had never met before handed him $5,000 in one-hundred-dollar bills, delivering the message, "The man says thanks."

When you have no bills to pay, $5,000 can go a long way. Can things be any better? Kevin marvels, as he leans back in a soft chair in Randolph's barbershop, a mini-Brooklyn an hour away from his country paradise. Kevin decides this is just like the Rockaway Avenue barbershop but out in the country. A grizzled man stumbles in from the cold with a bagful of bootleg jeans and tube socks, just as might happen in Brownsville. As the clientele, those waiting for haircuts and those just on hand to socialize, rummage through the traveling salesman's wares, Randolph steps outside for a cigarette. Kevin hasn't seen Randolph in years, but a minute later, as he climbs into the barber's chair for a shape-up, he can tell that something is amiss.

"Randolph, you all right?"

"No doubt. No doubt."

Kevin can smell cigarettes on Randolph's breath. The barber is fidgeting, fumbling with the electric razor, going to the counter to study his reflection in the mirror, his face just inches from the glass, returning without cutting any hair.

"I'm holdin' it down, Kev. Holdin' it down," Randolph says as he finally begins the task of trimming Kevin's hair. But the whites of Randolph's eyes are rosy from stress or drink or worse. Observing the scene, a stranger would think that Kevin Davis, relaxing in the barber's chair, smiling and nodding to people calling his name and meeting his outstretched fist with theirs, is the owner of the establishment, the one who had already gained a foothold out of Brownsville, and that Randolph was the man without a home.

Randolph had always been conflicted, while Kevin Davis had been whole, firmly encamped on one side of every divide. Kevin was on one side of the racial line and one side of the law. Despite stories of his fearless great-grandmother, there was no outward physical evidence of Cherokee blood coursing through his veins, certainly no visible whiteness from the seed of a South Carolina slaver. And, except for brief periods when he was behaving himself so he could get trailer privileges, he had always been a straight-up outlaw. Life could be hard for Kevin Davis but up to this point it had never been very complicated.

Randolph was different. He had shrunk from the combat of the ghetto, resisted the personal battles. Spent most of his time walking his dog and listening to music. Randolph didn't even like to argue. Eventually, though, both Randolph and his younger brother had slipped into the rhythms of the drug trade.

Unlike his brother, who had been murdered, shot down on the street by a Brownsville thug named Eightball, Randolph had lived through Brownsville, done his time in prison, wrenched himself away from the old neighborhood, and gained a niche in Binghamton. Life should have been good. But it wasn't. As he dropped his children off at school and headed to his barbershop every day, Randolph wondered why he had lived and his younger brother had perished. Was he any more deserving? Was there anything he could have done that would have saved his brother?

He had known that the trigger-happy Eightball was gunning for his brother and had done nothing about it.

Maybe Randolph had missed his opportunity to stand up for his brother in 1992 but Eightball was still alive, had been sentenced to eight to fifteen years for manslaughter in another killing and moved through the prison system much the way Kevin Davis had. While Randolph was in prison, he had done his time quietly, never hatching a plan of revenge.

When inmates mentioned to him that Eightball, who everybody knew had killed his brother, was in this prison or that, Randolph just shook his head and looked away. He never plotted with other inmates, offering to do an inmate with a life sentence a favor, almost any favor, if he would slit Eightball's throat. No, he had merely shaken his head sadly and passively. The message from Randolph had always been, *That was in another life.*

But it wasn't in another life. Randolph carried the burden of loss and guilt with him, even after he came out of prison, started a family, moved to Binghamton, saved some money, and established his own barbershop. He had realized his modest dream but he had never laid down the weight.

"Yo, Kev," Randolph says, after a few moments of silent cutting. "You know Eightball's back in The Ville?"

"Na, I din't know that."

"Snake is out."

"Word?"

"You know what he's sayin'?"

"Nah, I ain't heard nothin' about Eightball in years. I heard he was in Collins before I got there. That's all I heard."

"Grimy motherfucker is talking about he's . . ."

"What?"

"Fuckin' Kev, you know I love you, Kev. You was always straight up. A good dude. You was real. But that . . ."

Randolph is shuddering with anger. He isn't worrying about how loud he speaks now, isn't concerned anymore about who hears him.

Kevin understands. Once he had let an insult go and suffered for months until he caught up with the guy who had disrespected him and beat the guy senseless. Kevin knew the emotional cost of inaction. He had vowed not to put himself into that state again, and he never had. He did not want to be like Randolph, who looks now as if he were about to shatter into pieces.

"Kev." Randolph is gripping Kevin's shoulder with his left hand now, gesturing with the clipper, punching it in the air. "That fuckin' snake walkin' around Brownsville talkin' 'bout he's on zero tolerance. First person looks at him funny, he's gonna clap."

The very idea of Eightball making proclamations is driving Randolph out of his mind. It would have been one thing if Eightball had come out of prison quietly, ready to lead another life, the way Randolph himself had. Maybe, just maybe, then Randolph could have let it go.

"The fuck does he think, I'm a fuckin' faggot? Thinks I won't do nothin'. Just sit back and listen to him talk shit after he killed my brother. Who does he think I am?"

A bell over the front door jangles and Randolph's daughters charge into the barbershop, each holding a piece of brown drawing paper aloft. Red and green crayon streaks cross one paper. Stick figures dance under a happy yellow sun on the other.

"Daddy, look."

On the bus ride back down to New York City, Kevin sits next to another stripper, an Asian girl from Rochester who is traveling to New York, to begin a new life. She is tiny, just the right height for Kevin. She will probably find a job right away and she would be easy to control, Kevin thinks. He could just lay up in the hotel room in Manhattan while she hustled up a couple of hundred a day. Kind of like being a pimp. The way the girl is looking at him, gazing for long moments into his eyes, it is almost as if she is asking him to step up and be her man. When they get down to New York, Kevin spends the afternoon with her, hefting her two bags while she searches for a hotel. But this is not for him. He hasn't been out of jail six months, and he is going to settle for being a half-assed pimp with some stripper bringing home the money?

As he rides the subway out to Mill Basin where he is still staying with his mother when he is in New York, Kevin curses himself for not paying more attention to the local girls who came to visit the inmates while he was in the Elmira prison. The only contact he had made was Wanda. She is driving him up a wall. It was bad enough when he would visit putting up with her and her son. But now Wanda's mother, Libby, no older than forty-five, has had a stroke. She is laid out on a hospital bed in the living room, breathing through tubes and begging Kevin to make the trip to the nearby store and buy her cigarettes.

A month later Eightball has already been locked up again for homicide. Cousin Ben has been captured by the police and is facing life for one of his murders. In his trips up and back from Brownsville to Elmira, Kevin notices that the two regions are like two wheels that move at different speeds. The Elmira wheel rotates slowly. He can leave it for a couple of weeks and come back and it is as if nothing at all has changed. He can almost interrupt an Elmira conversation, go down to New York, and pick it up when he gets back. Meanwhile, the Brownsville wheel spins out of control. One day his friend who owns the barbershop on Rockaway is telling him about a mutual acquaintance of theirs who has been killed, and on the next visit the owner of the shop is dead himself, victim of a homicide. So it is no surprise Eightball lasted only a month in the world. He is back in prison where he belongs and Randolph is feeling quite a bit better.

CHERYL

||||||||||||||||||||||||||||||||||||||||||||||||||||||||||||||||||||||||||||||||||||||||||||||||||||||

On his next visit to the barbershop, Kevin glances in the mirror as Randolph nudges him on the shoulder and cocks his head. Behind Kevin stands a middle-aged white woman in a white spaghetti-strap T-shirt and tight jeans. Her weathered face is scored with lines, some fine, others, high on her forehead, deep and furrowed.

"That's a nurse," Randolph whispers. "Makes crazy money and she loves black dudes." Kevin is about to ask Randolph why that is news. It seems as if all the girls in this area like black dudes. Then the nurse turns around and Kevin understands the reverence in Randolph's voice. This middle-aged woman has nothing less than the perfect ass. Kevin rises up in the seat of the red leather barber's chair like a jockey in a stretch run as he studies the image in the mirror.

"Goddamn!"

Cheryl turns around and smiles. In fact, she has come into the barbershop today specifically to meet Kevin Davis. Outside in the parking lot, Kevin stands beside Cheryl's SUV, talking, flirting. It feels so strange to be flirting with a seriously old-looking woman, but Cheryl makes it easier by making sure to pirouette every few moments so she can check on her brood of children in the car and so Kevin can marvel at her miraculous figure. Cheryl has three children ages six to sixteen, and all three are in the backseat. All three are biracial, offspring of black men Cheryl has lived with over the years. They are sparkling clean, well dressed, and soft-spoken, Kevin notices, as he rides with the family over to Cheryl's spacious ranch home in a subdivision on the outskirts of Binghamton.

It is clear from the very beginning that Cheryl has a taste for rough-necks, black ones. She has even gone with ex-cons before. Two of her children are from the same former inmate. It is also clear that without meeting him, Cheryl had measured Kevin Davis for the position as her next live-in boyfriend.

Kevin is chirping. There had to be a better way to get a start in the area than doing hard time with that knucklehead Wanda. Maybe this is it. Cheryl's house is on a tree-lined street at the base of a range of steep hills. Every street, it seems to Kevin, ends at the foot of a mountain. When he peers out the kitchen window Kevin can tell right away that the neighbors are factory workers and corrections officers working a variety of shifts. Stone rednecks. But that doesn't matter at first. Cheryl's home is a tightly run operation, with all the kids doing their chores. Kevin's task, to be performed several times daily, is to have sex with Cheryl.

It isn't bad at first, a merry experience. But to Cheryl, sex is no joke.

In less than two weeks, Kevin begins to tire of the damp and rumpled sheets, the chafed skin. It is more than weariness or boredom that irks Kevin. It is a matter of control. In bed and out, Cheryl is the shot caller. While she is at work, Kevin has nothing to do but watch television and stare out the window at the high clouds and the locals driving past in their pickup trucks. He has no car, of course, and there is no way he is going to take a stroll in a neighborhood full of COs, who he is sure keep shotguns close by. Kevin calls a friend in Brownsville and tells him he has been kidnapped by a nymphomaniac and is being held hostage in a camp full of Ku Klux Klan members.

When Cheryl arrives home one afternoon, Kevin glides clear of the bedroom.

"Yo, lemme borrow the car for a minute."

Cheryl has seen that look before and isn't about to let Kevin slip away.

"Why?"

"I dunno, just drive. I wanna go down to Elmira to the Y and work out. I *am* a boxer, you know."

Cheryl looks Kevin up and down. The next day she has a local handyman put a chin-up bar up in her backyard so Kevin will have no reason to leave.

Kevin does manage to get away on what he calls "business" to New York. Cheryl and the kids stand at attention in the parking lot waving as the bus pulls out of the depot. It is such a strange world, Kevin muses. He is lying to Francesca, whom he still sees occasionally, telling her he is traveling to Elmira on business, and then he is lying to Cheryl about going back to New York on business. What he really needs is some actual business. He also needs a friend. As much as Kevin prides himself on being able to leave prison behind, he misses the stories, the laughter. Even more than that, stuck in his remote love den, he misses being admired by other men.

On one of his trips back to New York, he passes through Brownsville and crosses paths with Main, short for Maniac, an eighteen-year-old who as a boy looked up to Kevin, followed him around before Kevin went to prison. Main had been the first person Kevin recognized in Brownsville when he got out of prison. He still can't get over how tall the boy has gotten. As Main stands fidgeting on Blake Avenue, Kevin recognizes the symptoms immediately. The five-foot-eleven youth is unkempt and unhealthy, coughing and scratching himself as if he hasn't had a shower in a week. Besides his physical condition, the kid looks mentally exhausted and depressed, hangdog. Kevin guesses that Main is homeless, probably on the run.

Main had been a small-time dealer and a minor player in the drug game but he had hooked up with a few stickup men and pulled off some robberies of other drug dealers. In the four-man crew's latest "jux," a street term for robbery, they had invaded a room at a motel near the Belt Parkway. The idea was to interrupt a drug deal and make off with the cash and the product. But the robbery had gone wrong and now both the victims, a recently constituted band of dope peddlers out of the Cypress Hills Houses, and the detectives from the Seventy-third Precinct were steps behind Main, who had spent most of the last three weeks sleeping in stairways and abandoned apartments. One of the few things Main can count on is some food and a few hours' rest in the homes of stupid young girls, when their mothers aren't home, teenagers deaf to the warnings and mesmerized by his sapodilla-brown skin and soft hair.

Still, it is a matter of time before he takes a lengthy jail sentence or more likely a bullet to end his short stay on the planet. In Main, Kevin sees himself.

Just as with Kevin in the early nineties, Main's cases have begun to mount, which means the stakes for every new arrest are higher, and the beefs have begun to proliferate so it takes an encyclopedic memory to keep track of all the players, all the permutations that can trigger disaster. Kevin can see that Main does not have long to live.

Looking for a protégé and a partner in his Elmira project and anxious to add a page to his Good Samaritan résumé, Kevin proposes a solution.

"Come up to Elmira. The white chicks will love you up there. You can lay up with one for a while and if you don't like her you can switch up. There's mad bitches up there, you heard. Mad bitches."

"Umm. Naah. I'm cool."

Main believes that in all but a few rare situations it is best to be passive, detached, unconcerned, uncommitted, and unresolved. To be cool.

Not Kevin. He knows that thought, planning, and commitment are the keys to safety and success. He is willing to forgive his young friend's posture because he has seen it so many times, has benefited from the advantage that it has given him over the legions of cool slackers. He has gotten the drop on so many guys who believe thinking is for the white man. He can forgive Main because he understands.

"Nah, you ain't gonna be cool. You on a danger trip. You gonna be dead up."

Main's story is familiar. The final chapter, as yet unwritten, is so standard it can be recited by almost anyone but Main.

Kevin knows it won't be hard to capture Main's imagination. Young men are built to follow orders. Kevin will just substitute his word and his energy for those of the guys who have been leading Main toward death's door.

"I'm telling you. When I first got to Bing I was in Randolph's barbershop. You know Randolph's niece Reshawn. And this white chick is lookin' at me in the mirror and she is like a little bit old-lookin', then she turns around she has an ass like you wouldn't believe. Word up. And she was all up in my shit. Smilin'. Bing bam, Randolph tells me she likes black dudes. She has like three kids by different black dudes and, boom, next thing you know I'm livin' in her house up in the woods. Big house. She's a nurse, drives a Navigator, and all that shit."

Main is suddenly smiling broadly now and nodding his head. Being a kept man is even more appealing to him than being a stickup man.

"No, no, listen, listen. You don't understand. This shit is real. I swear to God. This bitch's body is kickin'."

Kevin's eyes are wide and his voice rises and almost squeaks as he relives the wonder of finding himself in a kind of heaven on earth.

"Word?"

"Word! Word! She tells me. This bitch tells me after I fucked her the first night. She tells me, 'I got to go to work. I want you butt-naked an' in the bed when I get home.' All she wanted to do was fuck. She fucked for hours. She fucked so much she hurted my dick. She wore me out so much I started getting sick."

Kevin is so carried away with his amazing story that he forgets his intention and plunges forward, telling of the downward arc to his relationship with the nurse. Kevin's voice is husky and intense as he describes his dream turned nightmare, relives the experience of being trapped and beaten down by sex.

"Main, Main listen. Listen to this here. The bitch fucked so much . . ." Kevin hesitates to give weight to the amazing development that followed. "She fucked so much that, that . . . *I started to hate fuckin'!*"

Main cannot comprehend these final words. Kevin need not have worried about turning Main against the Elmira and Binghamton area with the grim conclusion to his story. All the empty-headed Main can hear is a story of a white woman with a great ass and big house who loves to fuck.

Nothing Kevin says or does can change Main's mind now. He is sold on Elmira, smiling and nodding his head. Kevin does not tell Main every detail of how he was trapped, a sex slave, surrounded by racists. How he had bad dreams. How he was afraid that one word or phone call from the nurse and the police would bust him as a thief or a rapist and there would be nothing he could do about it. Kevin does tell how he had to sneak out of the house in the afternoon when the nurse was at work and arrange for her to bring his clothing to a parking lot, where she wept as he told her that she should find another pastime besides constant day-in-and-day-out, hour-and-hour-on-end sex.

"That's what you get for fuckin' so much," Kevin tells Main he told the nurse. Truth be told, he had just kissed the nurse on her cheek and moved on with his life. Nothing of the sad ending to the relationship, nothing of what

Kevin had said for the final ten minutes of his story, had made any impression on Main whatsoever. After the opening pitch, Main just knew that Elmira was the place for a worn-out kid from Brownsville.

The detectives in the Seventy-third Precinct soon note Main's absence. They don't care that he robbed the Cypress Hills crew, who they were sure would soon track him down, shoot him, and fling his corpse out into the long weeds on Liberty Avenue. What the detectives are concerned about is their carefully monitored yearly precinct homicide total. If they can just stay under last year's total, they might just get that Unit Citation everybody in the squad has been talking about. They just don't want Main to die on their turf. Before he leaves town they are determined to stick an old robbery case on him and get him off the streets. Who cares if he gets killed in prison?

THIRD CIRCLE OF HELL

||||||||||||||||||||||||||||||||||||||||||||||||||||||||||||||||||||||||||||||||||||||||||||||||||||

B ut Kevin himself still has no acceptable place to stay in Elmira. He has no job. He has heard that Kennedy Valve, a sprawling cast-iron foundry in Elmira, and a major manufacturer of fire hydrants and water valves, is hiring. The work conditions at Kennedy, which has been a fixture in Elmira since 1907, have always been steam-room hot and dangerous, legendarily hellish.

As Kevin Davis sits on a plastic chair in the outer room of the Workforce Development Career Center on Baldwin Street, filling out an application for a job at Kennedy, he doesn't understand how hazardous work at the plant really is. Labor in the foundry was always difficult, but after 1988, when the company was purchased by McWane, Inc., in Birmingham, Alabama, conditions at Kennedy got much, much worse. Kevin has smiled at bumper stickers he has seen around town, PRAY FOR ME. I WORK AT KENNEDY VALVE, chuckled at rumors that a couple of men a year die in the plant and that bones had recently been discovered of a man who had fallen into a chemical vat many years before.

What he doesn't know is that the ghoulish whisperings are not far from the truth. Naphtali Hoffman, a professor of urban economics at Elmira College, calls the working conditions at Kennedy after the McWane takeover "the third circle of hell."

In June 2002 as Kevin writes his name and personal information on the short application form for the Kennedy Valve job, the *New York Times* is researching a series of lengthy articles on conditions at the Elmira plant and a handful of other foundries across the country run by McWane, Inc. The title of the article about Kennedy Valve published in January 2003 is "Deaths on the Job, Slaps on the Wrist."

The piece describes how federal and state agencies have leveled heavy fines against McWane for violating a startling range of environmental and safety regulations in the past decade. There have been thousands of burnings, maimings, and injuries at McWane foundries across the country and nine workers have been killed on the job. On January 13, 1995, inside the Kennedy Valve plant Frank Wagner was monitoring the control panel on the door of an oven illegally retrofitted to incinerate hundreds of gallons of old industrial paint. The district attorneys who prepared the case against McWane and Kennedy Valve noted in a memorandum that "even a child knows you don't burn paint in an oven." But documents show that Wagner had been ordered by supervisors to do exactly that.

When the oven exploded, he was crushed between the door of the oven and a pillar.

According to the *New York Times*, state prosecution of the case was thwarted by political pressure on then–New York State Attorney General Dennis Vacco. In a "position paper" delivered by McWane to Vacco, the company insisted that an indictment in the case would contradict Vacco's "business friendly policy" and warned of a possible closure of the plant and the loss of 320 jobs.

Vacco delayed prosecution so long, federal prosecutors stepped in. Ultimately, Vacco structured a plea that allowed McWane to deny all responsibility for Wagner's death, plead guilty to illegally possessing hazardous waste, and pay $500,000 in fines.

Even if Davis had known the threat to life and limb the Kennedy job represents, as he passes his application over the counter at the Workforce Development Career Center, he doesn't have much choice. The GE foundry on College Avenue closed its doors in the 1980s. The other two large factories in the area, American LaFrance and Ward LaFrance, which built fire engines less than a mile from the Elmira prison, both shut down over a decade ago. Corning, Inc., another large employer in the region, uses mostly skilled and semiskilled labor.

There isn't really anywhere else to go. Besides, Kennedy Valve is paying twenty dollars an hour, twice as much as Kevin has ever made, they provide benefits, and they hire ex-offenders. Further, Kevin believes the hard, dangerous work will provide the structure and some of the drama that he has been missing after prison.

Another obstacle to employment even at a place like Kennedy is Kevin's résumé. He lists his occupation as "Professional Boxer" for 1991–1993, the years during which he had actually been a professional drug dealer. The next listing is "1993–2001—Attica Correctional Facility Maintenance, Porter, Welder, Electric Trades." The only other entry is for assembly at the Visual Graphic Systems job in New York City, where his cousin Ben had gotten him fired. It won't be easy to find a job.

Dream Girl

|||||||||||||||||||||||||||||||||||||||||||||||||||||||||||||||||||||||||||||||||||||||||||||||||||||||||||||||||

Karen Tanski is changing. Since she graduated from the Elmira Business Institute, sometime in those snow-blasted winter months and the hard heat of the Elmira summers she lost some of her forward momentum. Her waitress friends chatted on about out-of-work boyfriends and marijuana busts and getting piss-ass drunk. They shifted to the black guys in town, who at least had some style. The black men talked a lot of shit and cheated like mad but they were tougher, more worldly; some were even from New York. If you couldn't live in the big time, Karen's friends figured, at least a piece of the big time could come to you. The black guys were selling more than weed, carrying guns. Even that wasn't so bad. At least there was some drama.

Karen had hustled through business school, but when she graduated and the doors of the work world were supposed to spring open, they never did. There was a job at a small auto racetrack outside of Elmira. With her Elmira Business Institute training in accounting, she was put in charge of the payroll. The books were a mess, with all kinds of sloppy notations and confusing shortcuts. The boss was a disorganized visionary who pushed more and more work her way. The employees, used to getting away for so long with scams, were peeved at the new regime and shunned Karen. She sat in her cluttered office and ate her lunch alone. Her tiny paycheck was gone the moment she looked at it.

This was no fun, she decided, and certainly there was no future. So she showed up late a few times, got laid off, and started to collect unemployment checks. It was so much easier being home. Karen slipped into the routine of sleeping late so easily. Betsy had always worked hard, but where had that gotten her? It seemed to Karen that Betsy was better off now with her disability check. Instead of working herself to death, at least Betsy could ride her bike around Elmira and watch television.

Karen simply had no family history of initiative or success she could draw on when things got tough in the working world, no inherited alarm that would jangle her awake as she dozed her mornings away. Then one evening at dusk Karen was driving down Lake Street, at the spot where Lake converges with Oak Street, and some man driving home from a local happy hour sideswiped her, ran her off the road into a ditch. Karen didn't feel the pain in her lower back right away but the next day she could hardly move. Tests showed she had a herniated disk, and just like that Karen had a lawsuit. Like so many of her friends she now looked forward to a court settlement instead of a future, the same way some mothers and their children did in Brownsville. She stopped looking for a job and started waiting for "my money."

Meanwhile, the back hurt like hell. It was an injury Karen had to rehab, both to bolster her case and ease the pain, and yet, if her back did miraculously heal, it would substantially reduce her upcoming payoff.

As her court case advanced glacially, the combination of the dead-end jobs Karen was offered by employment services and the pain from her accident put her in an entirely different frame of mind than she had been in when she moved to Elmira and enrolled in business school. In the mornings she shuffled around the apartment, then slouched on the couch. Karen Tanski was getting lazy.

Slowly, she was stepping into the world of those who sleep till ten a.m. and buy handfuls of lottery tickets, gossip, watch television, and keep track of the whereabouts of their man. She was drifting into Zebratown.

At about this time a bit of good news finally arrives for Kevin. He opens a letter from a prison buddy, Bang. The 350-pound drug dealer had been moved to Southport, another maximum-security prison near Elmira, on the south side of the Chemung River, soon after Kevin was released. Kevin had visited Bang in Southport and even put $50 into his commissary account. Kevin had

also told the big guy about opportunities in the city of Elmira and passed on
Marlene's number to him. Miraculously, when Bang was released, he dialed
the number and apparently had not been discouraged by Marlene's appearance. The two were already living together on Brand Street in a blue-collar
neighborhood on the south side of Elmira. Bang's letter to Kevin is penned
with exotic swirls and backward characters, a penmanship inmates use to
make their letters more difficult for prison censors to decipher.

> *Kev, It is so good to taste my freedom. I do not contact the Bloods at Southport.*
> *Due to the fact that they are prone to backbite each other I keep my words very*
> *short to them. So I was among foolish people! Now I trust I'm not. I will tell*
> *you that for some time now in order to ensure my success I've bend overlooking*
> *so much bullxxx it's unbelievable.*
>
> *I told D.C. to get in touch with you because he's people and he handles his*
> *business on the struggle side! By the way there is a white chick who lives on the*
> *first floor of my building here on Brand Street who likes black dudes. My initial*
> *reaction to her present situation is that she does not, I repeat, does not have a*
> *man.*
>
> *I remain strong*
Black Seed

Two weeks later, on his way upstairs to Bang's apartment, Kevin spots a
trim blond woman, smiles his boyish smile, and continues up. A few minutes
later, he wanders down and strikes up a conversation with the woman as she
stands in the grass and gravel driveway beside the entrance. By this time, the
woman has her six-year-old daughter in tow. Kevin's introduction is feather-
soft and shy. There is no way that the woman can guess that the five-foot-four
power pack with the sweet smile is now thirty-three years old.

"Whas up? That your daughter?"

"Are you my daughter?" the woman asks her child.

"Yes, that's my mother, all right. Who are you?"

"My name is KK."

Kevin remains quiet, his head cocked to one side. The woman lifts her
hand to block the sun and get a better look at the man in front of her. He is so
short, so black, and so utterly relaxed and sure of himself that she examines

him more closely. He doesn't appear anything like the black men she has seen in Elmira. He wears a red strap T-shirt and his shoulders and arms loom so large that she has to stifle an exclamation.

The girl breaks the silence. "Where did you get those gigundo muscles?"

"The mall."

"Liar."

"I used to be a boxer."

Yes, the woman is thinking, he looks like a boxer. Every man should look like a boxer.

"Are you a friend of . . . ?"

"Bang? Upstairs? Yeah, and Marlene too."

"Well . . ."

"Nice to meet you too." Kevin leans toward the girl. "S'your name?"

"Jewel, Julia. My mother's name is Karen T-A-N-S-K-I. KK, you wanna come with us? We're going swimming."

"We are not going swimming."

Kevin's stillness is drawing Karen to him. His burnished skin and his wide neck, the sharp clear eyes and the ease. There is no chatter, no idle gossip. Karen has never seen anything like it. This man acts like he is somebody.

For his part, Kevin Davis is controlling himself, paying attention to fundamentals. No woman worth having wants a man who is hungry. To maintain his composure as he gazes into Karen's eyes, he breathes deeply and slowly, the way he did in the ring when he was hurt. This is no slob or misfit. This is a white girl with class. For the briefest moment, Kevin recalls looking out that window in the shower room in I Block. A smile skitters at the edges of his mouth but he stays quiet. No ill-considered remark now. Kevin does a rapid calculation. The encounter has already gone on longer than it would have if the woman was not interested. He is about to consider the initial contact a success and go on his way when Julia pipes up.

"Mom, give KK your telephone number and let's go."

Kevin calls Karen a few days later. The day after that he comes by to visit. He sits, chatting in the living room, studying the apartment. Karen lives with her mother Betsy, Julia, and a cat named Twister. The place is neat enough, besides some dirty sneakers on the floor of the bedroom and the spilled kitty litter in the bathroom. The toilet is making dripping noises but there is food in the refrigerator and the dishes are done.

Kevin keeps the facts of his life as vague and wholesome as he can manage. He is a boxer from Brownsville, Brooklyn, trying to relocate to a more peaceful environment and restart his career. He had been incarcerated over a misunderstanding that turned violent but any attraction that he might have had for the street life has left him.

It isn't what Kevin says that impresses Karen. It is what he doesn't say, along with his manner. He doesn't brag about conquests or abilities. He doesn't relate any elaborate scenarios. One close look at him, Karen now realizes, and almost anyone can see that Kevin Davis is a boxer and probably an ex-con. Basically, Kevin has stated the obvious.

To begin with, Karen decides quickly, he is very attractive, nothing like the pockmarked Bill and the other Elmira lightweights who have drifted in and out of her life in the last few years. He is definitely more masculine than the preening pretty-boy Marine. If this is what prison does to you, Karen thinks as she hands Kevin a glass of ice water, every man should go to prison. He appears so healthy that Karen is reluctant to light a Newport in his presence. She notices the flick of his eyelashes when she does light up, and grinds the cigarette out. She hasn't been talking with Kevin Davis for half an hour and she is already concerned about what he thinks of her, already anxious to please. She smiles involuntarily, catches herself in the smoked mirror behind the television, and forces her mouth closed.

Though Kevin desperately needs a place to live and it seems like Karen has plenty of room, he believes it best to leave his clothes upstairs at Bang's apartment. This could be a great situation, the solution to so many problems. Karen is a bright, articulate "college girl," Kevin calls her, as he tells Bang about his progress with the downstairs neighbor.

Bang is quiet. Maybe he is thinking about his own hard lot in life, about Marlene.

This is too good an opportunity, Kevin decides. There is no sense rushing things. Two days later Kevin does spend the night with Karen and the lovemaking is polite. None of that slam-bang stuff like with Cheryl, the crazy nurse. It isn't the hunger and the feast that went on with Francesca either. But that is a good thing.

Upstairs, Kevin keeps Bang up to date.

"I could get bored. No doubt. I see that much into the future. Broad is so nice I could get bored. But listen up, that boredom could be good. You heard? 'Cause Karen ain't no freak. Some dudes get addicted to that freak shit but sooner or later you gonna have to deal with the downside of that freakishness. Been there, ya heard?"

No, this woman is the real thing, Kevin decides, top-of-the-line. This isn't one of those white Elmira lonely-heart losers the inmates lined up for room and board when they got out. This is a blonde with intelligence and class.

Kevin gathers up his bags the next morning and moves them down to Karen's ground-floor apartment. When he runs into Bang later that evening, the big guy summons him upstairs. "I got to tell you I heard that your broad be messin' with some crazy little Rochester motherfuckers." Then Bang dips underneath the cushion on his living room couch and pulls out a .357 Magnum. "Hold on to this joint for a couple days. Just in case a some stupid shit."

Before he goes to sleep in Karen's bed, Kevin probes Karen's past.

"I wanna get this straight. Tell me now. You not messin' with nobody. I just did seven years. I can't afford any shit."

As he nods off in the wide bed with Karen slumbering beside him, Kevin Davis cannot help but be a tiny bit intimidated. He reminds himself to make sure not to say or do the wrong thing and blow this one. Ask questions. Don't pretend to know shit you don't know. Don't be too nice to her friends and family. That's a sign of weakness right there. Kevin conjures Karen even as she lies beside him. The woman is something more than attractive. Her huge green eyes and fine ivory complexion—wait till Mom sees this shit. This is Elmira paying off.

Kevin isn't quite sure how he came to have this woman, the kind of woman he used to see the few times he traveled to Manhattan or looked through white people's magazines. This is the kind of lady he would have had if he had won a world championship belt in the lightweight division.

He guesses his good fortune has something to do with history, blacks and whites so long kept apart finally getting together. Probably has something to do with rappers too, he thinks. *Niggaz finally comin' into style.* He also feels it has something to do with Elmira, with the area itself.

The economics tell the story. If Karen hadn't been from Fresh Oaks, a backwoods eastern Pennsylvania trailer park, where people were almost as poor and desperate as they are in Brownsville, instead of lying in bed next to him she probably would be riding in some red convertible next to a wavy-haired lawyer.

Kevin had enjoyed top-of-the-line women before. When he was in his teens he was seduced by the ghetto star Shorty Dip, who would later become famous in the hip-hop world, shouted out by disc jockey Wendy Williams on Hot 97. "You drink champagne?" the twenty-something Dip asked the teenager. Kevin had forced himself not to hesitate. He was soon drunk, his lips next to the scar that ran along Dip's otherwise perfectly smooth cheek.

Then there was Francesca. In a world of zero tolerance for disrespect, Francesca had been just as ready as Kevin, even more explosive than he was. Kevin had loved the same things in her that he admired and cultivated in himself. Somewhere, he had known that to square those ingredients would be lethal.

But Amboy Street is behind him now. Kevin Davis has graduated from the ghetto and from the prison wars. He is ready to take the book he read in prison, *The 48 Laws of Power*, use all the wisdom and confidence gained in the ring and in the street and in all those correctional facilities, and take his game to the next level. Karen Tanski would be just perfect at his side.

The second night at Karen's, with his clothes folded neatly in the dresser, his prison uniform hung carefully in the closet, and the .357 shoved under the mattress, Kevin drifts off to sleep.

An hour later there is a tugging noise, then a small thump on the sill of the window in the living room. Kevin draws his knees up against his chest, moves the sheet toward the sleeping Karen, pivots, and rocks himself to his feet. He squats quickly and reaches under the mattress for the big gun. Then he pads silently across the room and ducks into the living room. A wispy young black man is already halfway in the window when Kevin shoves the .357 in his face.

"That's my woman in there," the intruder stutters, jerking his head toward the bedroom, trying mightily to avoid being shot for a burglar. "I'm just comin' in to get my shit. That's all I'm doin'."

"At two o'clock in the morning, motherfucker?" Davis restrains himself from slapping the gun across the man's face. "Walk out the front door and if I ever see you again I'ma air you out."

A wonder of agility in the dark, the man swivel-hips around a chair as he darts across the living room and out the front door.

Karen, sitting on the edge of the bed now, waits until the night visitor is gone to voice an explanation. "Yeah, he had some clothes here but I threw them out. I used to deal with his friend."

Kevin is thoroughly irritated but in another way he is relieved. Karen Tanski's isn't a new world after all. There aren't going to be tea parties and book discussions, college people talking about things he knows nothing about. This isn't going to be about politics and operas and ballet where he will be lost, a lame ex-convict sentenced to silence. No, this isn't a new world at all.

This is gonna be 'bout niggers comin' in the window in the middle of the night.

That is just fine with Kevin Davis. The feeling he had experienced just a few hours earlier when he was making love, the hesitancy, the worry that maybe he really didn't deserve to be in Karen's world, was gone. This clean-cut white girl was just a variation on all the grimy women he had known in the ghetto.

"What you mean is that you was messin' with him and his friend."

Karen's silence confirms his accusation.

"I'm tellin' you that low-life shit is over. You with me, you got to stay away from all that shit. And clean up that kitty litter and get rid of those fuckin' sneakers. They smell."

White girls might look cleaner, Kevin decides, but they undoubtedly have some stink ways. Don't always take care of themselves and come out of the house like they don't care what they look like. Kevin kicks a dingy sneaker across the room as he climbs back into bed.

"This hillbilly shit is over. It's a wrap."

But it isn't. A knock on the door a few days later and a narrow-faced teenager is stammering the message he had been sent to deliver.

"A guy sent me to pick up somethin' that he left here."

"Get the fuck outta here."

"He says it's in the bathroom."

"The bathroom?" Kevin knows every item in the bathroom.

"Yeah, it's in the ceiling."

Goddamn if there aren't twenty packets of crack cocaine above a removable foam square in the ceiling. The boy walks off with the drugs and Davis sits staring at Karen.

"Let's stop the Disney shit right now. You know I got *life behind me!* You understand? *Life behind me!*" Kevin says, using the phrase inmates with two felony convictions use for the possibility that a third could draw a life sentence. "Police come in the house an' find that crack shit, I'm down for body time, twenty-five to life! Case closed, no questions asked. All those years I kept myself alive, just so I could catch life 'cause a dumb white bitch. If you was a dude I'd a lit your ass up already. You ever lie to me again, I'm gonna fuck you up."

Karen watches Kevin's jaw muscles tighten and loosen. His face seems square now, not round anymore. But his voice is the same, low and level except when he said he would be sent to jail for life. She should be frightened, thinking about the terrible mistake she has made letting a muscle-bound ex-convict into her home and bed, thinking about her safety and her daughter's welfare. But she isn't. Karen Tanski is thinking about how Kevin Davis isn't so much dangerous as serious and how nice it is to have a man mean what he says.

Kevin strides outside and stands on the porch. The way he feels, he's no longer lucky to be here with Karen. Now he's just here.

FAMILY

|||||||||||||||||||||||||||||||||||||||||||||||||||||||||||||||||||||||||||||||||||||||||||||||||||||||||||||

Kevin continues to search for work, sending Kennedy Valve so many applications that he receives a letter from the federal government, which is launching an investigation into the hiring practices at the plant. Still nothing. There is no crisis just yet. Kevin wants to make a good impression as a partner and man of the house but without a job he doesn't have the resources to claim such authority. He peels off the hundred-dollar bills he was given eight months before for guarding that envelope and gradually accepts his marginal position as a live-in boyfriend. Meanwhile, the apartment rent is covered by Betsy's disability check.

Just to keep busy, in June Kevin begins mowing people's lawns in the summer, and when winter sweeps into the valley in January he puts on his gloves and gets his daily workout shoveling snow. He gets to know just about everybody in Elmira. Through Wanda, he meets dozens of white girls and their slacker boyfriends, black and white. He spends afternoons hanging in the projects, Hathorn Court and Riverview, kicking it with the hustlers and the would-be players.

From his very first day in town, Kevin Davis is a celebrity in Elmira. Anyone with a connection to the prison system carries confirmation of Kevin's lofty status behind the walls. KK is a "real nigger," they say, and pass it on. Kevin carts his dog-eared copy of *The Ville* around town and produces yellowed newspaper clippings of his handful of pro fights. But it is not the book or his clippings that carry the day. Once again, it is his manner. Just as Kevin had seduced Karen with his understated assurance, so he impresses the population of Elmira.

Winter has almost passed. It is early March 2003. In Binghamton, at Randolph's barbershop Kevin hears of some locals who are launching a clothing business, driving down to New York to buy the latest hip-hop fashions wholesale and selling them out of a storefront in Binghamton. Kevin helps consult on exactly which urban fashions to buy and plunks down $2,000 of his last cash. In a week, he collects his $2,000 back along with $700 profit without doing any work at all. The key to Kevin's successful partnership is his capital. However limited his cash, it is rare in Elmira to have even a few thousand dollars to invest. His other business assets are his good sense and his reputation. There is no way anyone is going to stiff him for his money. In fact, the clothing salesmen spend two afternoons running after Kevin to put his $2,700 in his hand.

Kevin is waving to people and chatting up everyone he meets, black and white. He even befriends the mentally disabled brothers who live in the house next to where he and Karen reside on Brand Street and sit on the porch all day, staring into air. He takes them fishing one time in Betsy's car and now when he steps out of the house the forty-three-year-old Monty rises from his seat waving. Kevin Davis is one of the few people who ever paid any real attention to him.

"KK. KK."

Kevin shuffles to where Monty sits on his chair on the porch.

"Monty, what's going on? How you been?"

"I'm depressed."

"The fuck you depressed about?"

"I think I want to kill myself."

In Kevin Davis's world weakness is repulsive. He is as kind as he can be.

"Kill yourself? I don't want to hear that shit."

"I got no friends."

"You got me. Don't I visit you once in a blue?"

Kevin sits on the sidelines and watches the penny-ante drug trade. Local tough guys, weight men, travel themselves or send their people down to New

York to cop a few ounces of cocaine. Sometimes the transporter will simply mount a bus to the Port Authority in New York, ride the subway up to Washington Heights or Harlem to make a connection, or buy the product off the street. Then he will grab a gypsy cab back to the bus station and ride the Trailways back up to Elmira.

Independent dealers in Elmira purchase the drugs from the weight men, sell it mostly in twenty-dollar bags from a street corner or crack house or through a delivery system, then re-up for more. There aren't any truly organized crews, with strict rules and structure. Men and women peddle the stuff on their own and use the neighborhood alliances to protect themselves and their turf. There are no real gangs either, but there are plenty of guns in Elmira and little reluctance to fire them. Local white methamphetamine addicts burglarize the homes of residents, in particular hunters, who often keep all manner of firearms in their houses. The junkies then gladly trade the valuable weapons to the almost-all-black area dealers for cash or whatever drug they can get. That's how Bang had procured the gun he lent Kevin.

No one has been killed yet but there have been several Wild West shootings, crazy shots lobbed in broad daylight and in front of the police along Lake Street, in the parking lot of the bowling alley, and in Riverview.

The Elmira narcotics investigators P. J. Griffin and Richard Weed are moving up to speed, identifying the players. There is Bushwick, T Money, Lucky, Philly Dog, Just, and Frankie, all with a handful of followers and out-of-town connections. Along with dozens of other small-time dealers there is a newcomer who moves between Elmira and Corning where he lives, selling nickels out of an apartment he shares with a white girl in a middle-class neighborhood. He is tall and slim, with a creamy tone to his brown skin and a sleepy look on his face.

Kevin, meanwhile, remains a healthy distance from the drug trade and the rivalries.

It is mid-April 2003. Life has not altered much here in the past six months; only the background has changed, from the red and orange foliage of tranquil fall to the white of arctic January—and now the hills are stark and colorless. A funnel of wind humps down off the hilltops and slams Brand Street. A standing metal sign is flipped on its back, aiming its HOUSE FOR SALE message at a cloudless sky while garbage can covers spin down the street like tumbleweeds. Spring is more than two months away here, but Julia, seven years old now, is determined to ride her new bicycle. Karen stands hugging herself on the sidewalk as gusts wallop the girl off her bike onto the cement. She comes up rubbing her knees.

"It's too windy, Jewel, come in."

"Nooo, Mommy, nooo."

"You're going to hurt yourself."

"I don't care."

"I'll put the training wheels back on."

Kevin, dressed in the spruce-green trousers and shirt of a New York State prison inmate, appears behind Karen. He wears heavy boots and a green wool cap pulled down over his forehead but no coat.

"You won't put no training wheels back on. I took 'em off for a reason."

Kevin trots to the girl's side and props up her pink and gray bicycle.

Julia is straight-backed and grinning now, perched on the white plastic seat, the tailwind lashing her blond hair. Kevin grips the handlebar with one hand and the back of the seat with the other and begins to run, head up. Julia shrieks as she gains speed, sailing down Brand Street. Kevin lifts his hands off the bike just as the wind rears, changes direction, and punches the little girl against the curb, where she lies, knees folded to her chest. Kevin hunches over the child, framing her face with his hands as Karen quick-steps toward the accident. But before she can reach the spot, Julia and Kevin are up and racing down Brand Street once more. This time the wind backs down, lying still somewhere up on the ridge, as Julia Tanski pumps her pedals and hurtles ahead screaming in joy. Kevin Davis, shoulders raised high, sprints alongside, hands ready to stop a fall. As the block ends, he grabs the seat and slows the bike till it stops. The sight of Kevin Davis marching back up the street, the bicycle carried so easily in one hand and Julia's hand held by the other, brings tears to Karen's eyes.

The home life on Brand Street is better than one would have reason to hope. Kevin is so natural and easy with Julia that the girl takes to him in a way that she never had done with her father. Karen comes from a world where it isn't really safe to leave lovely young girls with men, men who stare too long at them when they are sober, make comments about how sexy the child is going to be when she gets older, and then who sit too close and touch too long when they are drunk. But Karen notices right away that Kevin Davis is not such a loose individual. If anything, he is too strict. Kevin is interested in the child and alert, listening to Julia's stories and watching her carefully, more carefully at times than Karen. When a rowdy, door-slamming clan with several girls Julia's age moves in next door, Kevin is vigilant.

"Karen, you better watch Julia on that trampoline outside. And I don't want her talking too much with those crackers next door. They talk too much shit and Julia's gonna learn the wrong things. Just tell her to say hi and 'bye.'"

"Kevin, they're just kids. Stay out of their business."

"No, you supposed to be in they business."

The trampoline fills the backyard, so Kevin sets up his weight bench in the front yard next to the driveway. Wearing his state greens, he hoists the heavy bar. There is no spotter as there was in the prison yards, so he goes light on the bench press, grunting through ten reps with 250 pounds. After three sets, he peels off his shirt in the spring sun. Monty, feeling better, hollers from his porch.

"Oooo, Kevin you look like the Hulk. You seen the Hulk movie. I seen the Hulk movie."

Kevin glowers across the yard in mock anger.

"Don't be callin' me no Hulk. The Hulk is white. This is black power you seein' over here, Monty. You spread the word black power in Elmira."

"You're right, Kev. I got it. Black power in Elmira."

"To stay."

But not everybody is so happy with Kevin Davis, his glad-handing and his power-lifting in the front yard. A family of Puerto Ricans lives across the street. Whether from the language barrier or the cultural divide that keeps them out of the loop in Zebratown, they have not yet gotten wind of Kevin's reputation. Several of the teenage boys have been staring at Kevin, grilling him, from across the street. One lad has gone so far as to point and laugh.

Kevin has a long history of fighting Latinos in jail. Despite his alliance with the Puerto Ricans in the war over Capone at Collins, Kevin had always been ready to battle the "Germans," as some black inmates in New York prisons call Latinos because they remind them of the foreign-language-speaking enemy in the World War II movies.

Karen counsels from the front door, "Kevin, they are just kids. Ignore them. They are stupid idiots. Don't make no big thing of it. And besides, there are like nine of them."

Nine? Kevin thinks. There were hundreds when he had stalked the yard at the Wende Correctional Facility pointing up at the windows on the tiers above, performing, as he had done in the amphitheater of his Brownsville projects. At Wende he added a monologue. "Just one man here. Come on out, you punk pussy-ass bitches. *Maricón* faggots." But none of the Germans had moved. Nine!

The weight bench and the Puerto Ricans bunched up thirty yards away draw Kevin's mind back to prison. He is out on the yard again and the adrenaline switch goes on. Not a thumping pulse and a dripping brow like some people, but a coiling stillness. He can hear a whisper from across the street, see a finger move.

"KK pushin' mad steel."

If it isn't for Main walking up and yelling, he would be tearing up some Puerto Rican ass right now.

Main is already living in the area, twenty minutes from Elmira in the city of Corning, named for the giant glass company there. Kevin has set him up with Joy, a five-foot-ten nurse's aide with a touch of the Pacific Rim about the eyes.

Joy's signature activity is getting beat up by black women. Four or five times in the past few years, either alone or with her strapping friend Jennifer, Joy has blown into bars like Ramsey's Place on the east side and started talking loud, this and that about whoever and whatever. Joy loves to talk shit and Jennifer, at five-foot-nine and 160 pounds, likes to mix it up. But the two simply aren't prepared for the ready anger they provoke in black women.

In the first place, the local sisters don't like the sight of two tall white girls flicking their hair and switching their asses. And there is something else. Besides the usual irritants of poverty and race, the black women of Elmira have the daily experience of witnessing the sorry spectacle of their men with white women. Zebratown isn't a pleasing curiosity to them, the way it is to Kevin Davis and his buddies. It is a shame.

So, time and time again, just when Joy is about to stick her finger in some frowning black woman's face and just as Jennifer is ready to dispense some serious threats, the punches and kicks have already been thrown, the beat-down already begun. They had tried half a dozen times now, but even when they warm themselves up in the car beforehand, drinking and talking—"No black bitch better come out her mouth an' say shit to me tonight"—the twin Elmira toughies still can't seem to get themselves angry enough fast enough.

Main can't care less about Joy's scraps. He is just tickled with his new life. He has been smoking weed all day for two months and Joy hasn't even brought up the subject of a job.

But this afternoon Main has a problem. White Mike, a local hustler, has been accusing him of stealing a gun. Main, who has been flaunting a fancy new Ruger, acknowledges that the weapon may have once belonged to the porcine ecstasy salesman. But Main swears that he bought the weapon with money lent to him by Joy from a third party, who probably was the one who stole it from White Mike. Main also insists that he has no intention of giving it back.

White Mike rolls up to the house balancing his wide ass on a tiny bicycle. Main, Kevin, and White Mike retire to the living room to hash out the matter.

While he listens to the testimonies, Kevin continues to stare out the window at the Puerto Ricans, who are standing in their driveway across the street, examining the engine of a car. Something has to be done about them and Kevin is of a mind to stand up and take care of the situation right away.

"So, Kev," White Mike begins, "your man, this dude right here, stole my joint. I left it with this little bitch and then she stashed it with her cousin and then he took it. Simple story. I don't wanna start shit, specially since this is your man, but I feel mad stupid with a dude, even if he is your friend, walkin' around with my gun. How that make me look? Right?"

"Fuckin' Puerto Ricans," Kevin mutters. "They like to laugh and shit but they don't want to back it up."

"What Puerto Ricans?" White Mike wants to know. "This is 'bout the gun? My gun?"

Main is silent, his eyebrows arched. The Ruger is nowhere in sight.

"Right over there. Them Puerto Ricans got me tight."

Main brightens. "You wan' me to get the hammer? Light up the block?"

"Nah. Fuck that shit." Kevin turns away from the window. "Now listen up. Okay, this is this. Main, it's Mike's gun. I dunno who stole the shit but it's his gun."

Main tilts his head toward Kevin.

"But I go by Brownsville rules," Kevin says. "Stealin' people's shit is grimy but in Brownsville we don't ever give nothin' back, 'specially a gun. How you gonna feel when you get shot with the gun you gave back?"

Main's expression doesn't change as he rests back on the couch. White Mike too is silent, his tiny eyes cast upward in contemplation. He doesn't like the fact that he is not going to get his gun back. But who can argue with Brownsville rules? Not him. He has spent the last five years trying to mold himself, with his white skin and lank hair, into a facsimile of a black street hustler. Who is he to argue with Brownsville rules?

"So, that's it?" White Mike asks without rancor.

"No. Main, you stay away from Mike. Stay out of his square, and same with you, Mike. I don't wanna hear any more of this bullshit or I'm gonna get tight with both y'all."

As White Mike and Main leave, Main on foot and Mike by bicycle, Main whispers out of the corner of his mouth, "Yo, Kev, I got Corning sewed up, man. Hee-hee. Check this shit. I'm a playa!" Kevin's attention turns back to the Puerto Ricans across the street.

Kevin has a growing reputation in Elmira as a man of substance. But by now he is running out of money. The Kennedy Valve job would be perfect. But it is not going to happen. They probably don't hire ex-cons with violent backgrounds like his, Kevin surmises. At home, when he tells Julia to do something, she glances at Karen for a signal before she complies. It is Kevin's conviction that his simple lack of money to contribute to the household, the way he hovers over his small stake of cash, is limiting his authority in the family, undermining his status. Not quite desperate yet, he begins searching in earnest for a way to make money. Kevin doesn't need a lot. He isn't going to buy any fancy clothes or jewelry, at least not to wear anyway.

With the $3,000 he has saved from the clothing business, which has regrettably slacked off to almost nothing, and the $2,000 he has left from the job he did guarding that overstuffed envelope, Kevin pays low dollar on jewelry from some locals who need bail money, then sells the gold for a couple thousand more than he paid. But transactions like that are lucky and far between. Reluctantly, he turns his eye to the drug business in Elmira. Kevin knows the system and he knows the players. It is not hard to understand and the whole scenario moves in slow motion compared to Brownsville. With his background and his experience, he could slide himself right into the equation as a weight man. Use his contacts in New York to pick up some ounces and unload them fast. Kevin had always been a natural in the business.

Kevin jogs slowly through the dawn streets of Elmira with his wool cap down over his forehead, throwing jabs and hooks into the sharp air, considering his options. Is there a safe way to get back in the drug game?

There are no stray dogs at his side as in the days when he ran in Betsy Head Park, but he feels like an underdog the same as he did then. The wind knifes down out of the hills as Kevin dances around wide puddles, enjoying the looks he gets from drivers on their way to work.

One morning a few weeks later, Judge Thomas E. Ramich stops his car, waits as the stoplight on Water Street turns green, watches as Davis, hunched against the cold, passes in front of him. The judge lives on Third Street in a mixed neighborhood instead of the far west side where the affluent reside. He chose the neighborhood to be close to the people he sees every day in his courtroom, where he has sat on the bench in Criminal Court for twenty-five years. The thoughtful and open-faced Ramich calls the troubled poor, both black and white of Elmira, his "flock" and takes pains to offer useful advice and dispense the kind of justice that repairs lives. That's just what we need, he thinks when he spots Davis, a diligent black role model. Somebody for these young kids to look up to before they start listening to the gangster music and following the wrong path.

Kevin Davis is thinking as he runs. Drugs might be the answer but they might also be the final trap.

He understands that Elmira is an easy place to make money in the drug business. But there is real danger. The users and dealers here are so country, so amateurish, that there isn't the slightest criminal security. People are giving each other up so fast that in Rochester they call Elmira "Tellmira" because of the snitches. Word is people are giving up their friends and associates, not to get out from under heavy cases, federal indictments, or DEA-generated investigations, but to beat traffic tickets!

Kevin has to laugh at that one. But it would be no laughing matter if he got caught up in even a bullshit case. The system would love to see him with a drug felony so they could lock him deep as they were supposed to have done for Amboy. Even though he knows that the so-called three strikes law in New York State has many loopholes, "life behind me" haunts him just the same. Life in prison for a half-assed drug charge? No, he would do stickups before he would get involved in the drug trade here.

But what about selling such small amounts of a drug that it wouldn't be a felony? He could take a misdemeanor, do a year anytime. But in the law library on Lake Street across from the public defender's office, Kevin's research tells him that any sale of a controlled substance is a felony.

Then Kevin's phone vibrates against his rib cage. It's one of the guys from the Binghamton clothing business. Kevin slows to a walk and stops on the Walnut Street Bridge, faces away from the buffeting wind, and peels off one of his gloves so he can feel the buttons.

"Shit is slow, son."

Kevin spits on the street. "What about the sneakers?"

"Straight-up zero," Kevin's partner in the clothing hustle answers. "I think they be sellin' them cheap in the mall."

"Word?"

"Word up. Athlete's Foot undersellin' the street. That's the global economy. Black man got nowhere to run, nowhere to hide. Don't worry about yo money."

"I ain't."

During the conversation an idea dawns on Kevin that he might put some money into a deal and stay clear of it. Just like the clothing business, he would front a few thousand with no questions, no knowledge of how it is used. For all he knows, it could be a legit use. Then he would get it back with a few thousand more. Same principle as the clothing business, but with a product that Athlete's Foot couldn't compete with, where the global economy couldn't mess with the black man's head. *Hell, it would be just like a mutual fund. White people played stupid, didn't they? Go around saying they don't know if the company is making Pampers or land mines with their investment money.*

As long as they make a profit, then it's all-the-way good. It would be just like the stock market.

Kevin begins jogging again, headed for Brand Street, his stubby legs pumping, snapping his fists down at the ground and then straight out in front, his steamy breath running away with the wind.

In the next few weeks, Kevin begins spending time with Trip, a local drug dealer out of the Hathorn Court projects. A month later, Kevin is driving a clean ten-year-old gray Lexus, a used car but a luxury auto just the same, over the Madison Avenue Bridge, a small clump of bills in his front pants pocket.

Kevin parks the car carefully on Brand Street. As he opens the front door, Kevin conquers an urge to look over his shoulder back at his car. "Yo, Karen, I just volunteered to teach boxing at the Ernie Davis Center."

"Volunteered? Kevin, you have to get a job, a paying job."

Karen isn't sure where Kevin got the $6,000 to buy the car, or the money in his pocket. She is concerned about his association with Trip, who is not only a dealer but a womanizer. "If you're doing business with Trip, you're making a big mistake."

Kevin doesn't believe he has to say a word on the matter. It isn't a man's place to explain where money comes from, just as long as it comes from somewhere. There are no excuses accepted when the money isn't there, so there shouldn't be any explanations required when it is. Still, he explains.

"It was a gift."

"I'm not stupid, Kevin. Who gives away thousands of dollars? If you're gonna lie, don't say nothin'. 'Cause I'm not one of those fat stupid bitches you mess with on the east side."

"I got people who appreciate who I am. You understand that?"

"I got people who appreciate who I am too, Kevin. But they don't give me money."

"They give it to me."

Kevin's explanation is not as preposterous as it sounds. Local dealers and an array of criminals, perched in the woods in the heart of New York State, are so close to the prisons that the culture of those penal institutions overflows onto the street. Nobody in the prison system has a better reputation than Kevin. He is a celebrity and, as such, his friendship is worth money. Famous athletes are paid just to show their faces at events to give the moment some weight, and according to Kevin Davis there are those in the Southern Tier of New York State willing to break him off a few thousand just for the honor of being associated with Killa Kev, the "realest nigga" in town. Just to be seen in his company on a regular basis is a letter of credit, a personal refer-ence, and a security fence combined. Perhaps, just perhaps, Kevin Davis has found a way to make a living out of being himself, at least for the time being.

The problem is that Kevin's reputation was built on strict codes and enforced with violence, guaranteed retaliation. Even if he can keep his hands out of the drug till, how long can he trade on a reputation and a name like Killa Kev without hurting someone?

ON CAMPUS

|||||||||||||||||||||||||||||||||||||||||||||||||||||||||||||||||||||||||||||||||||||||||||||||||||||||||

Kevin has a new friend and associate, Cortez, originally from Fort Greene in Brooklyn, a slick-talking, well-dressed events promoter, a half-assed businessman who, among other things, lines up rap acts to perform at local colleges, particularly the sprawling Binghamton University. The man talks too fast, alters his stories, and makes unreasonable estimations. Kevin calls him "shady," but, paying too little attention to how he spends the valuable commodity of his association, Kevin likes him anyway.

Kevin Davis likes almost anyone, black or white, young or old. He covers it up but he even likes some of the police officers who watch him now, pull him over to make sure his paperwork is in order, trying to figure out how he fits into the local criminal community. He is even getting to know their names. When it comes to casual friendship, Kevin Davis is so interested in people, so sure of himself, that he will connect with almost anyone. One weekend, Cortez invites Kevin and Karen to a party he is giving for fraternities and sororities at Binghamton University.

Binghamton is one of the highest-rated institutions in the state university system. This is where the next generation of black success stories will come from. A lot of these students are from New York City but very few are from neighborhoods like Brownsville or Jamaica, Queens. If they are, they came from households with parents who herded them past the neighborhood gauntlet, handpicked their schools, and reviewed their homework. Though there are kids at Binghamton who are decked out in 'do-rags and T-shirts, who wear pants that drag along the floor and fill their sentences with obscenities, very few of them are children of the ghetto. Those men are down the road at the Elmira prison and across the Chemung River in Southport.

Kevin and Karen and Karen's friend Michelle arrive in two cars. The narrow-hipped Michelle has left her bubbling two-year-old with the wavy blond Afro with Betsy and Julia. The two white girls, each a few inches taller than Kevin, flank him as they enter the sprawling all-purpose room reserved for the party. Main is already on hand, slouched in a chair next to Joy. Cortez is duly impressed with Karen. It isn't clear exactly what Cortez expects to gain from his relationship with an unemployed ex-con like Kevin, but he is all smiles and winks, hand touches, even hugs.

There are few people on hand at ten o'clock, the publicized starting time. No alcohol is on sale, and there are no drinks or food in sight, as half a dozen singles wander through the brightly lit room. This is certainly no party. Kevin and his New York City buddies sit together at tables on a raised section at the end of the room and talk. They look and feel uncomfortable.

"Shit is squashed," Kevin mutters, looking around.

So this is college. Kevin never even considered going to college. He couldn't even sit still in elementary school and long ago set his mind toward making his mark some other way. What did these college kids have that he didn't have? He admitted to himself, they wouldn't spend years in prison. They would never be shot or hunted. They would have legit jobs that he might never have, homes.

But they would never know the sense of mastery that came from surviving the streets and prison. They would never know how sweet freedom really is. They would never be quite as proud of themselves as Kevin is of himself. Most telling of all is that while many of the young men in the school admire and mimic men like Kevin, he has no desire to copy them.

The campus has its own rhythm, it seems. Slowly, the hall begins to fill. Kevin's people relax as the students file in from their dormitories and from the library. Some carry backpacks or books. Main is intrigued. "Yo, Kev, whas this here?"

"I dunno the fuck it is. Do I look like a college dude to y'all?"

It is eleven o'clock, an hour after the Brooklyn men and their Elmira girlfriends arrived, when the lights begin to dim. None of Kevin's crew rises to dance to the heavy rap beat, but neither does anyone else. Instead, people stand in clusters around the edges of the room and talk as more students wander in. Kevin is dressed in an immaculate white dress shirt, with pearl-gray slacks. Michelle is actually wearing high heels. Joy is heavily made up. None of the students is dressed up, and sloppy jeans and wrinkled T-shirts abound. The atmosphere is so casual that this does not appear to be a social occasion at all, certainly not a Saturday night dance.

There are no flirtatious glances, there is no cruising. Just a bunch of people chatting.

"So this is how brainiacs party?"

Karen is annoyed at Kevin's remark. The couple began arguing a few weeks ago, bickering about the housework and then the decoration of the apartment. Lately, they have been arguing about everything, arguing as if it were a sport.

"I asked you if this is how brainiacs get down."

"How should I know, Kevin?"

"You white, ain't you?"

The couple are so evenly matched intellectually that their arguments are competitive, even entertaining. As with well-matched tennis opponents, one good shot follows another. Karen nods to the hall filling with hundreds of students, all black. "What the fuck does that have to do with it, Kevin? Do these students look white?"

"They act white."

"What does that mean? How can you act white?"

"Just look."

Main laughs, then exaggerates his levity and slides off his chair giggling. Karen looks at Main and wants to say something about acting black, wants to ask Kevin why he saw fit to drag a Brownsville gunslinger up to Elmira. But she doesn't. "Whatever you say."

Kevin and Main, even Cortez, are sure that these black college kids are too lame or too educated to get down and party. They lounge above the motionless dance floor and watch, exchanging glances.

Then something remarkable happens. In the center of the formless crowd of nondescript shuffling students seven or eight young men coalesce into a rapidly moving column. In exact synchronization to the rising bass beat of an invisible sound system, the line of men dips and struts, rises and falls, twists and stomps, thrusts and twirls. One at a time the dancers move from a full squat to a standing arch, down the row and then together, and then one at a time again back up the row. At the same time, the entire line glides snakelike through the throng. The virtuoso performance, and it is most definitely a performance, lasts just a minute until, as quickly as it was formed, the dance line melts into the crowd and is unseen. A moment later, another line materializes, thrashing and cavorting between the stationary bodies on the dance floor. The first line reforms and then a third, this time of women, snaps to attention and steps, then dissolves and reforms. The dance is unusual, so tightly choreographed and exuberantly executed that it seems the hall has been invaded by competing professional dance groups.

Step dancing, pure folk art, passed down from generations of black college men and based on the rhythmic traditions of Africa, is simply amazing to the Brooklynites, who are not smirking anymore. But Kevin, Main, and Cortez refuse to broadcast their admiration. They just sit still, watching.

"These motherfuckers have too much time on their hands," is all Kevin will allow. It is true: the inspired choreography and the practiced cohesion must have taken hours a day for months to master.

The group from Brooklyn and the proud tradition of black fraternities and sororities on display on the dance floor are two sides of the African-American experience, two sides of its culture that do not often mingle.

"Let's go."

Kevin and his friends head to a club in Binghamton for an hour of sipping drinks and then take the one-hour drive back to Elmira. On the ride, Michelle tells of bears that come down out of the mountains to pad around her home. Kevin is at ease, much more at home with these country people than he was with the black college students, laughing about the bears and the life of drinking and hanging out in the woods.

"Y'all would go into the *woods* to drink. That is the last place I would go. Word."

Thirty Days

||||||||||||||||||||||||||||||||||||||||||||||||||||||||||||||||||||||||||||||||||||||||||||||||||||||||||||||||||

It is late June 2003. The white moths of high summer haven't begun to swarm the streetlamps on the bridges over the Chemung River yet.

"Yo Kev," says Cortez, "I got this girl I want ya to meet. She goes to the college."

"Elmira College?"

"Yeah, she's getting her degree in law or criminal justice."

"Probably a Fed."

Kevin and Cortez cruise up to the tree-lined campus of the expensive girls' school. It's all there, rolling lawns and stately buildings, a pond and a fountain. When she arrives, the college girl is taken aback a bit by Kevin, almost invisible in the shadows and child-sized behind the wheel. But she knows Cortez from the Queensboro projects in Queens, and Cortez is deferential to the ex-con boxer, so she is careful to show respect.

Besides, she is glad to see some brown faces, at least. The women's college and this small country town have been getting on her nerves and it is past time for her to sample a whiff of the big city, and Kevin "Killa Kev" Davis is, by accounts, all about the big city.

In his baseball cap and oversized sweatshirt, driving his Lexus, Kevin Davis looks to her like a character from a movie. There isn't much of anything for the threesome to do in Elmira but visit the projects or someone's house, or to drive around, back and forth over the bridges.

"Yo, I'm 'bout to run out of gas, for real."

Kevin pulls into the Mobil station on the south side, just over the Madison Avenue Bridge. As he reaches for the handle to open his door and step out to pump the gas, he spots a splash of red light from behind.

"Motherfucker!"

"What the fuck is this?" Cortez whispers.

The Elmira College student pipes up from the backseat, "This is wrong. You didn't violate a law. They have no probable cause to stop you."

Officer John Hibbard of the Elmira Police Department is bent at the waist looking in at Kevin Davis. "Can I see your license and registration, please?"

"What?"

"I pulled you over. I am asking you to produce your license and registration."

Kevin raises and lowers his shoulders, like a boxer warming up in his corner. He stares up at the cop.

"You din't pull me over. I stopped to get gas. I don't got to give you shit."

Hibbard's voice is flat. "If you don't produce your license and registration, you will be placed under arrest."

"Ain't this a bitch?"

Kevin reaches into his back pocket, withdraws his wallet, and produces his license and registration for the Lexus. The police officer returns to his black-and-white and in a minute steps back to the passenger side of Kevin's car. The officer leans again to speak into the car. "Step out, please, Mr. Davis. You have a warrant."

"Warrant? There's no warrant. No way there's a warrant." Kevin steps from the car, raises his arms as if to submit to a pat-down, and then bolts through the gas station's parking apron, down the sidewalk on Sly Street, and into the darkness. Officer Hibbard plunges after him, sprinting half a block between two buildings and into the backyards. "Stop, nigger, 'fore I shoot you," Kevin says Hibbard bellowed at him. Kevin recalls that even in full flight he almost laughed at the epithet, thinking Elmira ain't so cool after all.

With his short legs and heavy muscles, Kevin Davis is anything but fleet. As he flees across the grass, he notes that Hibbard is gaining on him. He also eyes a gaunt three-story brick hovel with no curtains in the windows, a crack house. Then, from between the houses, he spots a cruiser racing up Sly

Street, then another. The police vehicles skid to a stop and splay red lights on the walls and trees. Screams and curses pour from the crack house. More exclamations as windows fly open. Caught in a trap, Kevin thinks, as crackheads slip out the front door of the house and scuttle into the night. But he just might be able to get away in the confusion. Kevin is just about to dart through the side door of a neighboring house when the police grab him. Good thing. Would have been a burglary charge, to be sure.

After the police transport him to the station house, Kevin learns there is no warrant for his arrest—some kind of a mistake—but there is a resisting arrest charge now. The police hold him for three hours and are about to let him go with a desk-appearance ticket for resisting when a smirking cop pops in the front door of the station house holding a packet of crack aloft, twenty grams.

Kevin argues that the drugs came from the crack house, that somebody must have dropped the packet as he ran or tossed it out a window when they saw the flashing lights. The police are unconvinced. They want to know what Kevin Davis is doing in Elmira. They want to know how he bought the fancy car. But they don't ask about those things. They do ask him why he ran from the police if he wasn't dirty.

"I been locked up a lot of times. And I just panicked."

To the police, Kevin Davis doesn't look like a man who panics. He does look like a drug dealer. "Tell it to the judge," they advise, as they charge him with criminal possession of a controlled substance in the third degree, a Class B felony, and cart him off to the county jail on William Street. He will stay there for thirty days before the preliminary hearing.

The shouting and laughing and bellyaching in the county lockup goes quiet when he arrives. Everybody, it seems, is glad to see Kevin Davis. Sick to death of lightweights and punks, even the guards appreciate the moment as Kevin Davis walks down the line of cells. A burglar, a former New Yorker, takes Kevin's arrival as an opportunity to taunt a guard. "Yo, yo, yo, Officer Smith. You wouldn't never make it in BK. They'd beat your ass on sight. Ha, ha, ha. You'd never make it in my hood."

"*You'd* never make it *your* hood," the guard cracks back. "That's why you keep your soft ass right here in Elmira."

Nodding, twisting his torso slightly to greet acquaintances, Kevin keeps moving.

"Yo, Killa Kev in the house."

"Get this party started."

Something makes Kevin stop and turn. Behind him, at the gate, waiting to be admitted to the floor from some other area of the prison, is a youth with slit eyes, a spray of freckles across his chestnut face. Kevin holds the gaze from that freckled face for a long moment. The man is grilling him, scowling for real. Looks like he wants to spit.

At a preliminary hearing, Judge Ramich asks Officer Hibbard why he stopped Kevin Davis in the first place.

"He was coming from a known drug location."

Ramich looks down at his notes. "You told me he was coming from Elmira College."

The officer does not respond.

"Are you saying Elmira College is a drug location?"

"No."

Judge Ramich has had enough. "Mr. Davis, you may, in fact, have had drugs on your person. You may have illegally possessed and then discarded those drugs. But I have one thing to tell you. This case seems frivolous to me. The stop appears illegal and therefore everything stemming from it is probably inadmissible. I cannot, however, because of your record of felonies and past involvement with drugs, dismiss this case at this time. You have the right to speak before a grand jury."

Kevin Davis nods twice to the judge. Davis doesn't listen much to rappers who rant about shooting people, about killing. Why should he? He has lived it. Unless the rap is about someone he knows, there is no value in listening to that stuff. What he does like, has even taken to memorizing the lyrics of, is a rapper named Papoose, who rhymes specifically about ways to beat the criminal justice system. Davis listens to Papoose's cut on grand juries again and again: "Gotta look 'em in the eyes as simple as can be / Make 'em believe you innocent, you could be free."

When Kevin follows Papoose's advice and insists on telling his story to the grand jury, the district attorney backs up fast. He has a puny case. On the other hand, he is aware of the disastrous downside for Davis of another felony conviction. That twenty-gram packet of cocaine on the wet grass outside the crack house on Sly Street could put Kevin Davis in jail for twenty-five to life. So what if the judge himself called the case frivolous, doubted the legality of the car stop? It is just too steep a downside to give Kevin Davis all the leverage, and the district attorney knows it.

The district attorney speaks to Kevin's Legal Aid lawyer as Kevin listens.

"In exchange for a guilty plea, we'll drop the drug possession felony charge to criminal possession in the seventh degree, a Class A misdemeanor, and give him time served on the resisting arrest," the DA says.

Kevin hesitates. It sounds too good to be true.

The young DA glances at a paper in his hand and turns to Kevin.

"Oh, yes, and there will be a six-month suspension of your driver's license and, since the vehicle was involved in a drug violation, we will require that you forfeit your automobile. Your—what is it?—2000 Lexus."

Kevin shoots a glance at the ceiling. "Shit."

"Excuse me?"

Kevin ignores the district attorney and speaks to his lawyer. "I'll take the offer. They can have the car."

At the sentencing hearing, Judge Ramich presides. The wide wood-paneled room is three-quarters filled with drunk drivers, petty thieves, and deadbeat husbands, along with several robbers and a wife beater. A nervous mother perches on the edge of her seat waiting for her son to be brought before the judge. Kevin Davis, as he stands before Ramich, already knows many of the people in the courtroom.

Ramich clears his throat. He has been a judge in Elmira for more than two decades and during that time has developed a reputation for being deeply concerned and precisely fair. He has turned down requests for so many special favors for the elite of Elmira, their friends and family, carefully worded requests for diminished charges on DWI cases and the like, that he has become a pariah among the city power brokers, who have already started raising money to unseat him when he comes up for election in a year. Ramich takes the time to get to know many of the people who come before him, giving many second chances and keeping a record of how much use people make of his generosity.

"Mr. Davis. I am mandated to sentence you to time served on your guilty plea to resisting arrest and criminal possession of a controlled substance in the seventh degree. But that sentencing does not tell the whole story by a long shot."

Ramich peers over the bench to get a better look at Kevin Davis standing in a light gray dress shirt and charcoal slacks, holding a pair of designer sunglasses in his left hand. "I know you are a boxer and I have seen you doing your roadwork and I am . . . I must say . . . I am shocked at what I see when I look at your record."

Up to this moment, Kevin has been a curiosity in Elmira, an outsider with a scent of danger and an aura of the big-time, a glad-hander who is as friendly with white shopkeepers as he is with the slackers and the troublemakers. Kevin has been a conversation piece and somewhat of a mystery.

"You seem like an intelligent individual, Mr. Davis. But I have never in my career on the bench had an individual stand before me with a record like yours."

Ramich holds up Kevin Davis's rap sheet in his right hand, then lowers it and reads while he speaks. "I see a record of arrests and convictions going back to 1986. I see possession of stolen property. I see criminal possession of a controlled substance. I see criminal sale of a controlled substance. I see assault. I see robbery. Gun possession. And I even see murder."

The dozens of people in the gallery, the scofflaws, the bullies, their friends and victims, stir in their seats, arching to get a better look at Kevin Davis. It doesn't matter that Kevin was never convicted of the Amboy Street murder; the word "murder" is right there on his rap sheet. Ramich's monologue couldn't have ensured Kevin's status in Elmira any more than if he had written it himself, any more than if it had been put up in lights and hung from the Madison Avenue Bridge.

"Quite frankly, I have never had anyone with as bad a record as you have in front of me. I am only hoping that you use your intelligence and your personality to make a good and peaceful life here in Elmira and that you contribute to this town in a positive way. Good luck, Mr. Davis. I will be watching you closely."

Kevin stifles an urge to wave or toss a thumbs-up to his gallery of new admirers. Instead, he plays it low-key like Dillinger or John Gotti would, nodding solemnly at Ramich, pivoting, and heading for the door, eyes aimed ahead.

RIDE

|||||||||||||||||||||||||||||||||||||||||||||||||||||||||||||||||||||||||||||||||||||||||||||||||||||||||||||

On Brand Street, the bickering has subsided. Kevin's troublesome case has been taken care of and Karen's insurance money for the car accident has finally arrived. Julia reacts to the lightened mood by positioning herself in front of Kevin while she bounces on the balls of her feet, begging for toys and trips to the mall, anything to take advantage of the celebratory atmosphere.

"Please, please, please. KK, please."

"Oh, my God. I said no, you little demon. All right, we'll go to the mall, but not till later."

Karen's money is not much more than $15,000 after the lawyer gets his cut. The first thing the couple do is take half of that amount and combine it with the few thousand dollars Kevin has and purchase a thirteen-year-old Mercedes-Benz sedan from a used-car lot in Binghamton. The car is black and as long as any automobile either of them has ever seen. "Looks like a car for a king or a fuckin' governor," Kevin marvels. Karen has to admit, it is one beautiful automobile. As they stare together at the Mercedes, Karen is engulfed by admiration. The car is like Kevin Davis himself. She has never seen anything like it.

In the middle of the next week, Karen and Kevin take the Mercedes across town where they will pick up Route 17 and head down to Binghamton to visit with Randolph and check on Kevin's clothing hustle. Kevin's license has been suspended as a result of the guilty plea on the car-stop bust, so Karen drives. She concentrates on the road, guiding the huge car, stopping slowly and gradually at traffic signals. Other than the gleaming silver twenty-four-inch custom rims, the car is factory issue all the way, no gaudy accessories.

"You drive this car like a little old lady."

"You drive it, then."

"Why you say stupid things?"

"You can't drive the car, then let me drive it, Kevin. Stop criticizing."

"Who's criticizing?"

"Besides, you and Main drove it last night till three o'clock."

"Liar."

"Oh, Kevin."

"I came in at twelve-thirty."

"And what did you do till twelve-thirty?"

"Ah . . ."

"Kevin, you don't have to know everybody in this town. You don't have to know every woman in Elmira. You have a woman."

Karen can see plainly that Kevin Davis is infatuated with his Mercedes SEL extended luxury sedan. He has already heard from the Mercedes dealer in Elmira that the windows are bulletproof and he has already noted the looks, the stares, and the fascination the car holds for almost everyone in Elmira, from teenage girls to police officers. Kevin and Karen pull up to a light next to a gray Ford Explorer driven by a woman with prominent cheekbones and her light hair drawn back, wrapped with a burgundy scarf. The woman stares through the tinted windows at Kevin, who is suddenly concerned with the air-conditioning controls, though the windows are half open and the afternoon is cool.

"Do you know her?"

"What?"

"What a stupid question. You know everybody. Keep it up till it's too late. Till you find out that I am not like these other losers out here. I will walk out of your life fast, Kevin. Very fast."

People continue to gawk, and two grown men on tiny bicycles wave as the big car rolls down Lake Street. The Mercedes is sublimely impractical. The 1992 model weighs almost five thousand pounds and, as Kevin will soon discover, it costs almost $80 to fill up the gas tank. The slightest repair demands a small fortune. But to the people of Zebratown, the waitresses and the unemployed, the slackers and weedheads, Kevin Davis and Karen Tanski look like a dream couple in a dream car.

To Investigator Richard Weed and his partner P. J. Griffin sitting in their blue Dodge Caravan in the parking lot of the Holiday Inn, watching as the Mercedes rolls past them toward the entrance ramp to Route 17, Kevin Davis looks like what they are sure he is, a drug dealer. Karen Tanski appears to be another local girl swept off her feet by big-city charm, a roll of bills, and the novelty of danger.

"Girls watch those videos and they think life is all about a rap video," Weed says, adjusting his brown Yankees cap.

"Is KK with Bushwick? Frankie?"

"Can't they see through a video?" Weed turns to his partner. "Nah, he smarter than Bush, Frankie too. Knuckleheads, 'specially Philly's man Puppet. That kid doesn't have the mental capacity to butter toast. Philly's not stupid, though. We can't pick up a thing, keeps changing numbers, droppin' phones every two weeks lately."

"Sooner or later KK's gonna make a mistake," Griffin says. "Lose his temper, do business with the wrong . . . Make a mistake."

"I feel bad for her, though."

"Why?"

"You're right. I should feel bad for us. Do we wheel a Mercedes? No, this here is a soccer mom's car. No wonder we don't get our props."

The black battleship of a car floats down the ramp and settles onto the highway, rolling east to Binghamton.

"I need options," Kevin says after a silence.

"You need to grow up."

"Fuck you."

"Oh, Kevin."

Kevin believes that if a woman begins to feel too good about herself, she will be trouble. He believes that it is important to keep a woman low and he works hard at the task.

"You not supposed to ride behind no big truck. That's why you get in so many accidents, 'cause you don't know how to drive. Pass that truck."

A gentle light tumbles through the sunroof as the hills of the Southern Tier float by. Creeks and rivers, yellow wildflowers. A used-car dealership. A motel far back from the road. Karen is in the passing lane now, gaining on an old blue and white bus with the thickly painted letters DOC on the white side panel.

Kevin is galvanized. "Pull up! Pull up!"

As Karen draws alongside the state Department of Corrections bus, Kevin lowers his window and raises himself in his seat, thrusting his torso out the window, arching his back, and hurling his arm up and his fist in the air.

"Freedom is a must! Freedom is a must!"

The inmates stir behind the wired windows. Davis trumpets again.

"Freedom is a must! Freedom is a must!"

There are audible cries from inside the bus. Shouts, as the inmates recognize Kevin Davis as one of their own, a once-caged soul now rumbling down the interstate in a Mercedes-Benz with a blonde beside him. The inmates are screaming now. Even the ones who cannot get to the window on Davis's side of the bus holler as they catch the feeling. Those who can see Davis cling to their latticed portals with one hand and bang the wall of the bus with the other as they drink in the sweetest of sights. Here is living proof that there will be better times, that someday the bars and the head counts will be behind them. Someday they too will ride the wave.

But like so many ideas running through the convicts' minds, Kevin's success is largely an illusion. Back in Elmira he is squabbling constantly with Karen, spending much of his time in the projects with the likes of Trip, the young drug dealer, even spending nights away from home with the secretary with the burgundy scarf and the gray Explorer. He met her at a club and spent the first night quiet and still in the bed beside her. The couple had simply kissed and fallen asleep. After that, in the weeks that followed, the sex had been delicious. Not once, though, did he think about leaving Karen. After Francesca, he wasn't about to trust a freak.

He has applied to Kennedy Valve half a dozen more times. He has taken out the letter from the federal government asking him about the status of his Kennedy application to read it so many times he can't find it anymore. Still, he drops off application after application to Kennedy Valve at the Workforce

Development Career Center across the street from the town's newspaper, the *Star-Gazette*. Thinks of calling up a reporter and having an article written about the discrimination involved. He even reaches for his phone one day to call. But as he does, he sees a police car sitting outside his house and changes his mind.

Driving with his suspended license, Kevin Davis rolls through the streets of Elmira in his thirteen-year-old Mercedes. Black, with sterling panels along the lower third of the body, it is in remarkable shape. The car is at the same time a symbol of his limited vision and emblem of his triumph over Brownsville and the state prison system.

As he glides over the streets waving and smiling, listening to music with an attractive young mate at home and any number of girlfriends, Kevin feels little remorse over his infidelities.

When he was twelve years old Kevin once made a quick stop with a friend to the other boy's apartment to grab sodas from the refrigerator. Together, the Brownsville buddies noticed Kevin's father's leather jacket thrown over a kitchen chair. At the same moment they looked up to see the door of the friend's mother's bedroom closed tight. Without a word the boys touched hands and headed back out to play, but a lesson had been learned.

Instead of feeling guilty, Kevin is thinking, Who could possibly have figured this shit out but me? Who could have come up with this town but a man who had confidence and focus, a man who had seven years to think and plan?

As Kevin waves to the daughter of a corrections officer who lives on his street, he notices that the heat gauge on the dashboard is indicating hot. Within minutes, the engine is steaming.

At the Mercedes dealership on the outskirts of Elmira, the floor is in a state of high polish. As far as the owners know, Kevin Davis, a retired boxer, bought the car with one of his last purses. Kevin is always smiling and chatty when he comes to price tires and rims, talk shop. They like him and he enjoys their company. In the month since he bought the Mercedes, he has made it a point to stop by every week, even if only to shoot the breeze.

"Got bad news and good news, KK."

"Yeah?"

"Oil problem. Somebody shoulda picked it up on a maintenance check. No oil, no engine. Bottom line, needs a new engine."

Kevin squints. He hadn't paid much attention to his classes during the year he went to Automotive High School, but he knows enough to notice an oil stain, if it was there on the pavement outside the house on Brand Street.

"Word?"

"We got one. Perfect fit. Drop it in for five grand." Kevin has no other way to get home, so he coaxes the Mercedes the few miles to Brand Street. The needle is already on hot by the time he gets there.

Karen has her back to the door, cooking. Ears of corn stick from a large pot. Twister the cat is frozen in a corner, looking at Kevin.

"Five thousand dollars? Where are you gonna get five thousand dollars?"

"Don't worry about it."

"Kevin. Take that car back to the man who sold it to you, who cheated you. Get your ninety-five hundred back."

"That's not gonna happen."

Karen has some idea how much the car means to Kevin, but she doesn't know that he is loath to confront the car salesman for another reason. Since childhood, Kevin has abstained from both complaint and negotiation. To seriously consider the possibility that the salesman knowingly cheated him might set off a bomb within him. An image of Johnny Blanco's hapless label rep on his knees in the parking lot, his hands to his bloody face, comes to Kevin.

Kevin steps off the porch and walks toward the Mercedes. He has spotted a smudge near the driver's-side front door handle. As he rubs the spot with a cloth retrieved from the trunk, his head barely reaches the top of the huge car.

A high-pitched cackle pierces the morning. As Kevin looks up, two Puerto Rican teenagers across the street, eighteen or nineteen years old, turn and head up their driveway toward their house. They are giggling, conspiratorially.

Kevin folds the chamois cloth carefully, lays it on the roof of his car. Then he walks across the street toward the young men. These are boys who once told Julia that Kevin was a convict who would soon be back in prison. In the front window of the house someone lifts a cell phone. As Kevin approaches, one of the young men turns to face him. Kevin dips his left shoulder, widens the angle of his elbow, and snaps his hips. The sound of the left hook is something between a smack and a thud as the young man topples to the grass. His friend backs up toward the house, hands up in front of his face, his fingers spread for protection. A small car wheels across the sidewalk onto the driveway with four men inside. Kevin walks to the car as the injured man rises, trips over a garbage can, and stumbles toward the house.

Kevin addresses both the driver and the man in the seat behind him.

"Just knocked your man out. 'Bout now, you supposed to kick *my* ass."

No one moves. Kevin walks back across the street, where Karen is standing on the lawn. Monty is silent on his porch. A black-and-white cruiser zips to the curb across the street. Kevin stops and motions Karen inside, then steps forward and waits to be arrested. Instead, Officer Michael Ross approaches the carful of Latino men. He has had a number of complaints recently about the house, about verbal harassment from the crowd of boys, loud music, and marijuana use. Somehow, he already knows about the punch.

"I want to give you guys a piece of advice. You can take it or you can ignore it. That man across the street is not somebody to mess with. You started up with the wrong person this time. The man is a killer and I strongly suggest you leave him be."

FELONY

||||||||||||||||||||||||||||||||||||||||||||||||||||||||||||||||||||||||||||||||||||||||||||||||||||||||||

Another worker has been killed at Kennedy Valve, decapitated after he stumbled onto a conveyor belt designed to separate sand from steel components. The snow is blowing sideways, howling across the frozen Chemung, stripping trees on the south bank of their last leaves. The Mercedes has been in the shop for over two months. Kevin doesn't mind. He thrives on deprivation. Let it sit in the garage for a year, who cares? Keep it out of the weather. Now that the ninety-day license suspension is over, he doesn't mind driving Karen's red Cutlass Ciera. Wheeling the little car reminds him to stay humble, makes him think about isolation, how he used to drink hot water and do push-ups to build himself up for more war with the guards. Makes him think, solitary confinement, about the box.

It was in the box that I started to feel for the quiet life. It didn't come all at once. It took years. Believe it or not, it was the isolation that made me feel superior. The more I was alone, the more pure my mind got. You don't know how it is to be alone for twenty-three hours a day every day by yourself. I started writin' my autobiography but the shit got so deep you would think that I'm a maniac, that's how deep it was. You actually look at yourself. I'm not talkin' about inside, I'm talkin' about your body. You examine every inch of yourself. You discover birthmarks and scars that you never knew you had and then you start to think deep thoughts. You begin to think that anything is possible. You got a square that you are in total control of. Everywhere I got boxed up and it became a habit. When I went to the medium-security prison when you are constantly around people I didn't like it. I'd rather be in my own square, my own domain.

At a red light on Water Street Kevin glances in the rearview mirror. The two men in street clothes in the front seat of the car behind him are DTs, detectives, nothing but cops. It's almost a joke how they can't hide it. The clothes, the look on their faces. The car. Is that the Lexus . . . *his car?*

Kevin twists in his seat and studies the automobile behind him. He eyes a tiny dent on the frame of the right headlight. It is his car. It takes every ounce of Kevin's self-control, every measure of his discipline, to restrain himself from pulling over and leaping from his car and snatching one of those police out of his Lexus. His beloved gray Lexus with the black leather interior and the police, looks like a couple of Feds, driving it around town like they own it.

"They do own it, Kevin," Karen says when he gets home. "You forfeited it 'cause it was involved in a drug arrest."

"You act like you happy. You act like you on the police side. Sometimes I forget you white."

Karen doesn't like the police either. They have never treated her with any particular respect and now that she is with Kevin, the cops seem downright hostile. They haven't said anything yet but they look like they want to. Still, she can't hide her amusement at Kevin's discomfort. She blames his cars for the fact that he never seems to be home anymore.

Karen stews at home. Sometimes her sour musings are interrupted by phone calls from Francesca. The messages from Kevin's ex-wife are far more bitter than anything Karen has on her mind.

"He's just usin' you, white girl."

"Then you would take him back?" Karen answers. After a few months the calls begin to taper off and then cease completely. Kevin and Karen have now moved to a better house, one wing of a full house, not just one floor, on Livingston Street on the south side. There are no Puerto Rican teenagers to deal with and this place has a wide porch. Best of all, the toilet doesn't drip.

The snow squalls have ceased but ice streaks the ground high up in the hills and the battering wind will not stop. It is February 2004, summer in Elmira a lifetime away. Kevin has been spending time in the Hathorn projects with Trip lately and money doesn't seem to be a problem for the time being. The Benz is out of the shop now with a new engine and Kevin Davis is rolling over the wide flat Chemung. Beside him is his protégé, Main.

Kevin Davis is enthralled by respect, has risked his life for it in Brownsville and suffered for it in prison, spent months on twenty-three-hour lockdown just so he could feel that wave of regard when he walked back into population. Kevin has found the mother lode of deference here in Elmira, in the woods, just miles from the Pennsylvania border, but he hasn't gotten away from the pressure. His phone bursts a hip-hop tune. It's Karen and she's crying.

"Karen, Karen. Whas the matter?"

"KK, Oakes, the cop whose father lives on our street, is following me."

"What?"

"He pulled out after me in his police car. He's following me."

"Drive back home."

When Kevin arrives back on Livingston, Karen is inside the house and Officer Oakes is up the block sitting in his patrol car talking with a neighbor. Kevin pulls up sharply beside the black-and-white. He and Main stare long and hard at Oakes.

Three years on the force, oval-faced and short, balding, the son of a retired officer, James Oakes is the kind of cop who believes in making a difference. He revels in the job, the status and the power. He also thinks he is just a bit smarter than the people he most often deals with.

As Kevin pulls slowly away from the patrol car, he reaches for his wallet and removes his driver's license and pulls his registration from his glove compartment. Officer Oakes hits the switch that activates his roof light, calls for backup, and flies down Livingston to the corner where Kevin is now pulled over. Kevin stares ahead as he hands his license and registration to the young officer.

"I know why you did that," says the cop. "You're mad because I followed your girlfriend."

"You harass her, I'm gonna harass you."

"I'm not harassing anybody. I followed your girlfriend because there is a lot of traffic coming in and out of your door." Oakes jerks his head toward the side of the street to where, through the branches of a stunted apple tree, Kevin's gray and white two-family rental sits.

The cop's statement about heavy traffic through the front door is laughable. Kevin and Karen and her mother and daughter moved in only weeks before, and since then have had almost no company. Oakes points to a door to the right of Kevin's, the entrance to the other wing of the two-family dwelling.

"Which house, which door?" Kevin demands.

Oakes points toward the door of Davis's gregarious neighbor. "You don't live there?"

"No, I live next door. Dodo."

"In that case, I apologize."

"Yeah, yeah. Save it."

Kevin Davis has enough money for appearance's sake, a few hundred or more here and there given him out of respect by Trip. He has enough to help pay some household expenses, help manage two, even three cars for the small family. The flagship Mercedes and red Cutlass Ciera and an $800 beater for Betsy to pick up her meds in. At times, he can even appear to be the head of a household, staying ahead of Karen on most practical matters. What it seems he cannot do is provide a future, a secure environment. There are always late-night calls, the threat of violence, and, through his association with Trip, the possibility of arrest.

One afternoon Kevin heads off to the One Stop to pick up a six-pack of Pepsi and returns nine hours later. But in spite of his disappearances, he is proving himself to be something of a family man. He is kind to seven-year-old Julia, who spins cartwheels to keep his attention. Anyone can tell that Kevin Davis has more than a thug's heart by the way the child is drawn to him, climbing on his back, squealing in his face, and talking back. Karen sees all that but it is not enough. She stalks into the living room, wringing a dish-rag and frowning. "Julia, get off KK."

"Yeah, get off me, you demon."

Betsy steps through the front door and stands clutching a piece of paper.

She is trying to sell her trailer in Gillett, has fashioned a flyer, complete with tear-off strips. She hopes to get $2,000 for the unoccupied mobile home.

Betsy squares her shoulders and reads out loud. "'For sale, two-bedroom mobile home Monarch, silver-top roof, completely covered and spouted. Vinyl windows. Sits in Fresh Oaks Trailer Park. Must apply with manager. One hundred fifty a month.'

"What do you think? It's got a ten-thousand-dollar roof," Betsy gushes. "My mother put it on. They must have seen her comin'."

Kevin rises and, headed outside, brushes past Betsy, as Twister darts in the door and straight across the room to where Karen stands. "Sometimes I think you is a cat," he says over his shoulder to Karen.

The Mercedes is parked at the curb. More than ten years old and so beautiful the cops, everybody, think he's rich. But he isn't. Karen thinks the Mercedes is a bad joke. It's all the way you look at it, Kevin decides. Just like Amboy Street. Kevin decides not to drive the Mercedes and stands for a moment considering the small car beside it.

Cutlass Ciera. What the hell is a Cutlass, and what's a Ciera? Little piece of shit. Kevin changes his mind, pivots, and steps into the Mercedes. He is smiling to himself as he heads downtown to mail letters off to Bang, who is back in prison on a parole violation, and some other inmates he knows across the state, words of encouragement. He is even sending $50 for Bang's commissary account. He makes a turn onto Sly Street.

> *Boom! I get ambushed by the police. Two cars. So I pulls over and sits there with the windows up. Police comes knockin' on my windows talkin' 'bout, "Get out. You got a Superior Court warrant."*
>
> *I tells 'em, "You don't got no fuckin' warrant. I ain't gettin' out the car. Fuck you." And then they start bangin' on my windows for real, hollerin', "We ain't playin' games with you." So I tells 'em, "Yo calm down, puppy." And I gets out of the car. "You better have a fuckin' warrant," I tell 'em. Couldn't arrest me in the fuckin' Cutlass. Had to wait till I was in the Mercedes.*

Kevin is out of jail in two days but the police have impounded his Mercedes. As he hikes over the Madison Avenue Bridge toward home, he mulls something more troubling even than the loss of his car.

The next day he stands at the front door of an apartment in Hathorn Court. His rap, rap, rap on the wood panel of the front door sends a message. Indio Mathison, a local Elmira gangster wannabe, one of Trip's friends, is inside seated in the darkened living room staring at the television. Mathison's girlfriend Arlene and their baby son, whom Kevin sometimes plies with toys and candy, are in the kitchen. When Mathison opens the door, Kevin shoulders past him.

"Yo, Kev, what's up?"

"I just got outta fuckin' jail. That's what's up. They snatched me up Tuesday on a bullshit conspiracy charge. Took my car. The Mercedes."

Mathison sits up wide-eyed. "Conspiracy. What the fuck is that about?"

"It's about they say that I conspired with three other individuals to pool our money and buy half an ounce of cocaine."

Mathison breaks out in high-pitched laughter at the idea that four people would get together to purchase such an insignificant amount of drugs, the price of which is between $350 and $400.

"Yeah, you right. That's stupid shit," he says.

"They got me on a Class E felony. One fuckin' step above a misdemeanor. They dickin' me."

"Yeah," Mathison concurs. But from the heavy-handed knock, the tone of his voice, Mathison knows Kevin Davis did not come striding into his house to complain about police harassment. This had something to do with him. Arlene appears and lingers by the entrance to the living room.

"Yeah," Kevin says.

"Yeah, that's bullshit," Mathison repeats, glancing at the television and waiting.

"And I wanna know how come I'm the only motherfucker got snatched up. How come nobody else involved been arrested. How come?"

"Yeah, how come?" Mathison seconds.

"Why me, when all the rest got Class A felonies and I'm the only one snatched and they took my fuckin' Mercedes? I'm a fuckin' get it back, though."

Kevin steps across the living room. Mathison stands up and accepts two sheets of paper stapled together. Under his shirt Davis has a black tape recorder the size of a candy bar. He is under the impression that a taped statement from Mathison will trump an affidavit or at least have some value in the legal process. After a dozen cases and seven years in state prison, Davis believes he is a few steps ahead of the game. Even if there is a trial and even if he is convicted, Kevin Davis will be prepared for the appeal.

"Read," he tells Mathison.

Mathison begins to peruse the paper.

"Nah, read it out loud."

Like a schoolboy, Mathison begins his recitation, knowing well that what he reads will not be good news. He clears his throat:

> The Grand Jury of the County of Chemung, by this indictment, accuse the defendant, Kevin E. Davis AKA "KK" of the crime of CONSPIRACY IN THE FOURTH DEGREE, in violation of section 105.10 of the Penal Law of the State of New York, committed as follows: . . . During the period March 23, 2004 through March 26, 2004 with intent constituting Criminal Possession of a Controlled Substance in the Third Degree, a class B felony, be performed, agreed with one or more persons to engage in or cause the performance of such conduct, to wit: the defendant agreed with Lawrence Williams, AKA Trip, Indio Mathison—

"That's me."

"Yeah, you right, that's you. Keep readin'."

> —and several other individuals to pool their money to purchase over one half ounce of cocaine, in furtherance of this agreement the defendant agreed to meet with Indio Mathison at the "Honeycomb hideout" for the purpose of splitting up cocaine that Mathison was bringing back from Binghamton. . . ."

"'Indio Mathison'? I can't believe this shit."

"They had your phone tapped."

"Shit."

"But I never even called you. Never called you at all."

"Naah. You never called me."

"Never."

"Never."

"Read."

Mathison continues. After a few lines, Kevin barks, "I never came nowhere. I never met nobody and I damn sure didn't split no cocaine delivery."

As if he is aware that the conversation is on tape, aware that Kevin is looking for an explicit exoneration from the man who may well be the government's witness against him, Mathison spells it out. "You didn't talk to nobody and you didn't split no shit."

"I got a important question for you. What is you doin' in my paperwork?"

"I fuckin' have no idea, Kev."

"And! And! And!" Kevin repeats as his anger mounts. "I got another question, an' you better have a answer to this one. How come *you* ain't been arrested? How come you ain't in jail?"

Mathison can only repeat the question as if dumbfounded by the mystery of it all. "How come they didn't come arrest me? How come they didn't get me?"

Arlene, still in the doorway to the kitchen, tries to help, desperate to add something that will take her boyfriend off the hot seat. "They probably will come get him." She nods her head to emphasize the certainty that the police will come to arrest her boyfriend. Her toddler wrests his hand loose from hers and runs smiling to Kevin, where he stands swatting Kevin's knee, looking up and giggling. Arlene walks to the window and studies the street, praying to see a patrol car. The calculus of the moment is simple. Indio Mathison's arrest for a Class A felony will ease the more imminent and extreme danger of being suspected of being a snitch by a man named Killa Kev.

"Why they didn't come get me?" Mathison is almost shouting as Davis grabs his indictment papers and heads for the door.

"That's what I want to know."

RAMSEY'S PLACE

|||||||||||||||||||||||||||||||||||||||||||||||||||||||||||||||||||||||||||||||||||||||||||||||||||||||||||

It is three weeks later. Kevin is alone in the living room on Livingston Street. "Ahhh. Check this shit out on television. Karen. Come. Come!"

Despite the problems with the Mercedes and despite his empty job prospects and the maddening conspiracy case, Kevin is on his back laughing and screaming, yelling for Karen, who drops her attitude long enough to hurry into the living room.

The six o'clock news is on, the screen flickering with a video of a rangy young black man in a long white T-shirt being led into a police station in handcuffs. Beside him is a tall young woman with the same style white T-shirt. "Last night Corning police arrested a couple for selling crack out of their ground-floor apartment. Roger Smoot, twenty-one, and his girlfriend Joy Peters, twenty-two, were both charged with criminal possession of a controlled substance in the third degree."

Even Karen has to chuckle at the sight of Main grimacing into the television lights.

"Now I know why I never saw the little nigger. Now I know why he was always smilin'. Ahh. Now I know what the fuck he was doin'."

"What's so funny, Kevin? I thought he was your friend."

"He is. He is. But how stupid can you be? Joy too. One of the only black dudes in Corning in the middle of all them rich white people an' this nigger think he's gonna sell crack out his kitchen door. Ahh!"

Julia is halfway down the stairs when Kevin takes up the chant. "Free Main! Free Main! Free Main!"

The child is tempted to join in the fun until she sees that her mother is not amused.

"You know what I'ma do? Serious. I'm getting FREE MAIN T-shirts and wear them to the courthouse. Julia, you wanna FREE MAIN T-shirt, don't you?"

"No."

The next court date for the Indio Mathison conspiracy charge is more than a month away. When the day arrives, another delay is mandated. The matter likely will not be resolved until after the summer. Kevin tells everyone he meets that it is a bullshit case and he knows from his long experience with the criminal justice system that delay works in his favor. But still the case is driving him crazy.

He doesn't even have the mental energy to joust with Karen. Julia tugs on his hand and drapes herself around his neck as he sits pondering his case. He spends hours a day in the law library at the courthouse researching conspiracy cases. He's even on a handshake basis with a man he met there, Weeden Wetmore, a sharp defense attorney in the area, who knows Kevin is a boxer and has taken a liking to him. "I would love to take your case, Kevin," Wetmore tells him in the hallway outside the reading room of the library, "but I can't. I have so many other things going on. Besides, I'm too tight with the judge, Jim Hayden."

In the third week of May, Kevin drives the Mercedes a couple of hours away to Rochester to meet with a lawyer Weeden Wetmore has referred him to. The attorney wants $10,000. Kevin Davis doesn't have that kind of money and is about to walk out of the office when the Rochester lawyer gives him a valuable tip. "I talked to Weeden about your case and we both thought that you should think about *People vs. Schulze*. Tell whatever attorney you do use about *Schulze*."

Back in Elmira, Kevin looks up the case, which hinges on the prosecution's burden to supply the defense with a copy of the warrant within fifteen days after arraignment or it is grounds for dismissal. Kevin finds some measure of peace in *Schulze*. His mind switches back and forth. One hour his mouth is dry with worry, and the next he is feeling good.

It is July 2004, a glove-soft evening. Kevin sits on the porch and listens to the silence. In many ways this is the life he had conjured when he was in jail, the life he had bargained for. The payoff is measurable in the peaceful shadows beyond the front porch where he sits chuckling at fate and the prospect of long life. The price is simple boredom. One woman, one wifey, one road. No more adrenaline.

I'm just chillin' on the porch. I had did my workout and even have my slippers on. Then Black and Sunshine roll up in a burgundy joint. Expedition. I step down off the porch and start kickin' it.

"Whas up?"
Kevin knows little about the two men in the front seat.
"We got the joint. Son, we rollin'. Get some birds. Find some chickens."
"Na, don' feel like it. Just chillin'."
"KK. Just hang. We got the joint."
Kevin changes his mind. He'll hang for a short while, take his mind off the case. He goes into the house and soon emerges dressed in black and white. A black baseball cap with ROCAWEAR on the crest, a black sweatshirt, black jeans, and glistening white-on-white Nike Uptown sneakers. He sits slouched in the backseat, on the low, his head barely visible from the outside of the car. The Expedition rolls over the Madison Avenue Bridge, over the Chemung River, into downtown Elmira.

Like Kevin, the two men in the front seats are from New York City, Black out of the Bronx and Sunshine from the Sumner projects in Brooklyn. Both are ex-cons who have lived in the Elmira, Rochester, and Binghamton area for several years. Big fish in a triangle of small ponds.

In the gulag of the New York State prison system, in the street world of New York City, and now even in a backwater like Elmira, associations can elevate your status or cost you your life. Black, in particular, has been anxious to hang with Kevin Davis, who he has heard through his prison connections is one of an increasingly rare breed, an absolutely "real nigger." Nothing less than a warrior.

So we head over to Willows. Nothin' poppin. So, boom, we jump back in the joint. Over the bridge to Ramsey's. Maybe we find some bitches in there. We make a right on Fifth, a left off Fifth, and pull up in front of the bar.

Ramsey's Place is a square building with a square four-sided bar, a pool table, and a TouchTunes jukebox along the wall. It is a black-owned bar in a black and white town, the kind of place you might find on the highway out of town somewhere in Mississippi. Drawn to the white girls, even trailer girls, rather than the black women here in Elmira or anywhere else, Kevin Davis wouldn't normally spend much time in a place like Ramsey's. Despite the banter, Kevin isn't really after women tonight. Sunshine and Black represent a little break from the family life, a flashback.

Inside Ramsey's, Kevin listens to a local named Rufus.

"Dude, Hollywood is fuckin' my girl. Can you believe that ill shit? Straight up. Not a suspicion, K., the truth. Rufus ain't gonna lay down for that now."

"Word."

"That snake Hollywood's in New York now. Pickin' up his money, they say. Better spend all that shit, 'cause his black ass is mine when he get back."

Sunshine is at the far end of Kevin's side of the bar, conversing with a pair of girls. Black is at the corner closest to the door when three young men step in. One is tall and light-skinned, basketball-player-looking, and the other two are short like Kevin. One has freckles around his slant eyes and wears a shiny red jacket.

Me and son in the red jacket have eye contact and then I go over to sit next to Black. I remember the dude from somewhere but I can't place it. I order two Hennys on the rocks. Me and Black is polyin' and reminiscin'.

"How you know little Rob from Sumner? Black, I thought you was a Bronx dude."

"Yeah, but I know dudes in Brooklyn. Yeah, little Rob. He used to fuck with Foxy Brown."

"Yeah, yeah."

Kevin's eyes are rosy with drink. Four Hennessys in forty minutes. Maybe it is the stress of the conspiracy case. He doesn't usually drink. Doesn't even belong here. There is no money to be made in this place. No progress. In prison, Kevin vowed he would treat each day like a military campaign, making only smooth essential moves, always gaining some kind of ground. Still, the air here at Ramsey's, the flow, reminds him of Brownsville, Brooklyn, and prison, of his former life.

"Little Rob, yeah."

A cell phone chimes and one of the short young men, the one in the red jacket, no older than twenty, steps outside to answer it. Kevin watches him through the window as the youth paces in front of the bar. Kevin thinks again. He knows the kid from somewhere.

Kevin sips his drink and checks out a woman as she slides over and starts talking to the tall light-skinned companion of the man in the red jacket.

I'm not thinkin' about no woman right there. I'm drinkin' 'cause I know I'm goin' home and get it on with my woman. I'm a little fucked up, for real. Then the red jacket comes back and the two short dudes sit at a table right next to the front door. They look funny. Not like they're treacherous but like they uncomfortable 'cause I'm in there and they don't know me. They lookin' at me an' I'm lookin' back. I'm definitely under the influence of alcohol. If I wasn't I coulda seen what was goin' on circumstantially.

Kevin speaks to the red jacket. "Yo, whas up? Whas poppin'? Wasn't you in jail with me?"

"Yeah, county."

"Come here. Lemme holler at you. Come here."

"You come here."

"Na. Come over here."

Kevin's invitation is good-natured, designed to cut the tension. But it is also calculated to "son" the kid, establish his dominance. The red jacket holds back and then rises from his chair.

"'S your name?"

"Shiloh."

"This my man Black."

I reach out to give my man a dap. But he's still on point, avoidin' me. I'm rememberin' him now. He was on the gate in county when I was there, grillin' me and then later startin' shit with my man. Talkin' to my man about suck my dick. You tell a dude to suck your dick in jail you better be ready to kill or die.

"Yo, be safe, son. Stay outta jail."

The kid slides past Kevin on his way back to the jukebox as Kevin catches a grill from the other short guy at the table by the door. These are some bold-ass little motherfuckers, Kevin thinks, as he stares the kid down. As the half seconds click by, the kid's hard look changes from fearful defiance to pure challenge. In jail, in the projects, Kevin Davis had lived by his powers of observation and interpretation, his focus. He always made the first move. But in the glow of four Hennessys and the soft nest of Elmira, his instincts fail him.

As he locks eyes with the kid by the door, he catches a white flash out of the corner of his eye and then there is a crunching sound as the red jacket behind him reaches back and swings a ball-peen hammer down into the left side of Kevin Davis's jaw. Everything goes to flame. Bits of teeth and flesh fly back into Kevin's throat as the flash turns to searing pain.

The kid has swung the hammer with all his strength but Kevin doesn't topple from his barstool. In the hazy chamber of his mind there is no shock, no fear, little confusion. Like a firefighter trapped in a blaze, Kevin knows exactly what is going on and what has to be done. He ducks, tucks his chin against another blow, and reaches for the only thing he can make out, a red jacket moving fast toward the door. Thousands of rounds in the ring assert themselves as Kevin Davis, Killa Kevin, trained boxer and thug, does the only thing he has ever methodically taught himself to do: fight.

Even as he sinks toward the floor, Kevin holds on to the red jacket with his left hand and throws slow, mechanical uppercuts with his right. The kid twists and ducks, yanks and squirms, but he can't wiggle out of the jacket or Kevin's grasp. Shards of pain rocket from his jaw into his brain but Kevin has regained his balance, is standing now. With full leverage from his legs, he drills uppercuts till the kid's head snaps back again and again.

But a bar is not a boxing ring. A street fight cannot go on for more than a few seconds before bad things start to happen, even for the winner. Kevin's back is to the door, near where Black is exchanging punches with the tall light-skinned guy. This leaves the other short guy, the one with the hard stare, to launch out of his seat toward Kevin.

I'm whippin' the dude out who had the hammer, hittin' him like four or five times. Bing. Bing. When I feel a pinch, another and another. Dude by the door is stickin' me with a little knife. A four-finger joint. I let the red jacket dude go for a second to deal with the knife, and the red jacket dude runs out the door. Boom, I'm right behind him. He's runnin' so fast he's kickin' himself in the ass. He runs over one block and out on the Clemens Parkway runnin' against traffic an' I'm right behind him. He runs right out of a sneaker. He gets away and I walk back in the bar with his sneaker, a red and gray Adidas. Still got that shit.

Black and Sunshine are comin' out. I'm laughin' at the way the dude ran outta his sneaker but at the same time I'm furious.

"Let's go back in."

Black and Sunshine are like, "Be easy." And I'm like fuck that. I got three stab wounds in my back and I'm spittin' mad blood and teeth. I'm askin', "Why ain't y'all fucked up?"

"We can't go back in there. Yo, dudes got knives and guns in there."

"I don't give a fuck about that."

Whoop! Whoop! Whoop! As the police tramp into the bar, Kevin, Black, and Sunshine mount the Expedition and start tracing the area. "Dude got to be around here somewhere."

Kevin demands a ride back to his house, where he runs into a back room. With his "izoint," his gun, now in hand, he dismisses Sunshine and Black.

"Get the fuck outta here 'fore I kill one of *you* motherfuckers."

Karen drives him back to Ramsey's, screaming at him the whole way.

"How fuckin' stupid can you be, Kevin? You don't know what kind of beefs those two guys have. You don't even know if they set you up. Why didn't you just stay home?"

Luckily for both Kevin and Shiloh, the attackers are not at Ramsey's. Later, at the hospital, a doctor removes pieces of broken teeth from his gums but Kevin refuses stitches for his back. Asks for just a bagful of gauze pads to dab his ruined mouth and plug the stab wounds. But while the nurse is getting the gauze, someone calls the police. Kevin is shirtless, leaning forward in a chair, as the police approach.

"What happened?" a detective asks.

There is no answer.

"You have anything to say?"

"Yeah. Ouch."

"You're bleeding pretty bad, Mr. Davis. Who stabbed you?"

"Don't know."

"You don't want to say?"

"Nope."

The attack is a mystery. Was it mistaken identity, a setup, or a simple barroom brawl? Interpretations pour Kevin's way from Rochester, Binghamton, and from surrounding prisons. One account has Black in a beef with a former drug partner in Rochester. The attack was a planned assault on Black, and Kevin had been at the wrong place at the wrong time. From locals comes word that Shiloh, the guy in the red jacket, is a mad agent with a case of lethal stupidity. Kevin had frightened him into a first strike. Whatever the truth, Kevin knows that the second attack will come.

"This shit is real," he tells Black. "Whoever did it knows I don't play. They gonna try to finish the shit. Don't be drivin' around here like this is la-la land. This is Elmira but this is serious. I don't sleep on people when it comes to shit like that. Don't be bar-hoppin'. Put your car away and stay in the house till you find out what's goin' on."

The next day a call comes from Trip, who is in New York City.

"I don't want to talk."

Kevin is suspicious of Trip. He has heard that Trip's name appears in the paperwork of two guys arrested for shooting two cops during an armed robbery in Pennsylvania.

Trip promises Kevin, "I'll talk with you tomorrow in Elmira at your crib."

"No, let's go to your crib."

Karen drives Kevin over to Trip's apartment at Hathorn Court the next day. Sunshine is on hand, standing against a wall, nervously shifting his weight, as Kevin rehashes the attack. Trip is incensed. He knows the freckle-faced kid. "What! What!" Trip bounces off the couch, ready for action. He bangs his hand on the coffee table for emphasis. "Let's do this shit right now."

"Be easy," Kevin responds. "I can't do it like that. The police know."

But Trip will not be deterred. He uses his cell phone to call a couple of girls. Holsters, gun keepers. "Bring my joints, my ammo."

With a smashed lip and pain in his mouth as points of his shattered teeth scrape his tongue, Kevin is still mindful not to let some trifling local girls know his deadly business.

"Yo, don't be lettin' chicks in on this shit."

Karen, outside in the Mercedes, tired of the heat, climbs from the car, walks across the front lawn, and steps through the front door into the darkened room. Trip and Kevin see her and they move to the kitchen. Sunshine follows. As they slide through the shadows, a hand presses an envelope into Karen's. Drugs or money, she guesses. She squeezes the envelope under the plastic band of her slacks. So what? She'd held things for people before.

"Yo, son," Trip continues. "I can't let this happen."

"No, be easy, I said. The police already know what happened. They already know what time it is."

Bam, bam, bam. Windows at the front of the apartment shatter. A gust of wind blows past Karen's face. She dives to the floor as a "flashbang," a stun grenade, blasts against the living room wall. Trapped and expecting a platoon of gangsters to pour in one door or the other, Kevin and Sunshine squat and scramble out the back door.

"Police! Police!"

Relieved, Kevin lies down on the ground and stretches his arms out over his head. He hears a police officer's voice as he stares at the blades of grass inches from his face. The voice is oddly solicitous.

"Kevin was hurt last night," Investigator Weed is explaining to a uniform. "Kevin, you all right?"

Kevin Davis is thinking, This is some small-town shit, and wondering, What the fuck they doin', treatin' me like I'm a king?

Inside, they are not treating Trip or Karen nearly as well. Trip is searched and arrested for possession of crack cocaine. In an upstairs bathroom Karen is strip-searched by a policewoman.

"The lady cop is just standin' there starin' at my titties," Karen tells Kevin later. As Karen and the policewoman exit the bathroom, a policeman notices vials of crack on the bathroom floor where they must have fallen out of Karen's clothes and Karen is arrested. Outside, a most unusual conversation is transpiring.

The police hoist Kevin Davis by both arms and sit him next to Sunshine on the steps to the first-floor apartment. "Kevin, one of my brothers knows you," a cop is saying.

"So what? I don't know you."

"He's a CO at Southport."

"Yeah?"

Then Investigator Weed comes up with a bizarre demand. "I don't have to let you go," he says, "unless you promise not to retaliate against anybody for what happened last night."

"What kind of a law is that?"

The police are frustrated and determined to stop what has been a season of gunfire on the streets of Elmira. Weed is trying to get inside Kevin's head. "I'm serious, Kevin," he says.

"This is some hillbilly bullshit."

"If you don't promise not to kill anybody, I'm gonna have to take you in."

"Fuck that, I ain't gonna kill nobody. I ain't about that." Amazingly, on the basis of a promise not to commit murder, back at the police station Killa Kev Davis is uncuffed and set free.

Black heeds Kevin's advice. Two nights after the attack in the bar, the day after the police have shot a stun grenade through the window of Trip's apartment, he drives over to Hathorn Court to see his girlfriend and pick up his clothes and belongings. His plan is to travel to Tennessee with a friend and stay there until the danger in Elmira subsides. At two a.m., when Black and his friend step out of the burgundy Expedition and approach the girlfriend's apartment, a man comes out of the shadows shooting. Some residents report five shots. Others are awakened by two gunshots and a woman's scream. Wounded in the head, Black dies face down on the sidewalk beside a straight birch tree.

Kevin gets a call an hour later. "Your man Black just got twisted."

"I Can't Go to Prison"

||||||||||||||||||||||||||||||||||||||||||||||||||||||||||||||||||||||||||||||||||||||||||||||||||||||

Karen is released the next day, after Kevin calls in every favor he can from acquaintances in Elmira and New York to raise the $1,000 cash payment on $5,000 bail. Trip is given a $25,000 bond. Outside the courthouse, Karen is not relieved to be free. Instead she is hysterical, weeping and shaking from her ordeal and from the realization that there is going to be no easy way out of this difficulty. She had been holding the drugs for someone, but shifting the blame is probably out of the question.

"They told me, my lawyer told me, that I could get off if I told them that the drugs were yours. They were mad when you bailed me out," she tells Kevin.

"They wanted you in jail for the weekend so they could scare you."

Kevin speaks softly but he is fired with rage. The way he looks at it, with Karen's charge the downside is a year in jail, most likely probation, and quite possibly no indictment at all. When they point the finger at him they are talking about decades in prison. They are threatening his life.

The following Monday morning, Investigator Weed is standing in the courthouse hallway among a group of suited men who look to Kevin like federal agents. Inside an office, Karen's lawyer is exhorting her once again to give Kevin Davis up and avoid being charged. When she comes out of the meeting, Karen is again shaken.

"Kevin, they are still trying to get me to say that the drugs were yours.

They say that is the only way that I am going to stay out of jail. They want to send me to prison for years, Kevin." Her eyes are brimming and her voice reedy. "Kevin, are you listening? I can't go to prison."

Kevin Davis does not believe that the prosecutors really want to send a white girl who has never been arrested to state prison. Furthermore, he knows that if she does go to prison it is not the end of the world, that she will survive and probably be out in a matter of months.

"Where the fuck is your lawyer?"

Investigator Weed overhears Kevin's question. "I think he just walked out the front door."

Kevin trots downstairs. On the street, he is heaving with anger as he stands face-to-face with the Legal Aid attorney.

"Why you tryin' to get Karen to say the drugs was mine?"

"I didn't say that. That's what the district attorney is saying."

Kevin struggles to prevent an unplanned explosion. *Cops, judges, DAs, and lawyers. All the same. Fuck them all.* He smiles through the broken landscape of his mouth. Someone will pay if he is sent back to prison as a result of the backroom machinations of these suited men.

"Only in Elmira can you do shit like that and walk the streets," he says.

The attorney says nothing. He is used to small-town cases and petty losers, has gotten used to being a comfortable witness to catastrophes in others' lives. He is not accustomed to worrying about his own welfare, not used to being threatened by killers. Twenty feet away from the steps of the courthouse, half a dozen white men wearing dark glasses see Kevin glaring at the lawyer. They are lawmen. To them, Kevin Davis, dark-skinned and scarred, heavily muscled, wearing the cloak of his New York City reputation, is a grim threat in the area, a harbinger of future horrors. Kevin wheels and faces the handful of plainclothes officers, Feds, or whatever they are. To him it doesn't matter. They are the enemy. He walks straight at them. The flood tide of anger is receding now and Kevin uses what is left to taunt the police.

"Hello, coppers."

But like so much that he does, this challenge is oblique, theatrical, and calculated. He hasn't threatened the lawyer directly and he isn't exactly throwing the gauntlet down to the cops right now. But his tone is pure challenge and he is moving straight ahead. The cops have never seen anything like it and they don't enjoy the experience. They rely on their own mythology to bolster their courage and their argument. This isn't the big city, where thugs and punks run wild.

The biggest cop steps down one step toward Kevin. "We don't tolerate that shit around here. We will kick your ass right here and now."

"We?"

Kevin spits the plural pronoun back out as if a bug had crawled into his throat. Then he veers off, heading back up the stairs into the courthouse where Karen is waiting, balanced on the edge of a bench in the second-floor hallway. Investigator Weed is talking to several other men a few feet from her.

Kevin aims his words at the assistant district attorney who spoke for the state at Karen's bail hearing.

"You the DA? How you gonna get the fuckin' lawyer to say the drugs is mine? I'll tell you what. You all want me that bad? You drop the charges on her and I'll leave town. And I won't kill nobody."

Investigator Weed speaks softly. It is as if the authorities are enjoying the drama. "Kevin, this is not the place to talk. We can work something out but not here."

"You don't want me in town, I'm goin' back to New York."

A week after the attack at Ramsey's and five days after Black's murder, the police come looking for Kevin Davis to question him. "You tell him to come and talk to us," they tell Karen, "or we will charge him with murder. He can help you by telling us who did it."

"He left for New York last night," she tells them. "He told you he was going to leave."

With Black's murderers somewhere in the shadows and the police resolved to stick a drug or murder case on him, Kevin is indeed out of town.

He is in New York with Paula, the secretary with the burgundy scarf, the woman he has been sneaking over to see a couple times a week for the past several months. Even though they had a vicious blowup the night Karen was in jail, Paula has inexplicably agreed to take a week off from work, drive Kevin to New York City, and help him pay the cost of living there for a while. The two slipped out of town late Tuesday night in Paula's Ford Explorer.

When the detectives leave Karen, she immediately calls Kevin. When he reaches for his phone he is seated on a bed in a hotel room just over the Brooklyn Bridge in downtown Brooklyn. Paula is across the room sprawled in a chair. Kevin checks the number of the incoming call, holds his cell phone in his right hand, and lifts the index finger of his left hand to his lips. Paula sniffs. "Yeah, Kevin. Sure. Whatever you say. You're the man, aren't you?"

Kevin lays the chiming phone carefully on the bed beside his leg and looks at the woman. The skin below her right eye is fish-scale green and blue. The night Karen was locked in a cell, Kevin had hit Paula.

It had taken all Kevin's strength and accumulated wisdom not to retaliate for the attack in Ramsey's. He prides himself for making the unprecedented, the unexpected choice. He even reckons that his mysterious inaction has added to his reputation, rendering him even more frightening by virtue of his unpredictability. But Kevin has doubts, for him an unusual and uncomfortable feeling. He is certainly not afraid of Shiloh. He has already beaten the little punk's ass. Kevin has pulled a trigger many times before and he will do it again if he has to. He isn't afraid of war. But he is concerned about the legal consequences, and concern is the cousin of fear.

Smart and crisply attractive, Paula has her own troubles. She has been sick to death of backwoods Elmira for a long time. There isn't a man in town who can do a thing for her but Kevin Davis, the only exciting thing that has happened to her in years. And she is resolved to either stay in Elmira as Kevin's lover, his woman, or gather her toddler son and get the hell out of town.

But Kevin Davis isn't making even the smallest step to leave his girlfriend around the corner. Won't talk about telling Karen, won't even lie and say he is thinking about making a change. All that heat, that grinding, heart-stopping sex flies back at Paula. It was all fake, and so was Kevin Davis, as far as she is concerned. There is nothing left but to find another black man in Elmira and taunt Kevin Davis with him, make Kevin feel as bad as she does.

That night with Karen away in the county lockup, Kevin had taken the opportunity to question Paula about the other man he had heard about. She had laughed in his face. "Why should I worry about you? Why should *he* worry about you? You ain't nothing but a fake-ass nigger." Jealousy and self-doubt connected in the back of Kevin's mind and he threw the left hook with purpose. Kevin knew the punch was a bad sign, an indication of weakness and confusion; still, he was not ashamed. Striking a woman for him was simply not the taboo it was for most men.

The physical conflicts between him and the rugged Francesca had been fights, not beatings. Sure, he had whipped Shorty Dip's ass once, but most everyone in Brownsville respected him more for it, even Shorty herself.

Neither did Paula consider the punch an outrage. She never called the police and here she is with him in New York.

"How'd you like the beach?" Kevin allows the phone to continue chiming as he changes the subject. That afternoon, the two had sat at a table on the boardwalk at Jones Beach on Long Island, watching the pale people on the white sand and the foam-flecked gray-green Atlantic behind.

"Fucking beautiful," Paula answers, lighting a cigarette. "If that was Karen, call her back, Kevin. Don't worry about me."

On the phone to Karen, Kevin is insistent that the authorities don't want her. "They want me. They don't want you. They ain't gonna indict you."

A grand jury indicts Karen seven days later.

Besides implicating Kevin, there is another way for Karen to beat the drug charge. The idea of pointing the finger at Trip comes up. But Kevin is adamant. Clinging to his perverse integrity, he will have nothing to do with informing on Trip.

"I don't even get involved in that. I won't do that. It's not my category."

The maneuver would not involve Kevin Davis informing on anyone. The person cooperating with the state of New York would not be Kevin Davis. It would be Karen Tanski, a citizen, nonparticipant in the criminal world and beyond the code of the street. But, as chivalrous as Kevin Davis portrays himself to be, a man of honor and protector of the weak, he is also startlingly selfish. Not only is it unacceptable, unthinkable, that he would say a word to the police to gain advantage, it is also forbidden for Karen to avail herself of any advantage as a result of providing information. All because she is Kevin Davis's woman.

"Nah. No. No. It can't happen. I can't have it all over the state that my woman is a snitch. No. That is impossible. It won't happen."

Even if the drugs were Trip's, who was stupid enough to have them in his house in the first place? Even if Trip is himself a suspected snitch whose name appears in the paperwork in several recent cases?

"No, not even then. Not any way. Not any how."

Two weeks later Kevin is back in Elmira at Livingston Street with Karen. On the surface it looks as if the attack at Ramsey's and Karen's arrest had never happened. The pain in Kevin's mouth has subsided. The three shallow stab wounds in his back have all but healed. Kevin watches as Karen tap-taps idly on the keys of her computer and studies the screen that displays Kevin Davis's résumé. She has told Kevin over and over that he must find a job. Not only for the money but to keep him out of trouble. She is sure his inactivity leads to his association with friends who are involved in illegal activities and his affairs with women. She has a hard time understanding Kevin's attraction to men like Trip. "Those people bore me," she tells Kevin. "Besides, if you're tired from workin' you won't want to hang out all the time."

On top of the computer screen is Kevin Davis's statement of goals. "To obtain an entry level position that uses my problem solving, leadership and organization skills." On the wall above the computer is the diploma Karen got from the high school extension program in Elmira. "Karen Ann Tanski, Graduate. June 21, 2001." When she was twenty years old.

Kevin taps his foot on the floor and stays silent. This is a very delicate time for him. So many times he has congratulated himself on his discipline, his intelligence, and his foresight. But there is no escaping that he has stumbled badly. What is more difficult for him to swallow is that he has jeopardized someone else with his stupidity. What was he thinking, associating with a local hothead like Trip? There were always women around the young drug dealer and there was money, but it was not worth the risk that came with Trip's impetuosity, the absence of design in his relationships and his activities. Karen had warned him so often. Kevin cannot admit to her that she was right. Cannot permit the power structure in the relationship to be altered in the light of day.

But last night in bed, as he lay pondering his troubles, he heard Karen catching her breath, then crying softly beside him. He pulled her close, held her head on his chest, carefully removed a strand of her hair from between his lips, and whispered, "Baby, I'm sorry."

With a deep sigh, Karen turns off the computer and lifts herself from the computer chair. Dressed in a gray business suit with a white blouse, she heads downtown. With her steady gaze and no-nonsense tone of voice, Karen Tanski could be headed to a job in the financial district or to her position as a well-compensated executive assistant, but she is not going to work today. She has decided to plead guilty to the drug charge, no sense denying that she had the drugs, and her lawyer has told her that the judge will probably go easy on a young mother with no record. She is headed to William Street today for a meeting with a parole officer, an interview that will be included in a presentencing report that the judge will take into consideration when deciding if and for how long Karen must spend time in state prison for possession of eleven grams of cocaine.

She sits for half an hour in the waiting room. Kevin has convinced her to switch lawyers to a local attorney with the unlikely name of Richie Rich. Rich quickly convinced Karen to plead guilty to possession with intent to sell, based on the amount of drugs involved rather than any presumption of her actual intent, emphasizing the likelihood that if she got any time at all she would be assigned to CASAT, an anti-drug program that would shorten her actual time served to a matter of months. Kevin had agreed with the strategy. There was no telling what might happen at trial.

Rosa Calderone Clark, about forty-five, with short brown hair, is sitting behind her desk looking at Karen's paperwork. Karen's educational and work history are straightforward but not typical of local girls swept into the drug business in Elmira. She had been thrown out of high school at sixteen for poor attendance but she came back to school, got her high school diploma, and graduated from the Elmira Business Institute.

Clark adjusts her papers and examines Karen's work record. At fifteen and sixteen she worked at Wendy's. Then there were industrial jobs, Elmira Stamping, and an office job at the racetrack doing payroll.

Clark listens to Karen's description of her household situation and, when Karen mentions Kevin Davis's name, pretends to check the name against Karen's indictment. Clark labors to make her connection appear spontaneous.

The parole officer wants to discuss Kevin Davis. She warns Karen that Davis is not someone she should want to be around.

Karen Tanski stays quiet. Observant and sharp-tongued with Kevin, she is strangely passive with representatives of the criminal justice system.

Karen stares at the parole officer and says nothing. There is no turning away from Kevin Davis now. But he is making mistake after mistake. No wonder the police think he is a major drug dealer. He has the car; he is often in the company of men like Trip. But it is all an act. Can't they see that? He doesn't have any money. Had to call everybody he ever knew to get the $1,000 to get her out of jail.

Karen can't think of a thing to say. As smart and tough as she is, she is not equipped to fight the system. Maybe that is why she fell in love with a man who is.

Clark insists that whatever the reason Karen is with Davis, she has to rethink her decision. She presses on, explaining that Davis is thirty-five years old. Karen and her other codefendants are ten years younger.

Karen looks at the table where her indictment is spread, tries to make out the notes that Clark has taken in the margins but can't, as Clark argues that Davis went to prison for a long time and came out smarter, more calculating. In prison, she explains, he learned how to manipulate people, people like Karen, into taking the fall for him.

"You don't know him," Karen says.

The parole officer asks Karen if she had been in a bad relationship before she met Kevin Davis.

"No."

She asks Karen if Davis visited her when she was in prison.

"I was only in jail for one day."

Clark wants to know if Karen thinks Davis will visit her when she is in state prison hundreds of miles away.

"Yes."

Clark repeats her message, explaining again that Davis is the kind of man who gets others to take risks for him.

This is an echo of what the police and the prosecutors had said and even what her first defense lawyer had implied.

"Ms. Clark, I didn't take a fall for anyone. I had what I had and I took the plea because I had what I had."

Rosa Calderone Clark has a point. When Karen Tanski met Kevin Davis and was drawn in by his smile and self-assurance, she had just graduated from Elmira Business Institute. Two years later she is preparing to enter the state prison system. No accounting of Davis's qualities, from his charisma to his intelligence to his loyalty, can erase that one truth. If she thought it was hard to find a good job in an economically depressed region with an eight-year-old child and a degree from a business school, she will find out what her job prospects are with a prison record added to her credentials. Karen does not realize what an irreversible step she has taken.

"You don't know Kevin Davis," Karen whispers. Sensing an opening, Clark takes one final stab at getting Karen to consider rolling over on Kevin Davis, or at least breaking off the relationship.

She tells Karen that Davis is a seasoned criminal and he does not have her best interests at heart.

Karen wants to tell the woman that Kevin Davis is no kingpin. His Mercedes is thirteen years old and worth half as much as new compact cars all over Elmira. That the rent is paid by her mother's Social Security checks, and those who were arrested had been selling drugs long before Kevin Davis made Elmira his home.

"I'm not going to tell on anyone. I have to live in this town."

The parole officer, stacking her papers to signal that the interview is over, inquires offhandedly if Karen has relatives in other towns.

"No, I don't have relatives in other towns," Karen snaps. "I live in Elmira."

TEMPORARY INSANITY

||||||||||||||||||||||||||||||||||||||||||||||||||||||||||||||||||||||||||||||||||||||||||||||||||||||||||||||||||||||||||||||||||||

Karen is adamant. Kevin has to find a job right away. Driving around town in his Mercedes, wearing his crisp clothing, and pulling out wads of bills, no matter how much of it is a skillful act, is still a red flag to the police and prosecutors.

This morning the dispute is over a purpose statement on Kevin's résumé. He is against including one. He wants to let the facts stand for themselves. Karen thinks differently and she is sure she knows better. Hasn't she been to business school? Isn't she the "college girl" in the family?

Kevin genuinely loves Karen. But there is some resentment at Karen's status, and especially her supposed superior intelligence.

Kevin came of age in the Brownsville cauldron where the hot fire of everyday life burned off pretense, leaving only the residue of a person's worth. In a neighborhood where raw intelligence is prized as much as bravery, where a crowd will gather around a chess game nearly as fast as around a fistfight, no one gives up an inch when it comes to brainpower. Sure, there are concessions to education and book smarts, but when it comes to the basic ability to figure out the best course of action in any situation, Kevin will never cede the initiative. He has always taken an active part in his legal defense. Thinks nothing of telling men who have graduated from college and law school about the law and the best courtroom strategy. He certainly isn't going to allow Karen to dictate how he will present himself on his résumé.

"Leave it off," he orders as Karen slouches at the computer in the dining room. Betsy sprawls on a recliner watching television, while Julia pads around in the kitchen waiting for the Pop-Tart she is toasting for breakfast to appear.

"All right," Karen answers. "Leave the mission statement off. You're the one who's going to look stupid."

Kevin's mother sucker-punched his elementary school teacher, got her face on television for attacking the teacher who called Kevin Davis stupid. It is not an insult that he is inclined to laugh off or ignore. Kevin leans over and flicks a light but stinging smack to Karen's cheek with the back of his hand.

Karen has grown up watching her mother brawl with her father. She is a fighter herself, not about to turn the other cheek.

She sprints into the kitchen and grabs two knives, which she brandishes from ten feet away while Kevin chuckles. "What the fuck do you intend to do with those shits?" In her Mickey Mouse sleeping shirt, Julia stands barefoot in the doorway of the kitchen clutching her breakfast Pop-Tart. Twister runs past Julia into the kitchen. Julia hasn't seen the slap and isn't sure what is going on. But it isn't a game she is watching, because Betsy is sitting bolt upright now, her saucer eyes wider than ever with alarm. Still, it can't be too serious, because KK is giggling as he walks across the room and takes both knives away from Karen. "What you gonna do with those. Uh?"

Karen allows Kevin to take the knives but there is something else Kevin remembers about the moment, a memory that will make him move with more caution in the future. As he spins the knives around like six-shooters, so that the points are facing away from him, he looks into Karen's eyes for an instant. Her pupils are huge, dilated with anger.

"Temporarily insane," he tells Main later in the day.

What was Karen Tanski doing with Kevin Davis? Depending on the judgment of the court, in a month or two she could very well be packed off to state prison, leaving her daughter under the care of her mother and assorted relatives for what might be a year, leaving Julia to be counseled and nurtured by a schizophrenic and a notorious thug. Why?

What had brought Karen Tanski to this point? Was it love, boredom? Was Kevin Davis Karen's adventure, her rebellion? Was it simply bad judgment, laziness?

It doesn't seem to be sex that keeps them together. In bed, they show more affection than passion. Maybe that is part of the answer for Karen. Despite his infidelities and his temper, Kevin Davis, sober, precise, solid, is still the closest thing to a man that Karen has ever met.

The morning after the slap, Kevin just has to get out of town for a few days. As he guides the Mercedes onto Route 17 toward Binghamton, the thought crosses his mind that he has made a mess of Elmira. He has the conspiracy case hanging over him and Karen may go jail. Shit, even his little man Main is locked up. Then he snaps his focus back to the positive side, something he has done all his life. The knife wounds in his back and his lost teeth are nothing to him. Nothing at all.

He reviews the retaliation issue. A lesser man would be driven to strike back, forced by expectations, both in Elmira and throughout the prison world, to send a missile, somebody like Main, out after Shiloh. But Kevin tells himself he isn't just any man.

A Chevrolet Caprice pulls up beside him, falls back, then sweeps past. Kevin's fingers tighten on the padded steering wheel. There is only one person in the car, a middle-aged man. But the Feds use all kinds of people. They even use dudes pretending to be Jews with yarmulkes and this sure looks like the kind of car a Fed would drive. When he spots the car an hour later, a hundred miles closer to New York, Kevin is sure the Feds are on his tail. He looks up to the sky for helicopters. Then he slows down, lets the car pass, and pulls up fast to within several feet of its rear bumper. When the driver looks into his rearview, Kevin grins and points his finger straight and sure. No Feds will ever get the drop on him.

A few days later, Kevin is back home. Karen has something to say, Kevin can tell. She is staring at him in the kitchen, waits till Betsy walks out of the room, and is about to open her mouth when Julia pads in. When he walks upstairs, Karen is behind him. He steps into the bedroom at the top of the stairs and she follows, sits on the bed. Kevin is not anxious to hear whatever Karen has to say. Lately, all she has been talking about is how she can't go to prison, how she is not cut out to do time.

He regrets the stories that he has told her about jail, about the pressure of having so many dishonest and unhealthy people around you in a closed environment, about all the adjustments and strategies it takes to survive. Karen will be able to do a few months if she has to. Just stay away from too many people, Kevin tells her, do your own thing, and don't borrow from or lend to anybody. The rules are simple and Karen is a smart girl. Smart works in prison. That is, if she has to go. The likelihood is that she will get probation. So what is the panic all about?

"'S up?"

"I'm pregnant."

"Say?"

"*Pregnant.*"

"Finally."

Kevin Davis does not have to act happy. Normally he does not sing or dance, but he feels like jumping now. Instead, he squats down in front of Karen, wraps his heavy arms around her legs, and buries his head in her lap and giggles.

"Damn."

"You glad, Kevin?"

"We gonna have a beautiful baby, you know that. The best thing you could give me."

"I'm happy too."

"Think. Think what he's gonna look like. Or she. Gorgeous."

Kevin looks up toward the dresser and Karen looks too. They watch the mirrored image of themselves seated on the bed. Black and blonde. Marble muscle against pillow-soft skin.

"Like us," Kevin says.

Despite his dalliances, Kevin's affection for Karen has deepened. He truly wants a child, a child of their own to raise the right way, with plenty of love but with purpose and discipline. Not like Julia. There won't be any of that hillbilly talking back. But Kevin is delighted with the pregnancy for another reason. No way in the world is the judge going to send a pregnant white girl with no criminal record to prison. That's for damn sure.

Kevin can't bring himself to trust Richie Rich any more than Karen's first lawyer. Rich is touting CASAT, the drug program, to shorten any possible sentence. They promise a lot, Kevin tells Karen, but what program you get once you are locked up is another story.

Still, Rich isn't all bad. One day on the street outside the courthouse,

Kevin tells him about his own case, the Indio Mathison conspiracy charge. When he tells him about the strategy he got from the Rochester lawyer, about *People vs. Schulze*, Richie brightens. "Right. Right."

That very same day, Rich outlines the *Schulze* strategy for Jerry Defilippo, Kevin's lawyer in the conspiracy case, while Kevin listens.

"Kevin is right," Rich tells Defilippo, shaking his head at the simplicity of the idea, "*Schulze* it's got to be. They violate that fifteen-day time frame without permission from the judge and their case is dead, dead in the water. Hayden'll never let them get away with that."

"The Feds Don't Want This Case"

||||||||||||||||||||||||||||||||||||||||||||||||||||||||||||||||||||||||||||||||||||||||||||||||||||||||||||||||||

Spring and early summer have come and gone. It is July 2005, a year since Karen's arrest, and delay has followed delay. Karen's sentencing has still not taken place. Kennedy Valve has not called. After much searching, Kevin has recovered the dog-eared letter from the federal government asking about his application to the company.

One afternoon, he drives over to the plant on Water Street and shows a lady there the letter. The men she passes the letter to appear to be alarmed and Kevin predicts he will be called to work soon. But still no call. Maybe they really do have a rule against violent felons. Both Kevin's Indio Mathison conspiracy case and Karen's sentencing are set to come up this month, but most of the family discussion has been about new beginnings, possibilities, about the baby.

Kevin drives Karen to the Twin Tier Women's Health Team on the west side of town. She is five months pregnant. Cruising on this bright and cool July day in the Mercedes, the young couple seem the picture of health and comfort. Perhaps it isn't blindness or laziness or even bad judgment that has kept Karen with Kevin. Karen has noticed that Paula, the secretary with the Ford Explorer, has disappeared from Elmira. Maybe being with Kevin Davis is a good thing after all, because in times like this when he is not running around with other women or lashing out, when he is taking care of family business or playing with Julia, life is better for her than it has ever been before.

A small fountain sits outside the freestanding three-story house that is home to the clinic. A car in the parking lot bears the sticker CHOOSE LIFE: YOUR MOM DID. It is easy to see why low-income New York City transplants and country folk from the area would choose Elmira, where they can be seen quickly at a clean, friendly, and apparently efficient health center like this. Elmira sure beats the hellhole New York clinics and the backwater Pennsylvania hospitals. In the examining room, Karen, in pink flip-flops and pink cotton pants, reclines on the table and lifts up her white shirt, allowing herself to be smeared with green goo.

Kevin, in shorts and work boots, sits on a chair a few feet away with a privileged view of a second screen that will show the images that appear on the monitor. "Just like I can see through you, I can see through the baby," the technician explains to Karen.

"How is that little bugger doin'?" Kevin asks, holding his hands in front, checking the face of his cell phone while hoping to learn that he will soon have a son.

The pudgy woman with the wand explains the gray-green images on the screen. "That's the cerebellum." Another image floats forward. "A hundred and fifty-seven beats a minute. That's wonderful."

"Can you tell if it's a boy or a girl?"

"We can when we get there," the woman says, with the intonation of an airline hostess.

Kevin points at a perfect picture of the baby's clenched fist and raises up both his fists in a boxer's stance, beaming. "He's gonna come out swingin'." Suddenly there is a close-up on the baby's face. Karen is silent. Kevin exhales. "Oh, my God."

Kevin's cell phone chirps a few bars from a rap song, "B-Boy Stance." The baby moves and the technician calls it a show-off.

Karen murmurs, "It's a girl."

"Damn," Kevin says. Then quickly, "It's okay. That's good. That's good. She's gonna be rough, though. I'll make her rough."

Karen turns and looks at Kevin, who smiles back. They both wanted a boy but the baby is perfectly healthy. Kevin raps his thigh and giggles. For a moment, Kevin Davis is not a big-city gangster with one foot back in the penitentiary. He isn't a slaphappy thug with no way to make a living and a penchant for other women. He is a father. He smacks his thigh again and holds the gaze of his woman.

"I'll name her Liberty."

Karen and the technician groan.

"She's gonna be with me all the time. I hope she comes out with blond hair and hazel eyes. I'm gonna get her one of those computerized Mercedes car seats. No hand-me-downs. Everything will be new."

In the car on the way home, Kevin is chortling about the baby's "white nose." But Karen holds up some of the still photos of the sonogram. "Kevin, she has a nose like you. Look how wide it is." Kevin is much more concerned the baby will look black than Karen is. "I can't wait to see what color skin she has," he says.

"I think that wide nose came from Julia. She got a nose just like Julia. She's definitely gonna have pretty hair. If my mother says anything about her nose, I'm gonna smack her."

Kevin and Karen pay $600 a month for their house on Livingston Street. Karen repeatedly reminds Kevin that the rent comes out of her mother's $908 monthly Social Security check. Karen is also on welfare, receiving $600 a month. Whatever the truth is about who pays the bills, Kevin will be more accountable if Karen goes to prison in August. He is trying another tactic at Kennedy. This time he has as a reference a man who works at the factory; maybe he can help somehow.

The next morning Kevin has his day in court. Kevin's conspiracy charge is apparently based solely on Indio Mathison wiretap transcripts. Defilippo files a motion to suppress the wiretap evidence based on the fact that the prosecution had not provided the defense with details of the recorded conversations within the allotted period of time. When Judge Hayden questions the prosecutor about why the legal time limit for disclosure has been ignored, the young assistant district attorney announces that he had been on vacation. New York criminal procedure law states specifically that "law office failure" is not good cause for delay. Hayden, a former prosecutor, immediately suppresses the wiretap evidence.

The question then becomes what other evidence the prosecution has. If they have testimony from informants, possibly Mathison and Trip, Kevin is ready with an affidavit from Trip and the taped denials from Mathison.

At the hearing, following the suppression ruling, the district attorney asks for a two-week delay to file an Amended Bill of Particulars.

Defilippo is doubtful that the state can come up with any "nonderivative" material, evidence that does not spring from the now-forbidden wiretap.

Still, Kevin is anxious about the case. He has been offered a deal of one and a half to two years for a guilty plea that would preclude any federal prosecution in the case and be served in the county jail, thus avoiding a state prison sentence that would trigger a harsh penalty as a persistent felony offender. He frets and wonders out loud about the Feds.

"They just doin' that to scare me. The Feds don't want some little-ass case like this, so they just passed it on and said, 'Here, you take this piece of shit.'"

Kevin believes that the local authorities may very well be planning to frame him. Aren't they threatening to send a pregnant Karen to jail on her first offense as an attempt to get at him?

Two weeks later, in early August, Kevin arrives for court, wearing his neatly pressed ivory shirt, sleeveless black sweater, and slacks. His only affectation is sunglasses with $800 Versace frames. "Ooh, what are those, lions?" Julia asked when she first saw the gaudy eyewear. Kevin parks his Mercedes directly in front of the county courthouse, slips two quarters in the parking meter, and heads up the sidewalk to the first-floor metal detector. Then he trots double-time up to the second-floor courtroom.

"I could do the year and a half, that's nothing. But you never know what could happen in jail. As many enemies as I have in prison, I don't want to go back to that savage-beast shit."

Davis is not happy with Defilippo's quiet style and has told him so the previous week.

"You have to bring things up so you have a basis for appeal. If you don't object, then the appeals people won't rule on it. I've read up on this shit."

On the wooden bench, waiting for his case to be called, Kevin Davis considers all the elements of his strange case, starting with the fact that he is charged with only a Class E felony compared to indictments on heavier charges for the others. Defilippo arrives beside Kevin and quickly advises him to keep his legal binder out of sight. "We don't want them to think you are keeping score."

Kevin is the picture of composure as he stands beside his lawyer listening to the prosecutor explain that he would like to drop the case.

Judge Hayden wants to make sure that he understands the prosecutor's intent. "Are you sure that you want this case dropped? That you don't want to appeal my ruling to suppress?"

The prosecutor repeats his request.

As Kevin strides down the aisle after the case is dismissed, he swivels his head from left to right, watching for federal agents to step up and arrest him on the spot on a more serious charge, the result of a more efficient, deeper, and wider-ranging investigation. The Feds were all over Elmira. Hadn't he seen them driving his Lexus? It would also be easy for agents to convince a couple of snitches to finger him as a weight man, a supplier, and grab him as he walked away from a case he just beat. He had seen that very thing happen in New York courtrooms. But when no such dark angels appear, Kevin steps into the narrow lobby before heading outside. Dizzy with relief, he shakes his head, marveling at his good fortune. Suddenly his eyes fill with tears. As Defilippo arrives, Kevin puts his sunglasses on and quickly wipes his cheeks with the back of his hand before the tears can track his face.

Both Kevin and his lawyer are amazed at Kevin's emotion. This is a man who has risked decades in prison, sometimes over relatively small matters. Why is he overwhelmed at the collapse of a case that hardly seems to matter? Is he so concerned about what might happen in jail, so reluctant to reconnect to the "savage beast" in him? Has he come to cherish the things that freedom offers, the fresh sheets and long showers and the love of a woman? Or is he a more deeply changed man, concerned about his unborn child and the destruction of his household should both he and Karen go to jail at the same time?

"I got to compose myself," Kevin whispers, shaking Defilippo's hand.

"Kevin, be careful, will you?"

It is almost ten in the morning when Kevin pulls onto Livingston Street and up to the gray stucco house with white trim. Inside, Julia is dozing on the couch, covered in a yellow blanket. Karen and Betsy are in bed upstairs.

"Sleep is the cousin of death," Kevin says, and yells, "Karen!"

When Betsy arrives downstairs, he asks, "Is she asleep?"

"Not now she ain't."

In five minutes, Karen comes downstairs, stepping carefully, wrapped in a white terry-cloth robe.

"They threw my case out," Kevin announces, and hugs Karen, his right hand cupping her left buttock.

Karen steps into his embrace and whispers, "That's great." But Kevin can tell Karen is not unreservedly delighted. True, it means she will have a partner who can help care for her daughter and maintain their home. If she goes to prison, she will have a man to visit her and to take care of her business. But she has lost a partner in crisis, a fellow victim of the system.

She alone will suffer for this latest episode in both their lives. The drug possession case was her own fault, as she has insisted so many times. When she thought about it later, she understood that she had accepted that envelope filled with tiny bags of crack in the darkened living room of Trip's apartment because somewhere along the line she had decided that Kevin should not have to take all the risks for much-needed money. Still, the incident would probably never have happened if she hadn't fallen in love with Kevin Davis. Now she might be going to jail while he stays home to conduct as many affairs with as many women as he can without her being able to do anything about it.

Anxious that Karen not put her thoughts into words, Kevin ignores her listless response to his victory and changes the subject.

"Why you come in so late last night?"

Karen turns away from Kevin. She had been out driving with Michelle, smoking, talking about the sorry state of their lives. Annoyed by a shriek from Julia upstairs and by Kevin's controlling nature, she answers, "Shut up, Kevin."

Karen and Kevin drive over the Chemung riverbed, wide and almost dry in the August heat. Karen squirms in the front seat and groans. Her back is throbbing and she is worried, not about her unborn baby, her daughter, or her own long-term well-being, or even her relationship with Kevin Davis. Karen Tanski is worried sick about going to jail. With all the fighting and backstabbing, all the shifty characters she had been with for the years before she met Kevin, even the Rochester drug dealer, Karen had been smart or lucky enough to stay out of trouble.

When they met, Kevin and Karen saw a world of possibilities in each other. The optimism had been understandable. They were young and smart, and more dependable than most people they knew. But as they both moved into Elmira, Karen from the Pennsylvania hills and Kevin from Brownsville and prison, neither spotted the young people streaming out, migrating to other parts of the country, almost any other part. Elmira was no longer the typewriter and fire engine manufacturing capital of the state and no new industries had shown up to take their place. The A&P food plant built in Elmira in the 1970s, at 1.6 million square feet under one roof the largest food processing plant in the world, had never operated at full capacity and was closed in the 1980s. There are thoughts of building a new prison on the site.

The unemployment rate in the region sits below the state average just because there are so few people left looking for jobs. Many of those you see on the streets of the city have gray hair or prison records. The ambitious young people have moved on and left behind those who stare at television sets and dream of money from lawsuits.

The high expectations the couple had were part of the problem. Unlike many around them, both Karen and Kevin had been smart enough to see the hip-hop-era absurdity of diamonds, hefty gold chains, and mansions. Still, the mainstream consumer culture had convinced them both that the good life was based on premium possessions. There was never going to be enough money for Karen and Kevin in Elmira to purchase late-model luxury cars and clothes and flat-screen televisions. No way to make much money at all. It was going to be a mighty struggle just to pay rent and keep food in the house.

It might have been possible for Kevin to follow his dream of a peaceful, dignified life without recourse to crime if he had remained alone. But he had a family to take care of and he had an excuse.

Now the tide had shifted, bearing him and Karen toward disaster. Instead of Kevin entering the middle-class world, Karen was headed to his world, to prison.

The couple struggled to keep their spirits up by reminding themselves that there was a chance for probation. Karen's good record and her history of work up till the time of her accident would stand her in good stead. And, of course, she was white.

Sunday. Julia is off with relatives and Kevin and Karen are taking a ride to Watkins Glen for a look at Seneca Lake, one of the Finger Lakes.

It has been a drizzly morning but the day is perfect now. The water on the slender lake is blue under a late summer sun. Even on this ideal summer weekend day there are not many people around the lake.

"I like this area 'cause of the seclusion," Kevin tells Karen.

The few tourists mill about as Karen and Kevin pick their way out to the end of a rock jetty. At lunch, Kevin studies the menu and wonders if they get the lobster for the lobster ravioli from the lake. Karen snickers. "They don't have lobsters in no lakes," she says.

Kevin moves to another chair so he can look out over the parking lot. "I'm too short to see the water, so I'd rather look at my car." In the restaurant the black and white couple draw no stares, not even guarded glances.

There are some, though, who are not-so-subtly opposed to such unions. As the couple pulls out of the restaurant parking lot, Karen spots her mother's sister, walking with her boyfriend. Karen lowers the car window and shouts a greeting. Aunt Grace waves back unenthusiastically, skirts the back of the car, and continues coolly on her way.

"Prejudiced bitch. She don't let her children play with black kids," Kevin says as he eases the big car into traffic and heads back toward Elmira.

"That's not true. She's just afraid of germs, that's all."

"Yeah, right."

When Karen tries to raise the power window the glass sticks, will slide no more than halfway up no matter how many times she presses her thumb on the button.

"Shit," Kevin growls. "You fuckin' dummy. Why you put the window down when the air-conditioning is on?"

"I just put it down for a second to wave to my aunt and it won't come back up."

"Jesus, that's all I need, a fuckin' five-hundred-dollar repair bill 'cause you're a fuckin' dummy."

Kevin stops the car and together, fingers gripping the glass, the two of them work to drag the window up. The sky is still clear and in the rearview mirror Seneca Lake is dotted with white sailboats, but the day has darkened.

"Why you always doin' somethin' stupid?"

"All I did was put the window down and try to put it up. A luxury car should be able to do that. This car is a catastrophe."

"You're a catastrophe."

"You ought to sell it tomorrow."

"Oughta sell your ass tomorrow."

"You never shoulda bought it."

"You the one who saw it first."

"That man cheated you. The minute it needed a new engine I woulda made him take it back."

"Nothin' wrong with this car."

"That's why you had to put ten thousand dollars into it. That's why the windows don't work."

Karen knows what the Mercedes means to Kevin Davis. She also knows as well as Kevin does that the car is a lie. And that anyone who believes it is some kind of a fool.

The next day Kevin drives the Mercedes fifty miles to Binghamton. His plan is to have the car repaired and to leave it in the shop for the rest of the summer where he will not be tempted to drive it and it will be parked under a wide awning, out of the elements.

On the drive through the verdant ridges of the Southern Tier, Kevin considers Karen's impending sentencing. Word has come through Richie Rich that Karen will not get probation. She has been mandated for CASAT, which Rich is saying will allow her to serve only six months. Still, the fact that Karen is headed to jail preys on Kevin. He remembers the look of disgust on Karen's Aunt Grace's face as she crossed behind their car the day before at Seneca Lake.

"Bitch."

Kevin drives carefully, using his directional blinker when he changes lanes. The fact is that he has to find a way to make a living very soon. He thinks about returning to the ring. At four wins, two losses, and a tie, he hadn't had much of a pro career. But maybe at thirty-six he could get in shape, line up a few more fights, and make a few thousand dollars. Maybe he could get a job as a sparring partner somewhere. He doesn't think about the detached retina he got as a child when he was hit with that stickball bat, or the collapsed lung he suffered a few days after he won his first pro fight. Or about the fact that he hasn't fought a competitive round in fifteen years. Purple wildflowers bloom on the shoulder of Route 17; bright yellow daisies carpet the center island.

Kevin is not headed back to the ring or to college. Kennedy Valve better call soon. His mind wanders again. They lose so many people at Kennedy, one a year at the plant, that there has even been a rumor that there is a serial killer on the premises. People say that the skull of a man who turned up missing at the plant fifteen years ago has just been found. No body. Somebody probably pushed him into one of those big-ass machines.

Maybe, Kevin thinks, he'll land a job at Elmira College. He heard the college hires ex-cons from the Elmira prison. Some type of program so the institution can say it is doing something for the community. Kevin has heard the ex-cons work in the college cafeteria under a strict rule never to speak to the female students. All it takes is just one word to a student, "Hi," and you're fired.

Back at home later in the day, Kevin sits on the couch rocking to the sound of Papoose and his album *Law Library Part 1*. Karen sits at the other end of the couch in a white robe, her wet hair wrapped in a red towel. Julia lies with her head on Kevin's lap.

"When you grow up, Jewel, you gonna marry a black man like me?"

"No."

"Why? You prejudiced?"

"No, I'm supposed to marry a white person."

"Who told you that?"

"Nobody."

"How come your mother is with a black man?"

"'Cause that's what she wants to do."

"Who told you not to marry a black man? Your Aunt Grace?"

"Shut up."

Karen leans her head back and moans. "What I need is a vacation."

Betsy, stretched in the recliner across the room, answers, "That's not likely."

That night, Karen sits alone on the porch. Betsy is upstairs and so is Julia.

Kevin is visiting the View, a project close to the river. Thousands of white moths swarm around the streetlights on the Madison Avenue Bridge and the spotlights over the used-car lot at the foot of the span. Hatched in the water and sprung to life by the heat, they spin in mad circles and crash exhausted to the pavement. Their white wings cover the road like the first half hour of a heavy snow. Kevin is out looking for a white guy who is selling coveted Nike Uptown sneakers for $65. Even Karen is interested in the sneaker sale. But the guy hasn't shown up at the View yet. Some boys at the project have been talking about robbing him. Kevin waits for an hour. At home, Karen rises and groans. She has been gaining weight. The slightest thing makes her tired. She shuffles into the kitchen, ties up the garbage bag, and carries it out, down the steps to the curb.

The next night Kevin is at the Ernie Davis Center, where he has volunteered to help with the youth boxing program. USA Boxing, a local youth program run by a gossiping, thick-handed former amateur boxer named Sandy, is holding its Friday fight night. There are seven bouts. Kevin is the corner man for one group of fighters. He dubs his team the Terror Squad and gives them a pep talk.

"I want y'all to relax in the ring. Don't be wildin'. Most of the thing you be dealin' with in the ring is in the mind. I'm gonna see what you doin' wrong. If you doin' wrong an' you not actin' sufficiently, two minutes is a long time. You gonna have to relax. Stay busy but don't overexert your ferocity."

Kevin looks out over his eager group. "I see winners here."

Sure enough, five out of Kevin's seven fighters win their bouts. Kevin glows with satisfaction. After scampering over to acknowledge the losing team, he chuckles with satisfaction over the performance of one of his young fighters. "I could work with him," he swears.

JUDGMENT

||||||||||||||||||||||||||||||||||||||||||||||||||||||||||||||||||||||||||||||||||||||||||||||||||||||||||

A week before her sentencing Karen sits on her bed, her back supported by two pillows, and writes in her new journal in an unwavering hand.

It looks like this next year is going to be really rough. I guess this is what every other hard point in my life has prepared me for. If I can make it through state prison pregnant, I guess I can make it through anything. It would be great if that don't happen but my luck says that it will. One good thing happened today—finally bought my dining room set. At least I got that to look forward to when I get my trouble done and over with. Another daughter on the way and I still didn't get my career up and going in the direction I need it to (and want). Almost 1 a.m. now it's the 13th tick . . . tock . . . tick . . . tock. Guess I will wait late for Kevin to crawl into bed with me tonight too!!!! Sometime I think about how much people regret the time they don't spend with people until they have lost that time & they are gone. Might be my last Friday of freedom for a long time and Kevin is sitting with some friends guys and girls (heard them all in the background on the phone) having some drinks while I lay here crying alone thinking and getting more and more nervous about the cards I've been dealt as a result of loving Kevin Davis.

I am so nervous and scared. I don't wanna go! My biggest worry is for Julia. I hope she is ok while I am gone when she realizes its longer than she thought. She will really miss me. I feel like I will be letting her down. Christmas, Hal-

loween, Thanksgiving, her birthday! O my God, I don't want to miss those things. I love giving her great memories and making her happy. I will miss her the most. I hope and pray that KK comes through for her. He is not her father, but he is really her Dad. He is all she knows and loves. I just hope he is there for her and gives her all the things I can't when I'm gone. I can't take Jewel sledding, maybe he will. I hope!

Still praying to God he finds a job soon and stays out of trouble. I love him so much and only hope and pray that he also stays faithful to me when I can't be here to fulfill his needs. This will be one hard thing to get through.

August 19, the day of Karen's sentencing, arrives damp and windless. With help, Kevin has written a letter and sent it to the supervising judge, signing it with Karen's name.

I have a degree from a business school, a good work history and a nine year old daughter. I have never been arrested in my life. I have not been considered eligible for probation or some kind of alternative to incarceration. I ask myself the question, "If I am not eligible for probation then who is?"

The letter is a bold move, typical of Kevin, attacking the system that controls him. But Karen is not nearly so sure it is a good strategy. The letter is sure to anger Judge Hayden, who will decide how long she remains in prison.

This morning there are only subtle indications of the tension at Livingston Street. The previous night, Julia hadn't gone upstairs to her room. Instead she watched television half the night and slept on the couch in her street clothes. Now Julia clings to her mother, following Karen around the house, as she selects a white linen dress with pink ribbon at the neckline for court. As Karen arranges her hair in the bathroom mirror, her pixie daughter stands a foot behind her. When she heads downstairs, Julia is on the step directly behind.

As mother and daughter kiss on the lips at the doorway, it is Karen who weeps. Karen has considered what she will say to her daughter and this is the moment. She holds Julia to her body, the child's face nestled at her rib cage. "Honey, what is happening to me is what happens to you when you hang out with the wrong people. When they go down, you go down with them."

Kevin, dressed in his dark gray slacks, black shoes, and a white T-shirt with the same black sleeveless sweater he wore on his own court date, holds the door wide open for Karen. She turns sideways, moves carefully down the porch steps, and walks toward the Mercedes.

Karen has things to say to Kevin Davis as well. She wants to tell him about betrayal. *A man is a man*, she wants to say. *But let me be in prison or let me come out of jail and find out that there is another baby and that will be it. I've left people before and I'll leave you too*, she wants to say. But she keeps her mouth shut for now.

Signaling carefully, Kevin makes a U-turn in front of the courthouse, parks, and steps from the Mercedes, then removes his designer sunglasses and reaches into his pocket. He has a supply of quarters at the ready to feed into the meter. He will be here only a few hours. There is a chance Karen will be gone for years.

Inside, Richie Rich mumbles about an adjournment, something to do with the pregnancy. The deal has been clarified. Technically, Karen will receive two years, but she will be admitted to the program, CASAT, that will allow her baby to stay with her in prison. After taking six months of classes on the dangers of drugs, she will be immediately eligible for a halfway house in Elmira.

Karen is not at all interested in adjournment, which could last as long as several months. She would rather have her baby in prison than on the outside, where she almost certainly would have to leave her baby behind when she goes in. Babies cannot be brought into prison, but the state policy is that babies born behind the walls can stay with their mothers for six months.

The courtroom is a newly painted eggshell blue with ivory trim. Two gold-painted fans twirl high above. On the left side of the large hall, under tall stained-glass windows, sits a faux fireplace fashioned with glazed tiles. An inmate in green, down from the Elmira Correctional Facility, is being sentenced for possession of contraband in the prison. "Are you the same person who was convicted of murder in the first degree in another county?" Judge Hayden wants to know.

"Yes, I am."

"I sentence you to three years to run consecutively on your sentence."

Sitting six inches from Kevin, Karen shifts her weight on the hard bench, leans forward, and stretches. She rubs her lower back with her hand. The short sleeve of her dress does not cover the tattoo on her right arm, a three-inch-high heart wrapped by a blue ribbon. Karen and Kevin do not hold hands or touch. Kevin, for the moment, appears helpless. A friend of Karen's sitting in the row in front turns. "This is all about revenge, Karen. They want you to do something that you just can't do."

Karen has a wad of tissue clutched in her hand and she dabs her eyes. Sensing she feels cold, Kevin reaches his arm around and rubs her bare shoulder.

Betsy's sister, Grace, a few rows ahead, aims a scalding stare at Kevin.

"Look at that bitch," he says. "She didn't buy nothin' for the baby shower."

Karen's face is pinched now. Her left hand slides under her belly. Unable to back away from any confrontation, Kevin will not give up the stare-down with Grace despite Karen's obvious discomfort. "Thanks for buyin' the baby present," he snarls.

Karen's aunt rises and walks over to a court officer. "Sir, I am being verbally harassed by that man right there."

Finally, with Richie Rich at her side, Karen approaches the bench. As she passes, her Aunt Grace hisses, jerking her head back toward Kevin Davis, "You gave up your family for *that*."

Hayden passes Rich a copy of the letter Kevin sent to the supervising judge. Then Hayden adjourns for the few minutes it takes for Rich to read the letter, while Karen wraps her arms around herself for warmth.

"When is your client due?"

"December fourth."

When directed by Hayden, Karen begins her statement by saying that she had never been in trouble until after her car accident. "I'm not saying . . . I know I was wrong. I take full responsibility for my actions. I was in the wrong place at the wrong time. I made a mistake. I would have been at work normally. That's not me. I wouldn't even have been hanging at nobody's house.

"I'm a hard worker. I've always worked. The only time I haven't worked is when I was going to school. And I worked my first eight months of my two years of college.

"I feel, I mean, I know I was wrong, and I take full responsibility for being where I was at, you know, at the time. I'm not—I don't feel that putting me in prison is going to . . . is really just, because, I mean, I'm not a violent offender. I've never gotten in trouble. I've never even been arrested."

Hayden interrupts. "That's all this is, you were in the wrong place at the wrong time? Well, you can keep telling yourself that. You can keep blowing smoke at the legal system." Hayden raises a thin folder, waving it in the air as he speaks. "I've read the pre-sentence investigation. Even then you're protecting your boyfriend. You were vague and guarded when your probation officer interviewed you."

Hayden refers to the police report that drugs were found on the floor of the bathroom after Karen was searched. "You seem to forget that the drugs on you fell out of your pants when you were being searched. You weren't just in the wrong place at the wrong time. The drugs were on your person."

Gray-haired and sharply angular, Judge Hayden looms as he stretches his neck, looks beyond Karen to where Kevin Davis sits, and what he sees is apparently enough to weaken his judicial reserve. "And you can choose to forget all these *characters* you're hanging out with. Almost every one of them are under indictment for drug possession or sales conspiracy. You can go on kidding yourself all you want, but the fact remains that you are wrapped up in this culture . . ."

Hayden appears to relax, puts down the folder, and places three fingers on his chin.

"Upon the conviction of the crime of criminal possession of a controlled substance in the third degree, you are hereby sentenced to a determinate sentence of two years, together with two years of post-release supervision.

"There is a mandatory surcharge of two hundred and fifty dollars, a twenty-dollar crime victim assistance fee, a fifty-dollar DNA fee, and your license to drive, if you have one, is suspended."

Karen rubs her eyes with the back of her hand.

Apparently irritated by Karen's tears, for being made to look like the bad guy for sentencing a pregnant woman on her first offense to two years in prison, Hayden's voice curdles. "All right, Tanski, it's time you stopped kidding yourself."

Slumped now in her white and pink party dress, Karen breathes with increasing difficulty, gulps air, and wipes her falling tears. She looks like she is going to faint.

In the third row, Kevin has been planning this moment for a week. He bounds to his feet and bellows, "Who is supposed to get probation around here? Huh? Who is? Fuck it. You're not a judge, you're a prosecutor."

As the court officers angle toward him, Kevin Davis steps to the aisle and begins to backpedal, shouting at Hayden, "I beat you in this courtroom before and I'll beat you in this case."

The court officers appear genuinely wary as they trail Kevin up the aisle, keeping their distance. Surely any other person who berated a judge in open court would have been arrested and charged with contempt. There is no signal from Hayden to arrest Kevin and the officers make no such move on their own.

Kevin's maneuver is exquisitely timed and planned for maximum effect and minimum risk. Kevin's idea is to show Karen that he is a worthy opponent of the criminal justice system, to take her mind off her pitiable position, and to reinforce the solidarity critical to both their relationship and her continued silence about the role Kevin may have had in the activities that led to her arrest.

Betsy and her sister, glancing back every few steps, walk out of the hall, leaving Karen alone on a bench shivering in her summer dress.

That night, half a block away from the courthouse, in the county jail on William Street, Karen begins her prison career sobbing in her cell. Though she has never served a prison sentence before, Karen has an advantage in this world of orange jumpsuits and bars. It is as if this place has been waiting for her. Her friend Michelle, recently in the same jail for assaulting an ex-boyfriend, has heard in a phone call from another inmate that Karen is in the middle of three cell units on the second floor in the rear of the building. Word is quickly passed to Karen that Kevin knows where she is and is rushing to the jail.

With Julia beside him in the Mercedes, Kevin speeds over the Madison Avenue Bridge and into downtown Elmira. He makes a quick left-hand turn on Church Street and then another left.

"Exactly what are we doing, KK?"

"I told you, we're going to see Karen. I'm taking you to see your mother."

"But KK, the jail will be closed. It's like, at night?"

Julia is even more confused when, as the two climb from the car, they head not to the front door of the jail but toward an area on the side of the building, a spot brightened by arc lights aimed from the jail.

Desperately lonely after only hours away from Kevin and Julia, Karen hears the sound of Kevin's voice: "Boo, I love you."

Then Julia's squeaky echo. "Mommy, I love you. Mommy. Mommy."

Kevin hollers one more time, "Boo, I love you forever."

He points to a shadow in one of two second-floor windows. "Jewel. Look! The window closest to the street. That's her!"

Julia squeaks, "Mommy, can I sleep at Maxine's house tomorrow night? Please."

Gripping the set of bars across a lower window, somehow Karen hoists herself and for a few seconds holds a position where she can see a lit patch of cement a hundred feet from the jail. But by the time she can see out, the spot is vacant. A corrections officer has already appeared and run Kevin and Julia off the property. "You wanna come in? Come back here and you will," he says.

On the way home, Kevin feels better, almost elated, as if he'd pulled off a coup. Then he turns to Julia, who is staring out the passenger window into the darkness.

"What the hell you talkin' about, sleepin' over?"

Julia sucks her teeth and lays her forehead against the cool glass.

"You know what? Sometimes I think you as crazy as Betsy."

Bedford Hills

||||||||||||||||||||||||||||||||||||||||||||||||||||||||||||||||||||||||||||||||||||||||||||||||||||||||||||||||

Three days later, Karen is awakened at four-thirty in the morning. She sits in her wrinkled court dress for two hours before she is escorted to a police car for the three-hour trip to Bedford Hills Correctional Facility in northeast Westchester County, forty miles north of Manhattan. Before the trip, the escorting police officers, a woman and a man, stop at the local Dunkin' Donuts drive-through. Karen, cuffed in the backseat, sees a girl she knows standing in the parking lot and another heading into the shop. "Oh, God," she whispers, and slumps low.

As the police car flies down Route 17 to Binghamton, Karen lies down in the backseat, twisting on her side so the cuffs don't dig into her back, and tries to sleep.

It is early afternoon when she arrives at the Bedford Hills Correctional Facility. The prison is just minutes from the highway and Karen gets only the briefest look at the town as the corrections car spins over narrow country lanes past stooped Victorians, fixer-uppers for the New York City professionals who purchase second homes here. The prison itself lies down in a grassy swale, surrounded not by a wall but an orchard of razor wire.

Beyond the razor wire sit fifty mismatched structures, some red brick, others stone and aluminum-sided, built in different eras since the prison was opened in 1901. The largest women's prison and the only maximum-security facility for women in the state, Bedford Hills houses about eight hundred inmates, from nonviolent drug offenders like Karen to notorious killers.

Beyond the visitors' entrance and just past the sally port is the front door to the prison itself. Flanking the entrance are neat flower beds tended by a platoon of middle-aged women who stretch and yawn while one of their number pokes her rake at a patch of red wood chips.

Karen is assigned a cell with a cellmate already comfortable on the bottom bunk. The guard points to the top berth.

"Is it possible that I could have the lower bunk because of the pregnancy?"

The guard does not bother to answer. A few minutes later, when Karen steps into the hallway to drag on a Newport Light, the same guard snickers. "She wants a bottom bunk. She cares so much about her baby she smokes."

Trouble starts the very next morning. Somebody has called the corrections officer a "nigger." The guard on duty insists that a younger woman told him that an older woman said it. The old con confronts the apparent informer in the line to the mess hall.

Kevin has given Karen lectures, emphasized again and again, that she must mind her own business, not engage in gossip, and above all avoid alliances with unreliable people.

During orientation there is no word of CASAT. The problem, Karen believes, is that Judge Hayden may have attached a note to her file not to give her the program because of her uncooperativeness and her relationship with Kevin Davis. "The judge don't know. He don't know why I did what I did," Karen tells Betsy on the phone from the counselor's office as black and Latino women, many in jail on life sentences, linger in the hallway. This is a maximum-security facility but the only prison in the state with a nursery. Karen would never have been assigned here if she weren't pregnant. "Judge Hayden was askin' me to do somethin' I can't. You should see what I am dealin' with. I could get killed in here for bein' a snitch.

"When Auntie Grace said that in the court, the thing about, 'You gave up your family for that?' She just doesn't know either. She has no idea what there is between Kevin and me. She just sees a black person and that's it. But I don't see that. I love him. He's a man. I like the way he looks and the way he handles himself. He has goals and plans and he is willing to do whatever he can to make them happen. Even if some of it was illegal."

It isn't as if Kevin has brought Karen Tanski from a country club to a women's prison. After all, there had been packets of cocaine secreted in her bathroom ceiling when he met her. She had even once been detained by the police before she met Kevin, when officers stopped her car and found two guns under the front seat. She had been released with a warning when the police determined that the weapons belonged to her Rochester boyfriend. No, Karen had already been edging toward trouble when she chose Kevin Davis, but it is his ill-considered connection to Trip that has brought her, eight months with child, to the state penitentiary, wearing her own green uniform.

The next week in the visiting room, Karen sits near a thin-lipped perky blonde with freckles up the left side of her neck who looks like a high school gym teacher.

"They say she's a great softball player," Karen whispers to Betsy. The ponytailed sportswoman laughing with her male visitor, tossing her hair and flirting, is Pamela Smart, played by Nicole Kidman in the movie *To Die For.*

In the film, and in life, Smart was a high school teacher who was convicted of seducing one of her students into murdering her young husband.

It is the second week of September. The morning chill in the hallway of Karen's wing in Bedford Hills lingers till midafternoon. In the dampness, Karen's feet have been swelling and her back howling, but the physical therapy the prison offers is nothing but a waste of time.

The food is varied, a good thing for the unborn child, but Karen isn't used to the fare, is nauseous much of the time, and doesn't eat much. "The women who hand out the food have beards and mustaches and when they talk spit flies into the food," she tells Betsy.

The first week inside, Karen launches a diary, inscribing the inside of the front cover of a standard black and white composition book: "Karen Tanski Personal Journal. Keep Out. Don't Violate My Rights!"

"*The first week is hard,*" she reports in a robust hand with no erasures.

Or should I say hell! There are seventy women and two showers that are either ice cold or burning h· :. We are still women. Not dogs. Ninety nine percent of the C.O.'s in here are black and they do treat white women different.

I was eating ice cream in the mess hall and this guard calls meal over real quick. So I take a shortcut to put the plastic spoon in the bin with the soapy water. He's standing there with his arms crossed. And he says, "Don't play yourself." Like he hates women. Especially white women. There's this girl here who's on her second bid, 3½ to seven and she's about to be programmed for CASAT. After three months she gets to go home. Let's see if they do that for me. Prolly not. I'm reading "If Tomomorrow Comes" by Sidney Sheldon.

While most of the other women head out for activities and programs, Karen sulks inside listening as two young women regale the CO with their gang stories.

I'm sure she's not supposed to promote their gang stories. The same C.O., I thought she called my name to go pick up my prescription but when I went to ask her she treated me like I was stupid. I'm an accountant. Not an eighteen year old gang member. Half of the C.O.'s prolly belong on the other side. That's not the first time she treated me that way. She treats me different cause I'm not the right skin color. I will never come back here. I don't want to be harassed by C.O.'s who don't know me.

That night the inmates watch the movie *Behind Enemy Lines*. Karen can't believe how excited the inmates get watching the film, laughing and clapping at the end. After the movie, Karen nibbles on a plum she got at the commissary. In her free hand she clutches a moist brownie.

"You're not supposed to have that," the CO barks, pointing to the brownie. "But I'm gonna let the baby have that. Not you. The baby."

The next day Karen tries to call Betsy but the phone is blocked. "I don't know why. How frustrating," she writes. "I put in a nursery application and a request for a new mattress. Another day in hell."

Soon Karen has been in Bedford Hills twenty days, and hopes and expects to be moved to the nursery before long. She has written several letters of application for the transfer but there has been no answer. Everybody seems to have different information. Just as Kevin said, there are loudmouths and intimidators all around her. Karen steers clear of serious conflict. But she overlooks the subtle current of sisterhood around her, is deaf to the voices of women who have learned important things about themselves in jail, things the outside world couldn't teach them. What Karen can't get over is the injustice of her incarceration. "There is a check forger in here who got three to seven years. Can you believe that?"

On Saturday night she watches a movie.

It would have been alright if the lesbos weren't in there. I don't really have a big problem with it, but I don't want to see it. It's not natural and it makes my skin crawl. Thank God I'm not that desperate for someone's affection. Even the ones you didn't think would fall for it are starting to be lesbos too! Eww! First the yard. Now the T.V. room and even the bathroom. I hate this place. They won't never get me! I don't need affection from other women. I am not ever gonna be that desperate. Once I get out of here I will not come back! I talked to Kevin today. He's being good. I'm a little leerie [sic] about why he needs two cells and who calls him so much. He says he be talking to his sister on the N.Y. number and his mother! And I tried to call the house phone and it was busy. He said it was his sister! We'll see! Better behave! I told him today he better not think he's gonna be going out all night when I get home. If parole says I'm in at nine, then so is he. No husband of mine will be running the streets.

The next day she attempts to make a call from the counselor's office. A pregnant white inmate leans into the room. "You call too much, girl. You got to remember. You ain't in no Holiday Inn."

Two days later, Karen does get through on the phone and that night gloats a little. Since just after Karen was arrested, Kevin has been promising to divorce Francesca so he can marry Karen. He now reports Francesca has signed the papers, has even had the tattoo with Kevin's name removed from her chest.

"She's thirty eight and I'm twenty six," Karen writes. "She isn't getting him back. LOL. It's Thursday and I'm praying to Jesus that I get moved into the nursery tomorrow."

Karen has a new cellmate with a history of violence sleeping below her now, wrapped in a dingy sheet and a tablecloth. "Every time I open my locker her googly eyes are all up in it."

Kevin drives to downtown Elmira and places a letter to Karen in the post office drop box. On the phone Karen has been railing about the COs, her cellmate, and the depressing conditions. He has seen inmates on that downward slide before and he is concerned that the shock of incarceration, the unremitting negativity of the prison, will cause Karen to crack.

He begins his letter stiffly, an echo of the hundreds of missives he has penned to prison officials and courts over the years, then quickly hits his stride with a review of the lessons he gave Karen before she went away, a refresher course in life behind bars.

I trust that this document will find you in the best of health. Stop letting these Correction Officers get to you. Do not deal with these dudes unless you really have to. Toilette, medicine, Doc, soap. Other than that, stay away from them dudes. Read, eat and think. They are not in there to like you. And you should not like them. They are still "po." Nevertheless, I got a good description of the faggot who disrespected you. They have no fucking idea who the fuck are your peoples or who you have ties to. I want you to know that I am looking forward to becoming a damn good father. The house is always clean. I put my Benz up for the rest of the year. Never let these dudes see you sweat. Hold your head up and smile at these cocksuckers through your beautiful eyes. Up here, the killings continue. Everywhere we go its there. It's not right that when someone like Black is killed that I get harassed. Now that I beat them on two conspiracy charges it makes them mad.

I'm so used to runnin shit and bein in control of my circumstances that I find myself tryin to diffuse situations that will make it better for you. As hard as it sounds, I cannot let your emotions dwell upon me because I am strong and YOU have to see THAT to be stronger! Remember how you wanted to go in the army. This is it baby. Bless you for not being a "Rat." You are a stand up individual and I bet that them cats in blue would of folded 100 times.

Betsy has been called in to talk with Jewel's teacher. The child's seat had to be moved. There was an argument with another girl and somehow a pencil flew across the room. Karen writes:

I need to get home before my absence really affects her learning and functioning healthfully. I miss her so much and feel like I am letting her down.

As autumn deepens, the sharp cold is another enemy.

They had cold water in the showers last night and when I woke up it was freezing in here. I wonder when they turn the heat on. Prolly when it's 20 degrees. Shit, the C.O.'s even wear their coats in here.

Kevin is indeed behaving more responsibly, announcing that the impending birth of his daughter has transformed him, but there may be other factors. He wants to make sure that Karen has no reason to doubt her decision not to name names in exchange for probation. And he has finally gotten a job, at Rynone, a vanity top and fixture factory just over the state line in Sayre, Pennsylvania. Karen is delighted that he will be working nights.

I hope the girls at the job leave him alone. I'm trying hard to put trust in his faithfulness. But Friday night my Mom told me that she woke up at 2:30 a.m. and he wasn't there. Didn't come in till nine the next morning. He admitted he wasn't there at 2:30. He said Joy was out of jail and he was helping her move. RIGHT! I was yelling at him and he hung up on me. Just another day down.

Now Karen considers Kevin's apparent infidelity with a growing sense of panic. She continues writing, pressing so hard on the pen she nearly tears the notebook paper.

He shouldn't be going out. I can't for four years. So it's time to grow up, especially since he wants me to marry him and I'm having his baby! I guess time will tell. What's done in the dark always comes out in the light! I better not hear anything about him cheating when I get out. Cause if he can't be true after all I've done and put up with for him I will prolly give up. Cause I can only take so much, an once I feel like a fool and betrayed by who I love I will start to question if I need love like that and eventually love can turn into hate. It's happened to me before. So, please God, guide him through temptation.

Near the end of September, on his first visit, Kevin hesitates over the visitor's application, then chooses to acknowledge his status as a convicted felon. Better to start out on the right foot. But he figures wrong. Officer Stanley, a lanky six-foot-three guard takes one look at the application and informs Kevin that he will have to wait to be cleared. The process might take two weeks.

Kevin paws the linoleum floor of the flimsy outbuilding where visitors are processed before admission. He blows his cheeks full and lets the air escape slowly through the toothless front of his mouth.

"Ahight, that's how it is?"

He places $40 in Karen's commissary account and sits motionless in his car for three hours while Betsy and Julia visit. But grandmother, mother, and daughter have no cash to buy refreshments during the long visit—the chips, cookies, soda, and even pieces of chicken from the vending machines in the waiting room.

Karen is not allowed to leave her seat without permission, so she signals to the guard behind a desk on a platform at the front of the room. The guard waddles forward, a tuna fish sandwich in her right hand.

"Is it all right if we use our commissary account to get some money to buy food?"

"Come again?"

"My mother and daughter are hungry. My boyfriend put money in my account. Can I get some of that money now to buy food? Here?"

The female guard shifts her weight and squints. Then she takes a bite of her sandwich and speaks through a mouthful of tuna.

"That won't happen. Nooo."

The next week, Kevin gets past the guard at the visitors' checkpoint. The female CO either ignores or overlooks the application problem and sends him inside.

"Have a nice visit," she says with a conspiratorial smile.

Kevin has been working at the vanity and counter top factory in Pennsylvania for over a month now, keeping a low profile in Elmira and speaking to Karen almost every night. Her welfare in prison is a major issue with him. He is still afraid that the woman he loves will fall to pieces, lose her mind or the baby, all because of him. There is also the unlikely possibility that she will call the prosecutors and talk about Trip's drug operation.

Julia is whining, doesn't want to go on another three-hour drive to Bedford Hills. Says she wants to visit her other grandmother. Betsy isn't going, either. It has always amazed Kevin how people can drift away from loved ones in prison. He saw his mother and his wife do it. He kept his disappointment to himself but he saw it all over the faces of his inmate buddies on visiting days.

Locked Out

||||||||||||||||||||||||||||||||||||||||||||||||||||||||||||||||||||||||||||||||||||||||||||||||||||||||||||||||||||||||||||||||||||||||

On his next visit, Kevin parks the Mercedes in a small lot and removes two bags of groceries from the trunk. Oatmeal, chips, juices. Karen simply can't stomach the prison meals. The fish on Fridays stinks and the mashed potatoes look green. Kevin actually relishes the role of supporter, being a valuable member of a team. But when he steps through the front door of the square outbuilding where visitors are processed, his heart sinks. The towering CO with the broad shoulders is there again and he is looking straight into Kevin Davis's face.

> *Now it's that fuckin' homo officer Stanley on the desk again and he's sayin' I got to write another letter to the counselor in charge of Karen's case. That's why I can't stand a black motherfucker. They the worst. I'm not fuckin' stupid. I know the deputy superintendent passed the letter I already wrote to the counselor.*

As he speaks to Kevin Davis, Corrections Officer Stanley stands and steps to the side of his desk to emphasize his height. Kevin shifts to the same side of the desk.

"You got animosity toward me, you shouldn't be in a position of authority," Kevin says, looking up into Stanley's face. "I was straight up with you when I told you I had been in prison. They don't even got Kevin Davis in the computer. I did my time as Kevin Williams, but I was real. Now you give me the fuckin' runaround."

"Don't raise your voice to me."

Kevin yanks his cell phone from his pocket and calls his sister-in-law in Queens, the wife of his brother Joe. She agrees to drive up and to bring the groceries in to Karen.

As he waits for his sister-in-law to arrive, Kevin sits on a folding chair and glares at Officer Stanley processing other visitors through the gate. He has spent so many years waiting to get out of prison and now his problem is how to get in.

Kevin's anger rises by the minute, matched by the steady hand of his calculating self. It would be satisfying but self-defeating to lose his temper here, to get arrested for assaulting an officer. Kevin knows there is nothing a CO like Stanley would enjoy more than to see Kevin Davis defeat himself.

A shorter, softer-looking guard sidles to Kevin's side.

"Look, all you have to do is write the letter and you will have no problem. The deputy superintendent is sure to okay it and you'll be fine. I know how you feel."

Kevin is not consoled. "Look in my eyes, you sorry motherfucker. Good cop, bad cop. Fuck that. Do I look like the person you should be playin' with? Do I? I should be playin' with you. Not you playin' with me."

Kevin catches Stanley frowning. The big cop knows how far prison-hardened inmates will go to retaliate against a guard.

"Go ahead, sue me," he purrs. "I don't care."

"Shoot you?"

When Kevin's sister-in-law arrives, Stanley tells her, "Your brother-in-law is pretty high-strung."

Back in Elmira, Kevin is bursting. "Where I been?" he says to Main over the phone. "I been in the crazy house."

He only begins to relax after he discovers a website for the Prisoner Assistance Center, a service funded by the Department of Correctional Services itself. Mario, an ex-con who answers the phone at the Albany help center when Kevin calls, reads off the regulations for visitation rights. "No person shall be denied visitation on the basis of past convictions or record of incarceration. The only way such visitation can be denied is if the superintendent informs the person seeking visitation in writing of special circumstances under which that person's visit would negatively affect the security of the institution."

Mario promises to contact Bedford Hills.

Meanwhile, Karen is desolate. The letter she receives from Margaret Davis, Kevin's mother, in the middle of October does nothing to lift her spirits.

I hope and pray that this letter finds you ok and in good spirit. It just saddens me when I have to write you in there, knowing your not suppose to be in there. You a very nice and sweet young lady. You didn't do none of those things they say. You was in a place at the wrong time with the wrong people. You don't even drink! Why they just throw you in there like that and you are expecting a baby. And a child at home. You have never been in trouble. The judge could have given you probation. I'm so hurt. I don't know what to do for you or the baby. Please tell me what I can do for you and my Grandbaby. As soon as this rain stop, I'll be able to visit you.

I'm thinking about selling this house in Mill Basin and moving to PA, or to Corning, New York. I see some nice housing there and very reasonable. Everything is going sky high in Brooklyn, everything. Travis just had a shooting at his high school, so I'm ready to get out of this place right now. Sell the house and all to save my son from harm. Don't cry because it affects the baby and the Devil likes to see weakness in people. And please don't smoke that's worse yet. I am closing now with a big kiss. I know they didn't like it when my son call Albany and went over their head. I know they will set him up anyway they can. But don't forget that the God I serve said, "No weapon that is formed against us shall prosper": Isaiah 54:17 And I serve a God that does not lie. And Karen, My God sits high and sees everything and no one is getting away with anything. I hope my son is seeing you as much as possible.

Love,
Your Second Mom

Late October. Julia is preparing for Halloween. She will dress as a Hawaiian maiden, a hula dancer complete with flowered skirt and lei. Her cousin

Carla will escort her trick-or-treating. But Julia hasn't told Karen, hasn't spoken on the phone with her mother for two weeks. There is a problem with the service that delivers phone calls from prisoners to their families.

It is the third week in October and Karen is spiraling downward.

Well, another Saturday of hell. It's been raining all day. It started early last night. And worst of all my car accident injury is really bothering me cause of the rain. My lower back is killing me, sciatica is causing pain to shoot through my leg and into my toes with numbness. I'm so regretting taking this charge and not telling them. . . . The pain is so great I have tears in my eyes, and the baby is moving a lot too. Why would they punish me so severely for something so small?! I want to go home now more than ever.

Karen watches a birthing video in her prenatal class.

Seeing how the babies' fathers were there to help and support their women made me really cry a lot. I only hope to God that Kevin can be there. But chances are very likely that he won't be allowed to.

I only hope that God will grant me this one thing and let me go home sooner or at least not have to do two flat and two post. If only they would change it to less than two years. But my luck don't seem to be that great. I only hope that Kevin can keep my home for me when I do get to come home to it. If that all falls apart, I don't know what I'll do!

Karen lifts her pen. Writing usually makes her feel better. Just putting the words down gives her a sense of control. Not tonight. She is drifting toward the bottom of some dark place when she is startled by her roommate shouting in her sleep.

"Thank Almighty God," Karen whispers when she gets the news in the first week in November that she will finally be moved to the nursery. From that new living space, not a cell but a room where they used to keep the baby strollers, she can see the front gate perfectly. She is by herself now, no roommate. Even with babies bawling in the cells around her there is blessed privacy. There are more babies and mothers in the nursery than Karen could possibly have imagined.

It's 10 P.M. (count time) and the babies are screaming. It don't bother me though. They are all so cute. So now I'm going to sleep happy tonight. I hope the phone is back on tomorrow morning so I can finally call home.

At Rynone, Kevin has been receiving compliments on his work habits. He has always aimed to stand out in a crowd and now he is doing just that. The supervisors have taken note of his upbeat personality and leadership skills, given him a clipboard to keep track of his four-man team. Kevin has been at work two months now and one of the owners of the company has noted the sleek automobile in the parking lot. He'll be damned if the classic Mercedes doesn't look better than his new BMW. The man inquires and learns that Kevin Davis is a retired boxer with some money left over from his career, marking time while he considers his options. A manager even offers to let Kevin park in a less crowded section of the parking lot so the mint-condition sedan won't get nicked.

The vanity tops that are manufactured in Kevin's area of the Rynone factory are made from five large forms. Each form is filled in turn with a fluid mixture that the manager calls "cultured marble." Kevin's task is to yank down the levers on the curing machines that bake each mold. There are two levers for this task so the worker cannot have a free hand caught in the machine as it closes. By the time he hauls down the levers of the fifth machine, the first form should be solid. Kevin then pushes the levers of the first machine up, muscles the piece onto rollers, where it slides toward an inspector, and sponges out the inside of the form with a gooey green solution, readying it for the next pour. Kevin's unusual strength is some advantage in this job, but his reflexes and ability to maintain focus for long periods make him really outstanding. The fast-paced system never stops churning and it takes timing and concentration to work it just right.

Now that Karen is finally in the Bedford Hills nursery, she sets her sights on the medium-security facility for women with babies, Taconic, across the parking lot from the main maximum-security facility. One afternoon, after Kevin's sister-in-law sits with her for an hour and a half, Karen goes back to her cell and bursts into tears. Her mood swings have become frequent and extreme.

Why can't they at least send him something in the mail telling him if he's approved or what he needs to do? He's already sent everything they said he had to. The baby is due in seven weeks and if they don't approve him soon, he won't be able to see his baby. I hope that the phone goes on, gets unblocked soon. I'm gonna go crazy not being able to talk to him. I need to at least hear his voice.

Her friend Tabitha moves over to Taconic but Karen remains stuck. Instead of news, all she hears about a Taconic transfer are rumors and guesses. When Ms. Young, the counselor, passes through the Bedford nursery, she is besieged with requests. Karen chooses to hang back, hoping her low-key approach and display of manners will impress the prison functionary. Still nothing. At least Karen's room is now warm at night. She has a sheet stuffed in the cracks in the window to keep the wind out, her door shut to trap the heat.

JUDY CLARK

||||||||||||||||||||||||||||||||||||||||||||||||||||||||||||||||||||||||||||||||||||||||||||||||||||||||||||||||||||||||||

One morning, Karen is staring out the one pane in her window not covered by the sheet. Her back aches and she is faintly nauseous. She watches a stray cat lurk near the corner of a nearby building, then bound through the morning sun to a pool of shadow. "Looks just like my Mom's cat Oliver that we lost when we moved from Brand Street," she writes in her journal. "We really miss him, he was Twister's brother."

Karen slumps and groans. It is not that she is any weaker than Kevin, who thrived on prison life. As a woman, she doesn't have ready access to the kind of mythology Kevin used to bolster himself. Kevin never felt abandoned because he was always the protagonist of his own never-ending movie in which he starred as one man against the world. There are no such reels in Karen's head. All she has is the truth. Julia is abandoned, Betsy half mad, and Kevin feckless. Sick and pregnant, she is simply locked up and helpless. It is all too much again. To stop herself from shrieking to the heavens, Karen hugs herself and rocks back and forth holding her breath.

"Can I come in?"

An inmate lingers in the doorway of Karen's broad nursery room. The woman wears a short-sleeve white blouse with her faded green prison pants. Her graying hair is chopped short. Karen can see that the white woman is an old con, in her late fifties, but with an odd air about her.

Karen inhales and moves to the edge of her bed as the woman sweeps a chair from beside the empty crib and sits facing her.

"My name is Judy—Judy Clark."

"I'm Karen Tanski. I just got here . . . on the nursery. About two weeks."

"I've been here, not on the nursery, for a lot longer than that." Clark smiles. Her teeth are white and perfectly even. She has a pockmark on her forehead and deep lines from the edges of her nostrils down to the sides of her mouth but her skin radiates good health. Clark stares into Karen's eyes, tilts her head, brown eyes narrowed in concern. To Judy Clark, Karen looks bedraggled, beaten.

"I'm sort of an elder around here," Clark continues, the *r*'s of her words so light they sound almost like *w*'s, "and I mentor young mothers. I was just wandering through and it looked like you could use someone to talk with."

Karen is mute, afraid if she speaks she will cry.

Clark does not break the long silence. She knows all about the sadness here, about the women haunted by their crimes, tortured by their bad luck and missing lives. She even knows who Karen is, has heard about her troublesome boyfriend, and understands well that it is best to wait, to listen right now.

Judy Clark has been in Bedford Hills for twenty-six years. A sixties radical, she drove a getaway car during the infamous 1981 Brinks armored car robbery by Black Liberation Army members that left a guard and two police officers shot dead. After her capture, Clark refused counsel, harangued the court with anti-racist and anti-imperialist monologues, and, while some codefendants accepted deals, was sentenced to seventy-five years to life in prison.

After years of solitary confinement and bitter self-imposed withdrawal, Clark began the transformation from revolutionary to humanist, eventually renouncing violence. She earned a bachelor's degree at Bedford Hills and a master's degree in psychology and began to spend her time counseling and nurturing her sister inmates. She launched the prenatal program here and wrote the curriculum for the parenting class. Clark's lifetime of good works behind bars is recognized state- and countrywide. Here at Bedford Hills, as she moves through the prison, sometimes leading a dog she is training as part of Puppies Behind Bars, a program in which prisoners train guide dogs for the blind, she draws approving looks from inmates and guards alike.

Clark sits waiting for several more moments. "Tell me your story," she says finally, sliding her chair a few inches closer.

"I'm here on a drug charge. I never used no drugs but I had some on me anyway." Karen hesitates and draws a breath that comes in shuddering stages. Then she exhales the same way. "They . . . won't let my boyfriend in for visits 'cause they're trying to get at him through me. So they delayed my move to the nursery. Din't put me in CASAT when I was supposed to be. So instead of the six months which I was supposed to do, I'm doing two years. I should be in Taconic. And—and . . . I'm sorry . . . just feel so low today."

Clark nods as Karen speaks. Still, she doubts that the system is punishing Karen because of her boyfriend. She understands that as one of the few pregnant women here in a maximum-security facility Karen probably just fell into a computer dead spot.

But Clark doesn't say anything at all, not a word of correction about the system or warning about troublemaking boyfriends. Instead, she gestures toward the grimy windowpane and indicates that she understands.

Fifteen years earlier, when Clark first conducted her parenting classes, she would often be counseling a dozen African-Americans and Latinas from Brooklyn and the Bronx. As the years passed, she noticed the demographic changing. More and more white girls from central New York towns like Rochester and Elmira were landing here in Bedford Hills. Most had been convicted of drug charges, and many of their boyfriends, partners in the drug trade, and fathers of their children, were black men. She had even had another white Karen here a year ago, when she conducted a class made up of only white girls, all from small Rust Belt cities. "My group of blondes," she called them.

"If I could just see him . . ."—Karen's voice trails off—"I think I'd be okay."

"What's he like?"

"A lot of people think that he's trouble. But they don't understand. He's black and he has been the victim of prejudice all his life. He is a good man and a good father." Karen stops and looks away for a moment, then turns back, adding with a touch of defiance, "Well, that's what he's like and I love him."

"And does he love you?"

"People don't understand, but he does. We have plans."

Clark knows too well that relationships with hardened convicts and drug dealers have been the downfall of many women in Bedford Hills. Karen probably would stand a better chance if she were to strike out on her own when she gets out of prison. Many of the city girls who are released from Bedford Hills go back to New York City, where they get jobs and an apartment through a church-run program and move on to better things. The upstate girls who leave here are not so lucky. They often go back to the same living situation, the same man, with the same result.

"Karen," says Clark, "I've looked at your record and I see you have a good work ethic and you are so smart. So smart."

"We don't need fancy things. We just want to work and raise our family together."

"You can make that happen," Clark says. "But you have to set your priorities. Your children have to come first. If he wants to follow the program you set, then that will be wonderful. But you have to set the path. You."

Clark knows all about women who try to impress men with how much heart they have, who try to save men. Knows all about twisted priorities. Twenty-four years ago, while she sat in an idling getaway car, trying to prove herself to a team of stickup men calling themselves a liberation army, her one-year-old daughter was in the care of acquaintances.

"Karen, what's his name?"

"Kevin."

"You have so much going for you. You say you want a simple life, that you don't need a lot of things, and that is so smart—so important. It can work. It can work with you and Kevin but you have to put your daughter first."

As Karen peers into Clark's brown eyes, she knows nothing of the woman's background, only that there is a lovely peace there and throughout the room, and that the weight of prison has somehow lightened. Here is the teacher who might have spotted her gifts, the mother she might have turned to. Suddenly the path ahead shines clear.

The children come first and Kevin can follow if he is able. She wants to hug the woman in front of her but both Karen and Judy Clark know that is strictly against the rules.

Karen will reflect on her brief meeting with Clark many times in the coming months. And she will remember the plan. The children come first. Set the path and Kevin will have to follow.

In prenatal class, the assignment is to write a letter to your baby. Halfway through the letter, Karen lays down her pen. Then she remembers the shining road. *Set the path and let Kevin follow.* Later that day, at the last session in prenatal class, there is a baby shower, with the room decorated, pink balloons bobbing against the ceiling, and crepe banners on the window frame.

At last, Superintendent Ada Perez appears at the door of the Phase I class and Karen rises quickly to ask her about the transfer to Taconic and Kevin's problems getting into the facility. The Taconic move is held up because there are not enough nurses for the facility, Perez explains, and she promises to check the whereabouts and status of Kevin's application.

Today was good. My Mom and Jewel came and visited all day. I seen Kevin out the back window. Well, I seen his car and he backed up into a parking space.

Betsy and Julia describe to Karen how Kevin was walking up to the visiting area with them when Officer Stanley emerged and ordered him off the property.

Finally, the Prisoner Assistance Center gets through to Bedford Hills, complaining that what Bedford Hills is doing to Kevin Davis is illegal. A few days later, as Perez leads a tour of outside visitors through the nursery, the warden takes a moment to tell Karen that she has approved Kevin's visitation.

On December 9, Karen scrawls in her notebook, "I am now going on six days overdue. Tired all the time."

KAYDAWN

|||||||||||||||||||||||||||||||||||||||||||||||||||||||||||||||||||||||||||||||||||||||||||||||||||||||||||||

Kevin is working a ten-hour shift, two-thirty in the afternoon to one a.m. It is nine-thirty and he has just returned from his break, getting back into the rhythm of the job. This is just like a boxing workout. Keep moving, watch your technique, focus, and move. He is hunched over an empty form, sponging out the inside, when he feels a tap on his shoulder.

"It's happening," a supervisor says.

Kevin turns and removes his goggles.

"That's right," the white man continues with a curious familiarity, "it's goin' down right now, brother."

Kevin shakes his head. "Huh?"

"The baby, brother! The baby!"

Kevin storms across the border back into New York State. The twenty-minute drive takes less than fifteen. He showers, changes, and hits the road to Bedford Hills, blazing through the night. He arrives at seven in the morning and dozes in the backseat of the car, waiting for officers to show up at the visitors' building so he can get directions. Then he drives the four miles to the Westchester County Medical Center. At the front desk, he is told that Karen Tanski is on the tenth floor and that she is already in labor.

A corrections officer sits on a folding chair outside the door to Room 1001. The policeman stands as Kevin approaches.

"Sorry, but you can't go in. That's the rules." The stocky officer chooses his words carefully. But a black female cop leans out from the hospital room, her face lit with charity. "You the dad?"

"Yeah."

"Shut up," she tells her fellow guard, "an' let the man in."

Karen is draped in a white gown with blue polka dots. Kevin steps close to the bed, leans from the waist, and kisses Karen on her cracked lips. Then he kisses her again.

"When I leave, you may have to leave," the female officer is whispering behind him. "The next people might not let you stay." At the three p.m. shift change, the female guard speaks to the arriving officers.

"We can't let you stay in the room but you can wait in the lounge across the hall," the arriving officer informs Kevin. "It has a couch where you can sleep and it has a television." In the waiting room, Kevin reaches for a copy of *National Geographic* and falls dead asleep.

Next thing I know, this police lady is pullin' on me. Tellin' me 'bout how she tried to wake me up so I could go in and see the baby born but she couldn't wake me up. So she takes me inside. Karen's sittin' up holdin' the baby, who's wearin' a little pink hat. She's got on Pampers and she's wrapped in a blanket. The baby still had a spot of blood on her stomach where they cut the tube. So Karen hands the baby to the police lady, who hands it to me. I was speechless, cryin', sympathetic. When I could, I told Karen, "Thank you. Thank you. Thank you for bringin' my world to me."

"You lucky you weren't here when the baby was born," the police said. "She woulda grabbed the hell outta you." Then the police lady said, "You got a beautiful baby." That was the truth.

It is 2006, a cold, colorless January at the Bedford Hills Correctional Facility for Women. The flowers are long gone from the flowerbeds outside the front door of the building that holds the visitors' room.

But Superintendent Perez has finally made good on her promise to allow Kevin Davis into the facility.

At a table near the front of the sprawling visiting room, Karen is smiling, deeply at ease, as Kevin squats beside her, hunched over his daughter. Kaydawn—*K* for Kevin and Karen, and *Dawn* for a new day—is the color of lightly cooked pancakes, with cheeks so full and chubby they droop. Father and daughter, face to face, blow air at each other and laugh. Neither tires of the simple trick even after they have performed it dozens of times.

"All right, Kevin. You are going to give her your germs."

"Me, I live cleaner than y'all. She's gonna give me germs. Babies got crazy germs. I feel like I'm gettin' sick already. Ahhh," Kevin yells, as Kaydawn blows a puff of baby breath at him.

Baby Kaydawn sticks her tongue toward a piece of glittering candy, one of her very first tastes of sugar. She stares in wonder up at her father's face and sticks her tongue back toward the sweet.

At the closest table, an attractive young woman with smooth brown hair and tawny skin, wearing a lime-green jumper beneath the forest-green of her prison suit, holds hands with a bespectacled man in his twenties, her age. The young man is nervous. She is not. With permission from the guard at the front desk, she leads her gentleman caller by the hand to the vending machines, where they carefully select items of junk food as if they are choosing accommodations for a honeymoon cruise.

Kevin has been working at Rynone, his minimum-wage job, for six months now and has even been hired full-time. His daughter is healthy and his woman is calm and smiling. The phone connection between Bedford Hills and home is even operational. There isn't much more he can ask for.

Karen will probably have to do another fourteen months. She throws the number off easily. Somehow, it seems that taking care of a newborn is so engrossing and time-consuming that it doesn't matter much to her where she is. Studies have even shown, she tells Kevin, that babies born and nurtured early in prison get more consistent care than babies on the outside.

The woman in the lime-green jumper is leaning close to her studious-looking visitor, a formerly discarded admirer perhaps, the only one of her suitors still willing to court her now that she is doing serious time. His hand creeps toward her back and she arches seductively.

"You know better than that," the guard at the front desk hollers.

Kevin and Karen exchange glances. The guard has never had to tell them to stop touching. They kiss each other quickly when they meet, no matter how long they have been separated. It was that way even when Karen was home. A few moments later, the amorous couple is in the back of the room, the woman posing for photos by an inmate photographer. The woman arches once more, throwing her head back and thrusting her buttocks girlie-magazine-style as she perches on the edge of a chair.

The guard, who had appeared to be slumbering, snaps to attention. "Knock it off!"

Kevin and Kaydawn are staring at each other, making faces.

"They might be moving us up to the third floor," Karen says after a few moments. "That's the old death row, Kevin. The building is like eighty years old? There's asbestos on the second floor where we are now. So I want to move. But, hey? The third floor has ghosts. At least one ghost."

Kevin scoffs, balls his hand into a fist, and holds it near his daughter's face. He is not nearly as domineering as he once was with Karen. "I got to be good to her. She gave up her life for me," he tells people. Right now he is all smiles. Even when he thinks Karen is being silly or superstitious he holds his tongue and tickles his daughter.

Technically, tiny Kaydawn is an inmate. She has a seven-digit number, the official identification of inmates in the institution, and is on the "count." "I can be burping her or she can be lying on my stomach and the guard comes in my room and asks me to turn her over to see if she's breathing. Every hour all night they check. It's so ridiculous. They got murderers all over here and they think that I'm going to kill my own baby?"

Karen has gotten a ticket somehow for twisting her ankle on a newly waxed floor and not reporting the injury to a guard. "That shit is crazy," Karen says. "No, let me say it's curious."

Kevin isn't listening. He is hypnotizing his baby daughter to sleep. A minute later, he turns to Karen.

"She ain't gonna turn out like Pamela, my first daughter. You know, last time I was down there she was at my mom's and she tells me my sister Tonya had talked to her about smokin' so much weed. I told Pamela right there, 'It's true. Your mother needs her ass kicked for letting you smoke so much weed.'"

Such concern is unlike Kevin, who has never been a father or even a friend to Pamela. Even when he was not in jail, he was absent from her life. In those years in Brownsville more than a decade before, when he would see his daughter walking toward him, his hand would reach to his pocket for some bills to send her on her way.

But Kevin just knows it will be different this time. He will be the central figure in this child's life. Kaydawn will have a real father.

The odds are against such a healthy relationship, though. Kevin mouths brotherly platitudes but does not have consistent contact with Travis, his teenage brother. Does not follow up, insert himself into Travis's life on a regular basis.

But how surprising is this, really? His own father had floated in and out of his life on the tide of his urges. Neither was Kevin's mother any kind of role model. The only time Margaret Davis was fully engaged with her son was when he was locked in a battle with the authorities, especially the police.

Kevin returns from the wall of vending machines in the Bedford Hills visiting room with a hero sandwich for Karen. The fresh-smelling bread means it must have recently been placed in the slot and Karen is delighted at her good fortune, chomping on her ham and pepper hero and gazing at Kevin and Kaydawn. The next day Kevin plans to return to the prison with Travis and Margaret. All is well in Bedford Hills.

But things don't stay that way long in Kevin's world. Two weeks later he misses a planned visit and Karen is beside herself on the telephone, accusing him of laziness and betrayal, infidelity. Kevin hangs up the phone but quickly pens a letter.

> *Stop the bullshit. You are my Boo 4 ever and baby moms. I knew that since I wasn't going to show up you will get all kinds of feelings. Expect me doing bad. It may look like that at times because you expect more than enough from me. I try. I want you and Kay to have the world. I got rolled over at Rynone! I am now a permanent employee!! However I only now will get paid every two weeks. But I'm concerned about Kay so health insurance will cover the family and now I have to manage this dough correctly. Feel me. These bitches around you in Bedford won't be laughin when I put thousands in your account. However, stop bugging out. I'm not going anywhere. And your not gonna do shit with no other Nigga cause I'll put you somewhere in the water. Smile. Now that we got that understanding, sorry for the hundredth time that I told you I was coming and did not. It won't happen no more baby. There were things beyond*

my control. Besides, Betsy is up here with Charles and some people drinking
beer all the time and would rather hang out than visit you. The same with my
family. But I am not like that. If the police snatch me up there will be no one at
all to visit you. It is two twenty a.m. in the morning so I better get some rest for
work. The money is nothing but I need to stay with it. I don't need to be rich,
just a stable life for my family. I will see you Sunday okay. Kiss Kay for me. She
looks beautiful in her boots and suit. I have the list you sent me so I will try to
get some items and money in your account. Be patient asshole. I love you. I have
to take a shower and get ready for work in another ten hours. Damn it's a dirty
job but I got to do it or else, Bang.

Love, your husband,
Kevin Davis

Karen reads the letter twice, reassured of Kevin's commitment to family
life. "I'm not going anywhere," she reads. But Karen pauses over two sentences
in Kevin's letter, not sure if she should be concerned: "And you're not gonna
do shit with no other Nigga cause I'll put you somewhere in the water. Smile."

The next day, on his way through the visitor processing procedure, Kevin
is asked to step into an adjoining room.

"You the one with the beautiful baby. I love that little baby," the female
guard coos. "That's *my* baby."

Kevin would later explain that the soft words threw him off guard, broke
his posture of wariness around the police. Just beyond the metal detector,
another officer appears. "Will you come with me?" Kevin is escorted to a utility room off the entrance area. There he is asked to submit to an ion scan for
drug residue.

"Oh, you did this before?" the CO asks.

"Sure," Kevin answers, even though he hadn't. "Let's do it and get it over
with."

Kevin sweeps his hands under a blue light and the guard frowns. "Well,
if you did it before it looks like you didn't do so well the second go-'round."

"What you mean?"

"Mr. Davis, you came up positive."

Kevin's neck tightens. "Either you made a mistake or you lyin'."

"No, that's the way it is. You can't go in for a visit."

"The fuck you talkin' about?"

"We are not saying that you have taken drugs. You may have been around the wrong people. You may have touched furniture or money that had been in the hands of someone who had been around drugs."

Kevin knows guards have ways of tripping machines. "Don't try to play me. You set me up."

The guard shakes his head.

Kevin spins and punches two quick holes in the flimsy plasterboard. Two guards from the other room are on him, twisting his arms behind his back and wrenching his thumb. Later, in the state police barracks, Kevin receives his charges. Disorderly conduct, criminal mischief, and resisting arrest.

Kevin will have to come back down to Bedford Hills to see the judge about the three misdemeanor charges. And he will not be allowed to see Karen or his daughter again until they are released from prison. Fourteen months.

Three weeks later Karen colors the outside of a blank homemade card with a crimson heart for Valentine's Day. Inside, a smaller rouge heart rides above the inscription "I love you," words brushed so they trail pink streaks across the paper. On the facing page is a printed poem she wrote herself.

I think about the sweet love we make
One thing I never had to do was fake.
You have made me feel so complete
Even when you rub my feet.
I love it when you touch my face
I belong with you I know my place.
I show your picture to people.
I say, "Look, isn't he fine?"
Then I say, "I'm so glad he's mine!"
I'v been away from you for too long
I'm sorry we did any wrong!
I cannot wait to get home and leave this State
Start over with a brand new fate.
We are going to do good and have it all.
This time we are not going to let each other fall.

Kevin is especially upset that Karen is in a maximum-security prison and sends Karen reports of his efforts to get her moved.

I called Albany, spoke to the Classification Movement Director. They are definitely considering your transfer considering you are Minimum Security Risk! If someone does anything to you while you are in there they will have to hand over the prison to me. Smile. A very good lawsuit is a good step. It don't make sense that you are in a building full of Maximum individuals and they have a Medium right across the street. I really think its cruel and unusual punishment. You have a good issue because I also spoke to a few of lawyers about your classification and they will point me in the right direction on how to find out who moved you there and why. You have to remain strong for the baby sake. You are a white girl with a black man in a majority black prison who do not approve of our relationship and they will try to make it hard. But I have to outwit these fools with my pen game. I have a very good pen game and take everybody to court. Smile. I want you to stay focused and remain positive. I want you to read this book I am sending you. You have to learn more about spirituality and warriorship. I still read these books at home because I am still locked up out here even though I work, got a house and can go anywhere I damn please! But I'm always aware of danger and I thwart a lot of situations before it escalates. You need some knowledge on life like that. You have a lot of disadvantages because you are a white girl in a black world! Please be strong.

Love always,
Kevin Davis, your husband

A month later Karen still has not been moved to the nursery at Taconic. She has been put into CASAT, though, the program that can shorten her sentence. But she is becoming more and more concerned that Kaydawn will be snatched away from her and sent home after six months. She writes a long letter to Kevin on the subject. As she writes, her concern turns to rancor.

Kaydawn is so attached to her mommy. It's gonna seriously hurt her if I have to send her home. You might think it's cool because you can spend time w/

her, but she is gonna be a handful if she wants her mommy. I mean it! The officer told me the other night that she came in the room through the night to check on the babies (which she does every hour) and Kay had her head lifted, looking for me and when she seen me, she laid her head back down and went to sleep! Today, she screamed when I was at CASAT and when I came up the hall to get her I heard her screaming. As soon as she realized I was holding her, she stopped crying and didn't do it again. How dare these assholes make us be together non stop 24/7 for her first 3-4 months and then decide to put me in CASAT, which I could have been done with by the time she was four months old! If I would have known that she could be sent home I would have had her at home and then left! Now if we get split up we will be lucky to see each other more than twice a month. Going from every day all day to a couple of days a month is absolutely going to fuck her up!! You don't even understand. I would never have put her through this. She is way too little to understand. She is going to feel abandoned and hurt. My poor baby. This isn't fair.

Must be nice to be you. Your life hasn't changed much! You don't know what it's like to be pregnant and feel her growing inside you, then labor and deliver. Seeing her come out still attached to me. The cord being cut, the bond of being together, just her and I sleeping beside each other every night, waking up every 1½ to 2 hours through the night to feel her next to me. Shit, you got it easy and don't even know how easy. You need to get on your job and get them to keep me and Kay together for a six month program or release without a program. You were on your job about your visits and now your just worried about a stupid lawsuit. But that isn't gonna matter anymore once Kay is home, right? And neither will I! You don't write much at all, so I assume you're not doing much to help my situation! You won't worry about visiting me if she is home. Plus she is going to cost you more money if she is home. And time! And so help me God, if you take her around other bitches you <u>will</u> pay eventually. Well, stop dicking those hoes and get on your job as a good man and father! Don't try to play me because you will be the one hurting in the end.

Remembering Kevin's written comment a few months earlier about putting her "somewhere in the water" if she ever messed with another man, Karen adds a lighthearted death threat of her own.

Shit, I'm scared you might flip on me if the baby goes home! LOL! No, you know I would kill you. Smile.

My tired ass is going to sleep.

Two weeks later Karen is finally moved to the nursery at Taconic and the threat of Kaydawn being sent home subsides. She writes Kevin, her printed words lighter, almost feathery.

Hello Baby,

You know how nice it is to be able to actually talk to you on the phone. It's better than writing. You actually tell me things more on the phone than on paper, and so do I. But it don't look like I'm gonna be talking to you on the phone anymore. They don't do that here. I still haven't gotten to go to Commissary. So I have absolutely no food or snacks and I'm hoping you will find a way to get me a package soon.

Kaydawn weighs fifteen pounds and some ounces now. Here the damn nurse comes to check on the babies every morning around 7:00 and it's annoying. They asked me her number and I told them she don't have no number. This nursery has so many rules because of accidents and lawsuits. For example, if you fall asleep with the baby in the bed beside you instead of in her crib at the foot of the bed, your baby will be sent home. I guess they're scared of somebody rolling over and suffocating their baby. They are like hawks watching over us! OK I got to stop writing. My finger is flat from the pen and my hand and elbow hurt. Why aren't you writing? Don't give me that "you don't have time" shit either. You got more free time then me and I sit up here late at night tired writing to you!

You seem to be drifting, hope your not spending the time you should be writing hanging around w/another woman or doing things that could get you in trouble!

Love always,
Karen

P.S. *I'm not writing again till you write back. Let me know what you've really been up to!*

Kevin is not about to tell Karen all of that. He does report to her that the three misdemeanor charges related to the wall-punching incident have been dropped, though he is still banned from visiting the prison. What he doesn't say is that he has quit his job at Rynone and has been seen nightly in the Elmira projects in the company of several women, including Joy, who has been released from jail after serving only a few weeks on the drug charge sentence. For Kevin, working is more like a sport than a way of life. He sees a job as a test and rises to meet the challenge, whether it be physical endurance, tedium, or plain disgust, as with the long-term care facility job in Queens. But once Kevin proves to himself, and in Rynone's case to Karen, that he can master the situation, he loses interest.

"I quit Rynone 'cause I was tearin' up my hands. They was goin' numb. And on top of that," he finally tells Karen after three months of unemployment, "I got to get things ready for when you come home."

Kevin does not seem to lose interest, however, in the Elmira women, who continue to see him as a luminary, and jockey for his attention.

SISTER TISA'S

||||||||||||||||||||||||||||||||||||||||||||||||||||||||||||||||||||||||||||||||||||||||||||||||||||||||||||||

It is November 7, 2006, election day and the date Karen Tanski is to be transferred from Bedford Hills to a work-release facility in Queens. Kevin spends the night at his sister's apartment in Brooklyn and rides up to be there when Karen steps out of Bedford Hills.

A silver cradle moon rides low in the morning sky as Kevin drives up the FDR onto the Saw Mill River Parkway, his trunk packed with clothes and a baby stroller. The jeans in the trunk are size ten and eleven, some old and others new. But they probably won't fit Karen, with all that weight she has gained in prison. A $100 car seat is attached to the rear seat behind him.

Kevin guides the Mercedes up the steep hill to within sight of the sally port and the front door of the visitors' building. He backs the car into a parking spot marked CLERGY and sits to watch the door from which he is sure Karen is about to emerge. A bald corrections officer tilts his head toward Kevin and shakes it.

Kevin smiles and waves at the CO and drives the Mercedes back down the hill to a lot where utility vehicles are kept. He won't get to see Karen come out the door after all. He walks over by a Dumpster and takes a leak. A moment later, Sister Roberta appears beside him at the wheel of her Toyota Camry, with Karen sitting up straight in the backseat.

Karen is wearing a brown wool jacket, cream long-sleeve cotton T-shirt, sky-blue jeans, and beige boots. Kaydawn, outside of prison for the first time, is strapped in a car seat at Karen's side, craning her neck.

Kaydawn's skin is a blend of cream and cocoa below ringlets of brown hair with sparkling copper highlights. It is the first time she has felt the sunlight and her eyes gleam like black olives. Karen has already shaken off the mantle of prison. This morning she is fresh-faced and crisp, ramrod-straight. Kevin quickly zips up his fly and lurches toward the car, delivering Karen a quick kiss through the open window. Then he trots to the other side of the vehicle, stumbling as he tries to stretch inside to kiss his baby daughter. The reunion is brief.

Kevin jogs to his car and follows Sister Roberta's car down the Saw Mill River Parkway toward New York City. The baby is asleep in seconds.

At the front door of Sister Tisa's Home, a three-story facility for women on work release, stands an alabaster statue of the Madonna. Beside it is a small garden that doubles as a kitty litter box for Sister Tisa's two cats. A wooden sign reads MY MOTHER'S HOUSE.

One step inside the front door, two light-skinned Latinas stand, feet wide apart, with black-haired babies on their hips.

Sister Tisa and Sister Roberta supervise as Kevin helps haul boxes of Karen's belongings up to her tiny second-floor room. As the couple enters the room, they see, balanced on the bed, a pink stuffed toy with MY FIRST TEDDY BEAR embroidered on its chest in darker pink. Eleven-month-old Kaydawn is entranced, gripping the teddy bear, holding the stuffed animal tight to her chest, snuggling and staring into its fuzzy pink face. As Kevin sprints downstairs for a second load of packages, no one, none of the residents or staff, steals a glance at the stocky black man and the country-looking white girl. Many, many such couples have come through here.

Sister Tisa tells Karen of a white girl from Middletown, New York, who passed through the facility with a beautiful baby girl, just a year old then, fathered by a young black man. The girl, now back in prison for parole violation, asked that her daughter, named Dawn, be raised at "My Mother's House" until she completed her sentence. "Another Dawn!" Sister Tisa hollers so loud mothers across the common room can hear, and flings her head back howling, her face set ablaze by whatever chemical is produced by the body as a natural reward for a lifetime of good work.

"This is the poorest neighborhood in Queens," Sister Tisa explains. "When we first moved in at our facility, around the block people started to put their homes up for sale. Now we have the best-kept building on the block and people have taken the FOR SALE signs down."

Sister Tisa heads across the street to her administrative office. As she tells Karen about the facility, Sister Tisa waves to office workers and assistants who fairly whistle at their chores.

After filling out the required papers, Karen is allowed to go with Kevin to lunch at a diner on Twenty-first Street, a busy Queens thoroughfare. On the way to the eatery, Kevin studies the neighborhood and frowns. Karen could have chosen to do her work-release in the Elmira area. She would have been close to home and would have been able to live in her own house a few days a week. But she would have had to live apart from Kaydawn on the days she was required to stay at the facility and Karen could not bear the prospect of such separation. Besides, she wanted to spend time in New York City. Though she had visited New York several times with Kevin, she had never been on her own in the big city. Maybe she would have some stories herself to tell when she left here. She imagined that maybe she would even take a job here and launch an entirely new life without Kevin.

Though she misses Elmira and her family, Karen knows the job situation has long been hopeless in the Southern Tier of central New York State. A year into her stay at Bedford Hills, she began to daydream about life as a single mother in New York City. No one here would care about her criminal record. There would be so much to do, so many opportunities. And though the sight of Kevin's strong face sent her heart beating this morning as he stood there alone in the parking lot at Taconic, so loyal and steadfast, there is also something in her calculations that whispers that there might be another way to raise her baby daughter.

Besides, there is no telling what the Division of Parole is going to say the next day when she has to take the subway to Manhattan and check in at the Bayview Correctional Facility on Twentieth Street. She has heard rumors in prison, but she has little solid information about what the state's attitude might be toward her continued relationship with Kevin. On the negative side is the anger of Judge Hayden and what she knows about many white people. To the outside world it certainly appears as if she is a tool in Kevin's hands, obediently following his orders straight into a prison cell. On the plus side is the fact that the black-white liaison, enough to make some people sick just a few decades earlier, is now almost commonplace. These days, some folks even smile warmly in their direction.

The negative reactions will be even less frequent now, she has learned in prison, because of Kaydawn. One look at the beautiful child and any notion that there is something unnatural in a black and white union is quickly dispelled, even in people with the most closed minds.

As the couple sits in the booth beside each other in the diner, Kaydawn is moved from the child seat in the aisle to her father's lap. Kevin places the napkin in his mouth and flaps it, looking like the Cookie Monster. Kaydawn could not be more fascinated. "Daddy! Daddy!" she squeals. Kevin keeps up his antics, lifting the child, bouncing her and holding her aloft like a prize. Kaydawn's eyes dart about as Karen settles into a steak-and-eggs breakfast. There had been neither steak nor eggs at either Bedford or Taconic, and now she cuts the meat carefully into tiny pieces, savoring each mouthful.

Kaydawn sits still for a moment as the waitress arrives with a coffee cup filled with apple juice and Karen helps her daughter handle a straw. At first Kaydawn tries to suck the juice through the straw as she had done with her baby bottle, but the long straw requires more sucking power and the baby eases up too soon, the sweet liquid sliding back down into the cup. Karen turns the straw around so the drops of apple juice fall into the baby's mouth. Then Karen turns the dry end of the straw back and Kaydawn sucks again, the immediate memory of the sweet juice providing inspiration for a stronger, longer pull. But there is still not enough suction to draw the juice up the five-inch straw. Three more tries, mother and daughter working together, and Kaydawn succeeds in drawing the apple juice up into her mouth. The baby sits dizzy with pleasure.

On the short drive back to Sister Tisa's Home, Kevin confirms his earlier impression. He's seen young men on the streets outside Sister Tisa's, recognized the dip and swagger, the laser eyes. Now he notices the sign RAVENS-WOOD HOUSES. This isn't a bad neighborhood; it is a very bad neighborhood, almost as tough as Brownsville itself. Sister Tisa's place is just half a block away from a substantial city housing project. And half a dozen blocks down on Twenty-first Street is the forbidding Queensbridge Houses, one of the largest housing developments in the country.

"Jesus Christ," says Kevin. "If it isn't one thing to worry about, it's another."

It is just before Christmas 2006, at Sister Tisa's Home, the weather unsettlingly mild in northern Queens, as Karen readies herself for Kaydawn's first birthday party. Though her friends and relatives outside Elmira are poor, relying on welfare and checks from lawsuits stemming from traffic accidents and lead paint poisoning just like their black New York City counterparts, there are differences in the intensity of their anger, the relentlessness of their competition, and the nature of their confrontations.

Karen first felt the difference in jail, where she followed her own simple rules. Don't gossip and don't lie. Don't trust too much. Don't let anyone walk on you, but don't rise to the bait.

But now, as Kevin comes down to New York to run errands, to shop, and to sneak time for making love to Karen, he has a chance to see up close how she reacts to the bad actors, the bullies, and the dominators.

Regina, a stocky black former convict, barges into Karen's room as Kevin plays with Kaydawn, holding the baby above his face and drawing her to him. Time and time again, Kaydawn squeals and grins as his face comes swooping up toward her. It is a dizzying display of fatherly affection. "You love your daddy, don't you?" he says. "You love your daddy, don't you? You love your daddy."

"Give me a cigarette," Regina growls to Karen, who is slouched in the only chair in the room. Karen throws her head back and laughs at Regina's authoritarian tone and reaches for her bag and her pack of Newport Lights.

"Hold on." Kevin lays the giggling baby down on the narrow bed and holds her with one hand as he turns and measures Regina. "Don't give her no fuckin' cigarette."

Kevin knows virtually nothing about history or politics or how one group of people or one civilization dominates another, though his life has been defined by that record of violence and exploitation, yet he knows exactly how one human gains control of another. "And step the fuck on outta the room anyway. Don't walk in here without knockin'."

"Yo, Kev, why you do me like that? I thought we was tight," Regina says.

"No, we ain't. What makes you think we is tight? Unless you stupid, you know that we had one brief conversation. Now you walk in Karen's room tellin' her to give you a cigarette, not askin'."

Regina is half crouched, with a clown's grin on her face. "It's all good, brother. My bad. My bad." She takes a step back, eyes locked on Kevin, as Karen protests lightly at Kevin's hard-core reaction.

"Kevin, it's all right."

But Kevin is not about to second-guess himself on any issue, much less on a subject he is so sure about.

"No, it ain't all right." He never takes his eyes off Regina. "Now get the fuck outta here."

Regina backs out of the room, murmuring soft protests. She too understands the rules of the game. But she isn't finished. The next day at Sister Tisa's Home, when she sees Kevin's sister, Tonya, helping the nuns in the kitchen and assisting with the decoration of the Christmas tree, she moves in with another probe. Her daughter is unattended upstairs while Regina prowls the common rooms trolling for conversation and cigarettes. She is looking for ways to insinuate herself into a slightly more dominant position in whatever environment she finds. It is a tedious employment but the only one Regina has ever known.

"Doin' your Christmas good deeds for the less fortunate?" Regina tosses at Tonya, who is standing on a chair with tinsel in her hand.

"Say what?"

"Helpin' out the poor?"

"I *am* the poor, girlfriend."

"You got it like that, I guess," Regina presses.

"Got it like what?"

"Never mind."

"No, let's mind."

"I'm just—"

"I know." Tonya steps down off the chair and tosses the tinsel on the lowest branch of the Christmas tree. "Let me tell you somethin'. I dress nice but I will take off my heels and start scrappin' in a minute, 'cause I go any which way I need to."

The warmth of the nuns and Karen and the Christmas season have convinced Regina that the whole world has gone soft except for her.

"Oh, so you go both ways?"

Tonya doesn't answer.

Regina lays down her only face card. "I only step one way, hard."

"Yeah," Tonya answers, moving forward, her voice honey-smooth. "But you know who to step to. Don't you?"

"We Gotta Talk"

||||||||||||||||||||||||||||||||||||||||||||||||||||||||||||||||||||||||||||||||||||||||||||||||||||||||||||

As Kevin walks into the bandbox gym at the Ernie Davis Center in Elmira, he is greeted by small nods and half waves from the cluster of young men and boys assembled in the gym. Their eyes flicker toward him and they nod if the moment is just right. Otherwise, they try to keep their admiration to themselves.

Kevin has changed in the four years he has lived in Elmira. In an effort to simplify his life and find clarity, Kevin has begun by shaving his head. But baldness makes him appear older and even shorter than before. Eight pounds lighter, he is still in top physical condition, but the girth of his neck and arms is no longer startling. Still, to the boys in the gym, KK—as they call him—is everything that Sandy, the man who runs the program, is not. Kevin is cool and quiet. Sandy is a loudmouth.

In a hallway off the gym where the makeshift ring stands, a teenager positions himself close, as Kevin wraps his hands in black strips of cloth to secure them and keep his fists firm under his gloves.

"'S up?" Stanton is one of the more talented of the boy boxers in the gym, blessed with fast hands and happy feet. It is sweet to see Stanton learn and develop as a boxer, but right now his stuttering and shuffling is annoying Kevin.

"Sandy was talkin' shit about you when you went down to New York," Stanton says finally.

"What he say?"

Stanton shifts around so he can see where Sandy is, hear him too.

"Sandy said, 'I hope KK's not going down to New York to pick up drugs.'"

"Who he say that to?"

"All of us. He said KK better not be a drug dealer. You might be a mule, he said. Or somethin' like a mule."

Of course, Sandy's fears are well founded. Kevin has already pled guilty to the possession charge two years back when the cops took his Lexus. He has been named in the indictment to purchase half an ounce of cocaine with Indio Mathison, the case that Judge Hayden later dropped on a technicality. He is known to police as an associate of Trip. Karen Tanski, his girlfriend and the mother of his one-year-old child, is at this very moment in a work-release program for a drug conviction. It is Sandy's duty as a supervisor of young men to keep his charges away from people who drive Mercedes-Benzes while they hold minimum-wage jobs or no jobs at all.

Still, Sandy's short speech about Kevin and drugs to his young boxers was way off base.

"We gotta talk."

Sandy takes one look at the scowling Kevin Davis and scuttles toward the equipment room.

"I hope you didn't say no stupid shit. You got anything on your mind? You say it now or don't say it at all."

Kevin waits, but Sandy is silent.

"I heard that you said I was a mule. Do you even know what a mule is? A mule is somebody who goes down to New York as a messenger for somebody else. If I was in the drug business, do you think I would be a mule? Give me some credit."

"I didn't say a word."

"Hope so."

It was foolish beyond words for Sandy to question Kevin Davis publicly, in front of the very kids who idolize him, in part, at least, for the very things that Sandy was accusing him of doing. If Kevin was the man Sandy was afraid he was, it was stupid of him to bring that up. If he was not guilty, it was just as unwise.

When Black was murdered, Sandy brought up the rumor that Kevin had killed him and Kevin laughed it off. But at least Sandy had brought it to Kevin himself. Now, after the two emerge from the room, Sandy goes about his coaching business. The boys are running laps around the small gym. "Hands up. All the time keep your hands up." But he is still disturbed by the short conversation.

The workout, four-thirty to six p.m., goes quickly, like a flash, especially for the boys hoping to get a moment of attention from one of the grown men there to teach them boxing.

"I'm gonna spar with KK on Thursday," a bigger boy brags to his buddies. "He say so?"

After the gym empties, a handful of boys stand mute on the sidewalk as the men linger talking. The boys wear only sweatshirts but none flinches at the sharp wind.

"I just remembered," Sandy begins after gesturing for KK to step a few feet away from the boys. "I did say somethin' about you goin' down to New York. But I didn't say anything that was accusing you. I just mentioned it."

Kevin tilts his head and says nothing as Sandy continues. Kevin even smiles weakly. In a couple of days, as the fear lifts, Sandy will be telling people how he had put it straight to Kevin in the equipment room, had demanded an answer. "I had to ask him: 'Are you dealing drugs or not?'" Sandy will tell people how Kevin had sworn that he was not in the drug business. But for now Sandy stutters and Kevin chuckles bitterly. What amuses Kevin has nothing to do with Sandy squirming in front of him. It has to do with his own life and his own lies. The day before, a woman in the Hathorn Court projects, with whom he had a one-night stand several months before, told him she is pregnant with his child.

HOME

||||||||||||||||||||||||||||||||||||||||||||||||||||||||||||||||||||||||||||||||||||||||||||||||||||||||

The next morning at seven, Kevin is awake and cursing. Karen's post-release supervision appointments at Bayview are over. She can leave Sister Tisa's and come home. He hoped to be up at four to get an early start down to New York to pick up Karen. Now that plan is shot. He looks at the phone but doesn't call Travis to wake him up for school, as he has been doing since his mother moved from Brooklyn with her new husband and son to Elmira in February. Since the move, the teenager has been annoying Kevin. It is Travis's passivity and sneakiness that irks his older bother so.

The boy is still a mystery to Kevin. Raised in white neighborhoods by a mother who changed from a ghetto party girl to a Christian. As a disciplinarian, Margaret has been inconsistent. As a role model she has shown her elder son and daughter a ferocious temper and underdeveloped sense of proportionality. Slight transgressions warranted swift and heightened responses. Her advice to her first two children—"Don't take any shit from anybody. Don't let anybody know your business. Get what you can from whoever you can"—is nothing less than the short and simple preamble to the constitution of the ghetto.

But Margaret's younger son has seen little of that anger and the self-ishness. Handsome and peaceful from his earliest years, Travis, along with church, has helped to calm his mother's raging spirit. She calls Travis "baby" and ignores his lapses, lets him coast in school and fiddle with video games until he is nearly a professional-level game player and a failing student.

Kevin watches his younger brother with mixed feelings. He notes the care and attention Travis receives that he never got. The flicker of jealousy is swept away by relief. At least the boy isn't shooting people and being shot at. At least he isn't in prison. He isn't by any means a thug, and that is undoubtedly a good thing. Still, he was left back in his junior year in high school. Travis is spoiled and Kevin knows that will exact its own price.

Out on the icy Route 17, Kevin pushes the big black Mercedes down a highway streaked with salt and littered with sand and pebbles from the snow trucks. It is going to cost over $120 in gas to make the trip. He has made the round trip fifteen times in the last few months.

A fucking mule, running down to New York to pick up drugs, driving on the interstate crawling with police with drugs in the car. Of all the stupid shit.

Eight hours later, when they step in the door at Livingston Street, Karen and Kaydawn have similar reactions. A nimbus of reddish brown hair floating above her forehead, eighteen-month-old Kaydawn gazes to the ceiling and up the staircase. She stares, amazed at the expanse of the room. Then she bursts out crying. Karen, who had dreamed for so many nights of sleeping in her own bed under her own roof, is struck by how small the rooms appear, how drab the paint job and worn the furniture. She feels like crying too.

"It's 'cause you got so many bags," Kevin explains. "'Cause everything is so cluttered. That's why it looks small. That's the only reason."

Julia, who did not make the trip to New York, stands to the side of the kitchen table, staring at her mother. Behind her, Betsy holds Julia's state test results aloft that show Julia ranks in the ninety-ninth percentile in language arts and only slightly lower in math. The two stand rooted as Karen steps up the stairs and hollers from her bedroom.

"Where is the comforter?"

"It's in the attic, I guess," Kevin says.

Karen's bedroom now holds a spacious crib that Kevin has bought and assembled. He has done his share of hanging out when Karen was in jail. More and more people in Elmira have heard the rumor that a white girl on the east side is now carrying his baby. But he has certainly held things together at home anyway. Like a plant that flourishes in poor soil, Julia continued to do well in school while her mother was in prison. Karen had received as many visits and about as much financial support in terms of commissary contributions as she could have expected. The incarceration had gone reasonably well. But what now?

The next day Kevin is upstairs when the parole officer first visits the house. He squats and listens from the second-floor landing, hears the name "Dolan." He knows the name, one of the better parole officers to have, an easygoing guy. Dolan steps through the living room into the kitchen and opens the refrigerator, checking for alcohol. Kevin breathes softly, waiting. A visit from a parole officer is no small matter. A violation of parole is like a jail sentence without the trial and the conviction. Now the police are going to be visiting his house on a regular basis. In a little while Dolan is gone.

Besides the friendly parole officer, there is more good news. The list of persons Karen can't associate with does not include Kevin. In fact, the only name on her list is her codefendant Trip.

With Karen at home, Kevin Davis congratulates himself yet again on his wisdom. Instead of landing back onto the streets and getting shot down or catching a quarter—a twenty-five-year-to-life sentence—for drugs or murder, instead of ending his life, he has managed to engineer a new one by using insight. Rather than trying to go big, to make a mark with money and fame, he has chosen to go small. It is like the new technology. Science doesn't make things bigger, it now makes them smaller. That's where the genius lies. He has learned that ego is a destructive force to be countered. Following the thirty-eighth law from his favorite book, *The 48 Laws of Power*, from this point onward he will be egoless like water; he will flow and react. He will be impossible to hold or capture and he will move wherever he wants. To him, it is an elegant strategy and even though he has left his job at Rynone and has almost no money, every day he continues to compliment himself.

A week after Karen arrives home, Kevin is riding down Church Street when he spots a cluster of unmarked cars. He wheels around into the bus station, and watches as a handful of Feds meet Hollywood as he arrives on a bus from New York. Two of the lawmen are checking his bag, while another handcuffs him. Snitches, Kevin thinks. Rufus from Ramsey's had probably finally made good on his vow to get back at Hollywood for fucking his girl.

Kevin reminds himself again to stay away from the drug game. No matter how easy it looks, sooner or later something will go wrong; there are snitches everywhere in Elmira. Besides, the Feds have adding machines; a hundred small sales would equal a charge that could not be bargained down.

Though Kevin does not want to admit it, in his heart he knows that as the shoot-first young guns come onto the Elmira set, more and more he will drift into memory, becoming an OG, old gangster, out of the game. He can already feel the spotlight on him dim as he hears about the beefs and the shoot-outs in Elmira, about Bushwick, Just, T Money, and Philly Dog. He is still remembered in prisons. But that could bring problems.

There has been a lull in the bickering, in Karen's bitter interrogations over the rumor that while she was in Sister Tisa's Home Kevin fathered a baby boy with a Zebratown woman. Then, when Karen comes across a letter from the court, a subpoena for Kevin to appear at a paternity hearing, she falls silent. Suddenly she does not want to know the truth.

In some ways, Karen is much like Kevin himself. After prison, she has come to believe that this family life, as limited as it might be, is better than some other fates. She has a job already at a packaging plant, her children are happy and healthy, Julia is blooming, popular, a whiz in school and a star of a girls' basketball team. Karen has even finally begun to lose weight. Kevin is strong, healthy, and sober, an adequate father by some measures. What can possibly be gained by badgering him?

When Kevin picks up his chirping cell phone one night at two a.m., Karen rolls over and falls back to sleep.

"Kev?"

"Who this?"

"Half."

Kevin is silent. He knows a short dude named Half from Brownsville whom he ran into inside the Wende Correctional Facility.

"Kev? 'S me. Half. Got your number from Bang."

"Okay."

"How's it goin'? Heard you doin' all right. Heard you wheelin' a Mercedes. Things good up there in Elmira?"

"Good enough."

"Yeah, Kev, I been in the world two months. You know, adjustin' to shit. 'S hard."

"No doubt."

"Well."

"Yeah."

"Just evaluatin', checkin' shit out."

"Got to."

"Lookin' to make some moves. Move some pieces on the board. Know what I'm sayin', Kev?"

Kevin Davis does not know exactly what his recently released Brownsville acquaintance is saying and he doesn't want to know. Not at this point. Not on a goddamn cell phone.

"Need to . . . you know. Deal with somebody real. Fake-ass niggers is more dangerous than . . . you know."

Prison drums are, it appears, still beating out the story of Kevin Davis. The legend includes his mastery of Elmira, the white girl, the car, the impeccable moves. Based on the prison narrative, a formerly incarcerated Brownsville thug, looking for a way to make a few dollars in the drug trade, could do worse than reach out to Kevin Davis.

Half is still casting about for some hint that Killa Kev is interested in making some kind of a deal.

"So, what you think?"

"What I'm thinkin' about is goin' back to sleep right about now."

Still, Kevin Davis isn't going to work for minimum wage anymore. He tried that last winter at Rynone when he lost the feeling in his hands after gripping those vanity tops for eight hours a night. He could hardly open his car door in the morning. The job was breaking his body down, not building it up. Besides, the checks were so small he didn't even bother cashing them for months.

The idea now is to get a job that pays some reasonable money. Fifteen dollars an hour, take home $400 a week. Add that to the money from Karen's new job at the packaging plant and Betsy's disability, and the family can make it without the specter of prison. It doesn't cost much to live up here. Not much at all.

But almost all the manufacturing jobs that paid that kind of money left the area years before. The last one to leave was the Toshiba plant in 2004. There are plans to convert the abandoned A&P canning plant into a Wal-Mart. Plenty of places to buy things, but nowhere to make any money.

One day, Kevin spots a black guy walking out of a building that looks like a factory. He is carrying a lunch box. The sign outside the metal fence says HARDING INC. The man looks twice at the lumbering Mercedes as it pulls beside him.

"Brother," Kevin says.

"Yeah?"

"You work in there?"

"Yeah."

"They hirin' blacks?"

"Looks like it, don't it?"

"How long you been there?"

"A year and half. Fourteen seventy-five to start."

Kevin drives off smiling. So there is another game in town besides Kennedy Valve. He's applied to Kennedy through the Workforce Development Career Center so many times he can't count them. He's even flirted with a middle-aged blonde in his neighborhood who says she works there and promises to hook him up. Nothing has ever come from it, though.

Kevin's latest idea is to acquire a skill, become a computer repair person. To get such a job he has to take a 435-hour training and certification course from March through January in the nearby town of Horseheads. To qualify for the course he has had to test on a tenth-grade level in reading and a tenth- to eleventh-grade level in math on the TABE, Test of Adult Basic Education, administered by the state Board of Cooperative Educational Services. He has tested at a seventh-grade level in reading and barely a fifth-grade level in math. That isn't good. The better news is that Kevin is confident he can raise those scores with some brush-up work. And there is a class that will do just that, held at the Ernie Davis Family Center on Baldwin Street every weekday from eight-thirty in the morning to twelve noon.

It is nine a.m. at the Ernie Davis Family Center. A dozen men and women sit around five large tables as a teacher and a teacher's assistant circulate, helping students with a lesson on fractions. The task is to find the lowest common denominator. Kevin Davis's workbook is meticulously organized.

The night before, Julia checked on Kevin's workbook and dissolved in giggles. "That's what we did in third grade. Ha, ha. KK's doing third-grade work."

"'Bout to do some third-grade work 'side your head."

As the teacher moves across the clean, neatly arranged classroom, Kevin labors at his math lesson. The large window behind him frames a sign for the bar across the street, RAMSEY'S PLACE, the east side Elmira juke joint where Kevin lost some of his teeth.

The scene captures Kevin Davis's dual paths. On one, he is determined to make his new life work, applying for jobs all over town and enrolling in courses to prepare him for a position that will pay enough to live on. On the other hand, he continues to travel down roads like the one that brought him to Ramsey's, paths that can only lead to trouble and even disaster. At a table on the far side of the room sits a nineteen-year-old blonde who shoots her eyes toward Kevin once every few minutes. She has told him that she is back from New York City where she went with her boyfriend and briefly worked as a prostitute. Her skin is as flawless and creamy as a child's, but her face is a miracle of vacancy, a match of the blank notebook paper in her hand.

There are twenty-eight people enrolled in the class, seven of them mandated by the courts. The girl looks up again and bats her eyes toward Kevin.

"It's okay to look in the back of the book to check your answers," the gray-haired teacher is telling the class as she bounces a piece of yellow chalk in her palm.

"I thought that was cheating," Kevin replies.

"No, you check every once in a while. There's a happy medium." The teacher pronounces happy as *heeappy*, in the accent of the region.

The former prostitute is already gone from her seat, cradling a cell phone, as she moves toward the door. She lobs one more smile in Kevin's direction. The sight of a winsome blonde nineteen-year-old straining to catch the eye of a thirty-six-year-old black unemployed ex-con with a smile featuring just one tooth in the corner of his mouth is a stunning testament of some kind. It might be the open-mindedness of Elmira, the fresh breeze of diversity. Or it could be the magnet of the hip-hop culture where white kids admire and imitate almost anything black. Or it could be a testament to Kevin Davis's masterful presentation. He has picked just the right town and fashioned his image to meet the constituency. Though he surely has some money, he has purposely chosen not to replace his front teeth, for the shock value the gaping hole of his mouth provides. While virtually every young man in the area seeks to look like a thug, no hard stare or gallery of gold teeth says "street fighter" like a mouth without teeth.

Kevin is satisfied that he has some things figured out just right. It wasn't hard to determine that the life of a thug had to end for him. The walls of the Elmira prison still rise above the city of Elmira, a reminder in case he has any inclination to forget how wasteful incarceration is. And all he has to do is follow the latest beef between Philly Dog and Bushwick, both Elmira transplants like him, the spate of senseless gunplay between their camps, to see the utter foolishness of the gangster life.

But for all his platitudes about family life, Kevin is still not sure exactly what form his self-reinvention should take. He is troubled by Karen's homecoming, the clutter and the noise.

Kevin slouches on the La-Z-Boy; Betsy is perched on a chair in the doorway to the kitchen. "There was a guy riding a bicycle by the trailer park and I called the police because he had this piece of his hair that was sticking out away from his head and his pinky was sticking out from the handlebars the same way, both in my direction. So I called the police and they took *me* to the hospital." Betsy breaks into laughter.

"Paranoid schizophrenic," Kevin says regretfully.

"That's the excuse they used."

Julia, without her mother for a year and a half, is begging for attention. She has even taken to hovering around Kaydawn to bask in the warmth cast toward the baby by Karen and Kevin. Right now Julia is lobbying her mother to bake peanut butter cookies. Kaydawn is dragging toys around the living room. Karen is at the kitchen table writing down all the things that the apartment needs, a high chair to begin with.

Kevin Davis is reduced to lying back in the soft chair by the front door with his hand to his forehead. He has been out of jail for six years now but there remains something in his nature that craves the order of one room, one bed, and no clutter. Now he must adapt to the needs of a stepdaughter and his own baby, his woman and her mother.

"Oh, my God," Kevin blurts, "this is fucking chaos."

He catches his reflection in the television as he rises from the chair. His shoulders, his back, have definitely lost size. Jesus Christ, it looks as if he's shrinking.

That night, he lies next to Karen in the bedroom as Kaydawn sleeps quietly in her crib by the wall. He has little desire to have sex with Karen, though the two have been intimate only a few times since she has been home. Kevin feigns fatigue, kisses Karen on the neck, hugs her firmly, and pretends to nod off to the early sleep of a father, husband, and working man. The difference is that Kevin is not a working man. Despite the personal statements and the job applications, despite the school attendance, the computer classes, and the job possibilities, despite the domestic scenes, Kevin Davis is still unemployed. The source of his trickle of cash is his last magic trick.

That night Kevin manages to slip away with Joy for a twenty-minute ride into Pennsylvania and a night out at Rock a Bot, a cavernous bar with a DJ. Young drunk white men leap and spin on the floor to the blasting music, sink to their knees and pump fists at the floor to the beat, then bounce up and reel toward each other. There are several near-fistfights. A tall girl stumbles to the floor and lies on her back laughing as her friends gather around and take pictures with plastic cameras. There are only four or five black men in the bar out of a hundred or so patrons, and no black women. Two of the blacks are dressed with bandannas under hats and baggy clothing. They aren't much bigger than Kevin. One approaches with exaggerated good cheer and loops his arm over Kevin's shoulder. The man was in the courtroom for what was perhaps Kevin's finest moment in Elmira, when judge Ramich delivered his speech about Kevin having the most extensive and outrageous criminal record of anyone who had ever stood before him. The youth yells into Kevin's ear for half an hour, telling stories of his own criminal exploits.

Though Kevin and the two bantamweights are much smaller than most of the bristling young white men, there is no hint of animosity, no testing. The black men here have somehow garnered a level of respect that has earned them the right to move comfortably, to talk to and even seduce women, relax completely in this rural Pennsylvania town. A snapshot of the scene would make it appear that great progress had been made in the last few decades. The civil rights movement and the accomplishments of African-Americans in all walks of life have made such easy interplay possible. But there is another reason why the black men are accepted so easily here, not challenged when they date, marry, and impregnate the daughters of police officers and corrections officers. The reason is sad and simple. They are feared.

"Thank God"

|||||||||||||||||||||||||||||||||||||||||||||||||||||||||||||||||||||||||||||||||||||||||||||||||||||||||||||

It is August 24, 2007, ten a.m. and cruelly hot in Elmira. Kevin Davis is feeling good. The air-conditioning in the Mercedes is pouring blessed jets of cold air on his forearms and neck. What's even better, he has just passed his Basic Ed tests in reading and math, gotten high enough grades to qualify for a state computer training program. He has heard from reliable sources you can make $25 an hour fixing computers. What this can mean is a steady check and health insurance for Kaydawn. With his test results on a slip of paper on the leather seat beside him, like a schoolboy Kevin is headed home to deliver the good news to Karen.

On Lake Street, he slows to check his gas gauge, which shows less than a quarter of a tank. Too much of his small stash of money has been going in that damn gas tank. Out of the corner of his eye he catches an unusual sight, a large unmarked yellow school bus parked in the courthouse lot. The chief of the Elmira police, Scott Drake, is standing in the street beside Investigators Weed and Griffin. Unmarked cars, which look like state police vehicles, are double-parked all up and down the street.

Karen is home early from work and Kevin trots up the front steps, his test results held high in his right hand.

"Thank God," Karen says, dropping her cell phone from her ear and staring at Kevin.

Kevin shakes the paper in the air. "You heard I passed the tests?"

"No. Congratulations, Kevin, but no."

"Ten-point-nine on the reading and ten-point-one on the math. Needed ten in both and got it."

"You don't know?"

"What?"

"Everybody in Elmira is in jail. This morning the police picked up Bushwick, Frankie, Just, T Money, Sosa, Havoc, everybody you know." Karen's voice cracks and she turns away, toward the kitchen. "I was so worried when you didn't pick up your phone."

Kevin sits down at the kitchen table and places the paper with his test scores a few inches from a puddle of spilled grape juice. The yellow bus, the police chief, Weed and Griffin, it makes sense now.

The six o'clock news and the next day's *Star-Gazette* tell more of the story, and over the next several months court documents detail the rest. Police discovered that Elmira drug dealers, almost all transplanted New Yorkers from Brooklyn, had been heading down to New York City to buy cocaine. In caravans of three cars, local girls as couriers in the middle vehicle, flanked by the streetwise dealers as guides and bodyguards, the crews would pick up as much as three hundred grams as many as three times a week, bring it to "the El," cook it, and sell the crack from apartments in Hathorn Court, three houses on Lake Street, and other locations on the west side. It made business sense. The dealers were peddling the product for more than twice what they could get for it in New York City and they didn't have to risk their lives to do it. Despite Black's murder and the occasional shooting, Elmira was still a sanctuary compared to Brooklyn.

Just as Elmira was a commercial hub in the early twentieth century, so it is now a natural distribution point for drugs. Surveillance tapes show cars arriving from Pennsylvania, from upstate, from points east and west. Tapes even catch a uniformed police officer and an Elmira College professor purchasing crack. Judge Ramich has issued the seven warrants, sometimes after watching real-time video of crack deals.

Seven teams of state and local cops have snatched up twenty-one people in dawn raids, all without incident. Thirteen of the cases have gone federal. The police have particular interest in Bushwick, who has been heard on a wiretap threatening Investigator Weed's life. "I was just blowin' off steam,"

Bushwick assures the police when he is questioned. "No one here got the heart enough to blast a cop up here." The school bus was brought in to transport the thirteen with federal cases to the Monroe County Jail in Rochester. The gravity of their situation, facing decades in prison—"football numbers," Weed calls them—has apparently not set in. The transportees were in good spirits, good enough to joke about "Snitchwick" and to cheer loudly when five-foot-three Frankie, the main man in the operation, was loaded on the bus last. Only T Money remained quiet. He'd read in the phone transcripts that others in the bus had planned to rob and kill him. Police were calling the sting "Operation Crack Hammer."

AMBOY

||||||||||||||||||||||||||||||||||||||||||||||||||||||||||||||||||||||||||||||||||||||||||||||||||||||||||||||||||

Just a week later, Kevin Davis, himself a free man, is in front of the computer in his Livingston Street apartment staring at the police blotter from the *New York Daily News*. The floor of the living room is littered with dozens of toys and children's books, but he is in the best of moods. Just a few minutes earlier he finished his workout. In his bare attic refuge, fashioned with a chin-up bar and equipped with dumbbells, a spot he has taken to calling "Attica," he punished his body into a state of near-bliss. Moaning and grunting, he had banged out dozens of pull-ups and dips, curls and presses, all with his baby daughter watching and waving at him from a tiny bench near the stairway.

The workout completed, he knows the euphoria will linger a couple of hours, at least until Karen comes home from her part-time job at Howell Packaging on East Fifth Street.

Kevin reads the *New York Daily News* crime stories every day to taste the drama and to keep track of old friends. The computer displays an article about a raft of recent murders in New York City: "Bullets Fly, Five Killed in Bronx Mayhem."

Just like when I was wilding out, Kevin thinks. Just like that piece in 1993—"It's So Easy to Die for So Little in N.Y."—that told of the Amboy Street murder.

As he reads on, Kevin shifts in his chair, rolls his shoulders. Beneath the headline, the words of a brief article dance from the page: "Cops said Kevin

Davis, 21, was killed about 2:30 a.m. at 181st Street and Third Ave. in Fordham. Responding to a 911 call, police found Davis shot several times. He was pronounced dead at St. Barnabas Hospital. Davis was a known gang member, according to police sources."

"Goddamn!"

Kevin reads the words again, leaning close to the screen: "Kevin Davis, 21, was killed . . . police found Davis shot several times."

That could have been me at twenty-one, Kevin marvels.

A lot of times that could have been me. Dead up. I'd be a spirit right now, outside lookin' in.

As Kevin sits back in his chair, an unfamiliar weight presses down in the darkened living room. What the hell is it? He flips through explanations for the unusual and unpleasant sensation: his fading notoriety, the endless Elmira winter ahead, the gloomy room?

The name, Kevin Davis, he wonders, me shot dead at twenty-one? That can't be it.

Then in the stillness, the truth falls upon him like rain.

It's Dupree. Dupree Bennett, the dude shot dead on Amboy Street. On the screen and there in the room. Him! Not me. Just a kid. Numerous shots. Same reckless shit. Same fuckin' tragedy.

When the Parole Board hit me they used to say I wasn't remorseful enough about Amboy and they was right. I wasn't. The dude brought the shit upon himself, beatin' on a kid, but there was more to it, 'cause he definitely did not deserve to die. And even though I did not pull the trigger, I was obviously involved in that stupid reckless shit.

Now I'm sittin' in Elmira and that article is spookin' me. After all these years. People die every day and nobody says shit. But to die premature, that's why it's in the papers. That's why it is a tragedy. That's what spooks me now. I'm readin' Kevin Davis shot at twenty-one but I'm feelin' Dupree.

I remember the day he died so clear. Believe it or not, that very same afternoon I saved a life. It was sunny. Breeze rollin' out of Canarsie. Perfect fuckin' day. I was on Rockaway and Blake just kickin' it in front of the store and I see my man Devine. Dudes used to call him Father Devine an' he was a straight-up gunslinger. He specialized in shootin' motherfuckers. That day he walks into the store behind where I'm standin' an' I hear a click, an' I look an' Devine's about to shoot some dude he has a beef with. 'Bout to kill him right there. I'm like, "Yo, Devine, don't do that." I'm talkin' to him like an authority figure, even though he was my same age. He say, "Wha'?"

I told him, "Don't do that right here and right now. In broad daylight." He just backed up and walked out. That's how I remember the day, the weather so good, that's what it was, some broad daylight.

Later on, about four-thirty, five o'clock, I'm out in front of my house, me an' about nine guys an' I'm laughin'. We just havin' a rankin' contest an' I'm laughin'. Francesca comes up an' her face is red and right away I'm like, "Oh, my God, what's this?" She tells me this Dupree dude was fuckin' with his nephew, her nephew too. Her brother was married to Dupree's sister an' they had this kid, Alfie. Dupree had kicked him down the stairs an' shit an' she intervened an' Dupree smacked her. She said somethin' about gettin' me an' he said, "Go ahead an' get your man." An' now she's up here whisperin' bold intentions. I'm thinking, Oh, my God. I saw it clear. I saw the whole thing comin'.

So I take three of my mans and I go over to talk with the little nigger. We ridin' on mountain bikes and Francesca is walkin' behind. So on the way over I tell her, "You ain't goin' with us 'cause you gonna make matters worser. So you go upstairs."

When we ride up, there is about thirty motherfuckers in front of 10 Amboy. Some go upstairs when we pull up. Others run inside. Some just walked away. About eight dudes just stood there. You could feel the friction. Ten Amboy and Brownsville don't get along nohow. So I asked 'em, "Where's Dupree at?" They say he went inside, so I just tell them to tell him to be easy. Stop hittin' on kids an' girls or I'ma come back an' tear his ass up. That was it. When I got back over to Hopkinson, I tell Francesca, "You don't have to be around there. Just don't go back around there."

So I went to the gym and after that I had my trainer drop me off at my mom's house at about nine-thirty an' when I got there they was tellin' me, "Your girlfriend just left." Oh, my God. I jump back on my bike and ride over to 10 Amboy. When I come around the corner there is like a hundred people standin' there. It was like a fuckin' block party. People in Brownsville love to watch fights. But this was crazy. I see everybody lookin' around by the back, by the parking lot, back there in front of 1400 East New York Avenue. I pull up to like forty feet away an' I drop the bike an' I'm tryin' to take control. Sayin' loud, "What the fuck is goin' on?" But there was no takin' control of this shit. This had a mind of its own. Dupree is on top of Francesca beatin' on her and just then as I run up, right then, shots start goin' off. Pop! Pop! Pop! I pull him off an' I see Francesca is passed out on the ground an' she has blood on her. The bullets went through him an' hit her.

But check this shit. The shots don't stop. They keep comin'. Another crazy thing is, when shootin' starts people always start runnin', duckin', and gettin' away. Not this time. Listen to this crazy shit. Nobody ran. Fuckin' people just stood there watchin'! They was amazed. Like this is a real-life shootin'. A killin' for real.

Dupree is steady gettin' hit, bam, bam, bam, in his leg and his shoulder and his back and he's like crawlin' up the steps in front of 1400. Then it all stops, silence, and I can hear him say, "Get my moms. Get my moms."

The police pull up an' I'm like, "They was two dudes in black hoodies on bikes an' they went that way," an' while the cop's writin' in his notebook I'm walkin' backwards to the corner. I start to run for real, haul ass, I can hear the people yellin', "That's him. He's the one."

When I did get arrested in November, I was in an apartment with my cousin Reggie, who just got out of jail. They lookin' for me for the homicide. No doubt. So up in the office the DTs come up an' show me a statement by Reggie sayin' that he was with me an' that I did the crime. Stupid. That right there was their big mistake. They was stupid an' they was crooked at the same time an' they wound up fuckin' up they case. 'Cause, for one thing, Reggie was in jail on October sixth, so he couldn't have been at 10 Amboy with me.

I did plead guilty to the gun for my own reasons and for the deal they offered. There were other things besides the false statement that played into the situation in me gettin' the deal that I got, the deal that gave me my life back. There was the type of individual who the victim was. The judge considered that. Not only was he beatin' on a kid, but he was not a good dude. He had a violent nature, so to speak, a criminal past, and the judge knew it.

So it all worked out for me. When my lawyer said they was offerin' me three and a half to seven to run concurrently with the three to six I had for the other gun, I couldn't believe it.

But it wasn't all good. Couldn't be. Once you involved in a murder, your life *is never the same. It's not like the movies where you got mad guilt that drives you crazy an' you toss an' turn in your bed, but it is always there. It never leaves you. You walk with shadows around you. I been thinkin' of movin' down to South Carolina. That's where my half-brother, Joe, moved after he broke up with his wife. That's where my father is buried outside a church. It's so quiet there. It's just nice. But that's where Dupree's people be. That's where he's from. People don't hesitate to shoot down there. Why stir that shit up? And besides the security issue, there is a feelin' of regret.*

I been livin' all these years since I was twenty-one an' Dupree Bennett been gone. He just missed all that livin'. That shit's not fair. 'Cause of some reckless shit. That's a weight.

Kevin Davis drags himself out of his chair, stares out the window for a moment at the sunlight on the peeling blue paint of the front porch. He's been out of prison for almost seven years. There is no .357 Magnum stashed under the mattress anymore. Dispatches from Brownsville and the Elmira drug dealers have slowed to a trickle. Main is out of prison and back in Brownsville. Trip and Bushwick, T Money and Philly Dog and Bang, are all in jail. Julia is at basketball practice. Kaydawn is seated on the rug at his feet, silent, studying his face. Karen won't be home from work for another couple of hours. Kevin rolls his shoulders, cocks his head right and left, then walks slowly upstairs and drags open the door of his closet. He stands still for a full minute before he decides not to put on his prison greens.

Strong-arm

|||||||||||||||||||||||||||||||||||||||||||||||||||||||||||||||||||||||||||||||||||||||||||||||||||||||||||||||||

It is early April 2008. The Mercedes is gone, damaged beyond a reasonable price of repair by an elderly motorist careening through an intersection on the east side. "Jesus Christ," Kevin mutters after the accident, "all there is in Elmira is gray-haired motherfuckers who can't see."

There should be $7,000 or $8,000 coming from the insurance, but that will take a while. Still, it feels good to Kevin to get out from under the expenses for the big car.

Karen is laid off from her factory job just before the company would have been required to hire her full-time with benefits. The day after she is let go she heads over to the Elmira Business Institute, where she remembers they promoted a "lifetime placement program." Before the interview at EBI, Karen makes a decision to reveal her felony conviction. "They're gonna find out sooner or later an' I don't want that hangin' over my head," she tells Betsy.

The man at Elmira Business Institute studies Karen carefully as she explains. "It was my fault 'cause I was with the wrong people. It was my responsibility." She looks the interviewer in the eye and sums it up. "That's just the way it was. But I have learned a lot since then."

The man runs his index finger down Karen's résumé, glances up, and smiles weakly. Two days later, a call comes to Livingston Street for Karen to appear at an interview for a job with a company that runs six dry cleaning franchises in the Elmira area.

There are two interviewers on hand this time but no mention of Karen's incarceration, no reference to her résumé even. The interviewers don't have any papers at all with them. They must be desperate, Karen concludes.

On the drive home, she comes up with a different explanation. The man at EBI must have gone out on a limb, she decides, made a decision not to inform the employers of the felony. That's a blessing. Karen sighs as she rolls over the Madison Avenue Bridge. Then she chuckles ruefully. She took a chance on someone too, overlooked a criminal background, and look how that turned out.

Two days later, Karen gets the job with the dry cleaning company. Her task is to keep track of the accounts payable. The company pays only $9 an hour, but it is not factory work and Karen is delighted to be doing what she was trained to do at the Elmira Business Institute. There is a bounce to her step as she heads down the front steps and off to work in Betsy's car.

Kevin is the one who is unhappy. His job is simple babysitting. After an eight-hour day of changing diapers and picking up toys after Kaydawn, when Karen arrives home from work Kevin doesn't even wait to hear dinner plans. He flies out the door.

Today he pauses. There is an image of Barack Obama on the fifty-inch television screen. The man has been running in the Democratic primaries for what seems like forever and now is locked in a struggle with Hillary Clinton. Clinton and Obama are vying now for the ballots of rural Pennsylvanians—the people who live in and around Gillett, Karen's hometown. Older, poorer, and less educated than the rest of the country, these are the same kind of folks who reside in the rest of the northern tip of the "Appalachian swath," as newspapers are calling it, which includes Elmira.

In some ways, Barack Obama is a mystery to Kevin Davis. In others he is not. The charm, the easy manner Obama has around white people, Kevin understands, because he possesses those same qualities. *Once white people see you aren't going to cause trouble, start wilding out, they are so relieved they are easier to deal with than black people.*

But Kevin, who has had almost no contact with the black middle class or black intelligentsia, cannot figure out what a man like Obama, with all that juice and all that money, is doing married to a black woman. More importantly, he can't fathom how Obama manages to turn the other cheek. Hillary and Bill Clinton have been saying all kinds of nasty things about him and Obama has been cool about it.

Now, on the television, the newsmen are talking about how Barack Obama has finally made a big mistake. On the eve of this crucial primary, in an interview on the West Coast, Obama observed that small-town Pennsylvania voters, frustrated with the Rust Belt economy and a changing society, "cling to guns or religion or antipathy toward people who aren't like them."

The pundits are speculating that Obama's comments will confirm charges that he is an elitist, and will activate latent racism, pushing Rust Belt voters further into the Hillary Clinton camp. They are guessing that Obama's negative characterization will spark a double-digit victory for Clinton in Pennsylvania and provide her with enough momentum to stage a successful comeback.

"Obama ain't gonna win," Karen says over her shoulder.

"Oh, yeah," Kevin responds. "Nobody want a woman for president. Oh, my God, what'd that be like?"

"You think people in Pennsylvania are gonna vote for a black man? Kevin, be serious. You said yourself they're nothin' but a bunch of racists. That's not true, but they're not voting a black man for president, either."

Kevin, in the doorway putting on his jacket, lifts his voice so Betsy in the kitchen can hear.

"What you don't know, Karen, 'cause you white, an' what Obama an' I know, is not that change is comin', but that change is *already* here. Just look out the goddamn window. This diversity shit is a done deal. It's a wrap."

Annoyed by Kevin's assurance, Karen is pulled further into the argument. "All you do is run around with sluts, you don't pay no attention to the election. Last time I heard, you was laughin' at Obama's ears, but now you're an expert. A political expert. Ha."

"An' one more thing." Kevin, delighted by the weight of his own observations, raises his arm and jabs his finger in the air like an orator. "White people is nasty but they not stupid. It's common sense to vote for Obama. Plain-ass common sense. Send the case to the jury. Election's a wrap."

When Obama loses the Pennsylvania primary by a narrower margin than expected, Kevin Davis calls it a "beautiful day."

Then there are bad days.

It is the morning of August 20, 2008, hot and still on Livingston Street. A Mister Softee truck parked at the end of the block bleats a musical invitation. Inside, Kevin is in the corner by the door to the kitchen, seated at the computer, when Kaydawn trots over to Julia and calls her stupid.

Not quite old enough to ignore the childish insult, Julia responds quickly, "*You're* stupid."

Kevin chuckles in satisfaction. Good to see somebody get under Julia's skin for a change. That will teach her to be so fresh.

"You're a dummy too, KK."

With no job to go to, no bills to pay, neither the inclination nor the sense of ownership to fix the porch or mow the lawn, with really nothing at all to do but monitor the online newspaper exploits of his criminal friends, Kevin is drawn into the name-calling game. He summons three-year-old Kaydawn to his side and whispers something in her ear. The child giggles and moves back across the room toward Julia, who squeaks in protest, "Ma. He's telling Kay to call me a name."

Karen answers from the couch, "Don't you dare call Jewel a bad name."

Kaydawn stops in the center of the living room. She turns to her father with a shrug and obeys her mother.

"Say it," Kevin orders.

"Don't you dare," Karen counters.

Kaydawn studies her mother's face.

"*Say it,*" Kevin shouts, a sudden rage catapulting him from his chair and across the room toward the couch.

With just a week of summer left, a handful of days before the start of school, neighborhood children are outside in numbers, a cluster of girls on the sidewalk in front of the house on Livingston Street and three pairs of boys by the curb, leaning on bicycles. Their heads whip toward Karen as she stumbles onto the porch, down the steps, and onto the lawn, with Kevin in pursuit. This is much more than the stinging slap Kevin had delivered a few years back when Karen had called him stupid.

Kevin would protest that it was a family tussle and that he followed Karen outside to stop her from calling the police. But it was far too late for Kevin's excuses. Karen had taken a lot from Kevin, had even gotten used to the threats and the occasional flicking smacks. This was abuse, plain and simple, and public humiliation. The police report would record Karen's claims that he followed her onto the street and struck her with a broom handle.

After the initial burst, Kevin is in control. He is calm because he is sure there is nothing really wrong with what he has done. For Kevin Davis, there is a measure of control that he will not concede, a line he will not let be crossed. He believes he has swallowed too much verbal disrespect from Karen and Julia already.

It is not merely the disrespectful act that must be quickly erased by action, it is the direction, the downward trajectory of one's status, that must be halted. This is the thinking that brings Kevin onto the street, manhandling Karen in front of his own daughter and the neighborhood children.

The police arrive in a blink, just as they did when Kevin punched out the Puerto Rican teenager on Brand Street.

Kevin is arrested, but ultimately no criminal charges are filed. Karen's parole officer, however, is informed and Kevin is immediately banned from the home, exiled to his mother's house a mile away.

The domestic violence had been a sad spectacle but not hard to predict. In recent months, Kevin had continued to mouth family values as he rankled under the restrictions that Karen's return from prison had imposed. He continued to call himself a husband and a father, but when he wasn't babysitting he spent almost all his time hanging out in the town projects.

Not only is the Mercedes gone, but with the police behind him at all hours of the day and night no matter what kind of car he drives, Kevin has picked up a handful of tickets and thirteen points against him for rolling through stop signs and red lights, following too close. According to state law his license has been suspended and he is on foot now.

There is a serious downside to residing in a small city setting like this, Kevin decides, as he hikes across town. When you are really down on your luck in a big city it is not so obvious; you can always get up enough money to jump on a subway. Hell, even the mayor of New York City rides the subway. But here in Elmira, not having a car makes you stick out like a sore thumb.

Ideas duel in Kevin's head as he walks. He will almost surely be able to slide back into Karen's life; his charm and her need will bring down her guard.

But what of the future, the fundamental issues, money and the clutter of relationships, the family over which he has no authority?

Kevin decides that what he needs is time away from all this confusion, a period to reestablish his purity of thought, the crystal vision that he had when he came out of prison, the clarity that helped him avoid the traps so many ex-cons had fallen into. Perhaps he will head down South.

No, that's where Dupree Bennett's relatives reside. No telling how they might react to his presence down there. Besides, there is really no way to make a dime in South Carolina. He'll save the southern strategy for a time when he is on the run from the police, if that ever happens. Maybe he should go back to jail where he can think. Go back to the disciplined life he led inside the walls. Kevin shakes the idea out of his head and snorts. That is a line of thought he scoffed at when he was in prison, when he looked down on the old cons that came back inside just because they couldn't learn to live in the world. What he really needs to do, he decides for the moment, is locate a monastery and do a Buddhist monk thing.

In his prison pants with a white sweatshirt and a frayed black watch cap pulled low, Kevin strides down Davis Street, past "the Hill," the prison, with that damn statue and thinks, "How you gonna put a statue with two naked men in front of a prison?"

Half a mile west down Davis Street, Kevin stops beside a small park nearly hidden beneath a thick stand of four-story spruce trees. There are two pull-up bars with red and blue plastic hand grips, parallel dip bars, and a push-up bench arranged on a bed of needles fallen from the cluster of trees. With abbreviated snapping motions, Kevin performs quick sets of twenty pull-ups. He needs to feel the blood rushing to his muscles, the thrust of his biceps and deltoids against the fabric of his sweatshirt. He needs to feel strong.

So does another man, another former Elmira prison inmate relocated here from Brooklyn. Six-foot-three, with shoulders like wings, the man arrives in a cherry-red late-model sedan, adjusts workout gloves, and hugs Kevin before he, too, begins his regimen of pull-ups. There is little speech between the two.

The tall man finishes quickly, hugs Kevin, and moves to his car. Their interaction is not nearly as jovial as other times Kevin has run into former inmates. There is something in Kevin's demeanor that is dull and slow. A shroud of disappointment hangs over him.

There is going to be no way to set the Karen relationship right, Kevin thinks, as he yanks his chin to the bar, seven, eight, nine, ten, eleven times. He had simply used the wrong strategy with the wrong woman. Thirteen, fourteen. Back arched, grunting up at a patch of sky between the branches, Kevin hangs, resting for another pull. There is no way he is going to change himself. Fifteen, sixteen. Never compromise yourself, Kevin remembers reading in prison in *The 48 Laws of Power*, because then you have nothing. Eighteen, nineteen, twenty. Kevin drops lightly to the bed of pine needles. Maybe he *would* be better off back in jail. A blast of noise, a single shrieking whistle. The ringing comes from somewhere, can't be the nearby church. Kevin turns as fifty twelve-year-olds, sprung from the Catholic middle school behind the church for recreation period, charge at him. The boys in white shirts and gray pants, girls in plaid skirts, arrive and stand stock-still, waiting.

Kevin looks into the gallery of eyes as a hatchet-faced white woman in a long gray coat separates the children and steps up.

"How are you, sir?"

"Good, good," Kevin says, brandishing his smile, then shutting it down quickly when he remembers his toothlessness.

"Have a great time, kids," he says, heading to the sidewalk and the route back to his mother's new house a few blocks away.

Fuck jail, Kevin decides as he walks. All life takes is some discipline.

Karen is busy, charging back and forth to her job and taking care of the kids. Just as Kevin predicted, even though her parole officer has officially banned Kevin from the house, he is able to insinuate himself back into her life by volunteering to babysit when Karen is at work. Soon, even the parole officer agrees that Kevin can return to care for Kaydawn if he vacates the house the moment Karen gets home. Before long, Kevin is sneaking back and spending the night whenever he feels like it.

One time, slipping into the house in the afternoon, he accidentally locks himself in the basement and has to wait there until Karen comes home to set him free. Sometimes, at night, Kevin drives Travis's car illegally, parks it a block away from Livingston Street, and weaves through the backyards to the rear door. The idea of beating the system is a constant pleasure to him. No good job available in this broke town, no ladder to success, he'll take what the world offers. He'll move like a laser through the night, savor the freedom and the pleasures of the womanizer, the outsider. The motion sensors that activate the floodlights in the rear of the house are turned off. Kevin had done that when he lived there full-time. What in hell did he want a motion sensor for?

One early fall evening, he stands in the cool shadows and watches Karen through the rear window as she washes the dinner dishes.

Working and looking after a teenager and a toddler, Karen doesn't have the strength to keep Kevin away. Instead, she leaves her future with Kevin to influences beyond herself. Kevin is just such a force. His determination is what drew her to him in the first place. When he appears in her bed at night Kevin is comforting and gentle. So what? she thinks. Plenty of people have marital problems. Besides, Karen is thinking long-term. If Kevin proves he cannot change, why not make a new start back in Pennsylvania, in Reading, maybe? Karen knows too much about Elmira to look forward to the prospect of raising her baby daughter here. The area has too many pitfalls; look at the ones she fell into.

The new job has been adding to her confidence. She has a small welfare payment, $400 a month in food stamps, and the money from the dry cleaning people. It is November and Karen has been at the job almost six months now. She conjures Judy Clark's words: "You're so smart and you are not afraid to work." Let Kevin do whatever the hell he wants, let him run with other women and come and go and tell lies about it. Let him be himself. She will figure out her own future and the future of her children and leave Kevin behind if she has to.

On the evening of the national election, as screams fly from a house across the street and distant car horns sound from both sides of the Chemung River, Kevin hoists a confused Kaydawn and points to the images on the television set. "That's the first black president. That is history in the making, baby." Then he turns the child's face toward his and kisses her. "Don't forget, Kay. Obama is *magnificent*."

Karen has finally realized that no amount of nagging, even the probability of complete separation, can stop Kevin. The power of her love, the value of their family, and her threats of vacating Elmira, disappearing for good, have done nothing to stop his nocturnal wanderings, his failure to get another job after leaving Rynone. But the flip side of this is that he cannot control her either. When her parole is over in January she will make a decision and a move. If Kevin Davis wants to do something about it, either by doing something good, like getting a job and staying home on a regular basis, or something bad, well, so be it.

One of the many differences between Kevin and Karen is the value of the counsel they have received. Kevin had been a star in prison, while Karen had shuffled through, suffering. But Kevin's focus had been on strategy, ascendancy, domination. His mentors had been the supermales. The talk had been about deception, lightning strikes, about disguising motives and pressing witnesses. Karen had no such conversations. She watched a group of caregivers, some of them convicted murderers, look out for each other and care for babies in the nursery. Her conversations had been about the true value of things and people, not about power. Kevin had listened to Walter "King Tut" Johnson. Karen had heard Judy Clark.

Kevin senses Karen's change of focus, notes that she is not as quick to react to his comments and his criticisms. It is as if she has decided something. Whatever it is, it cannot be good. As a deterrent, he begins mixing threats with his banter. "Don't even think about taking my daughter out of town if you know what's good for you."

One day in the last week of November, when the landlord visits, Karen complains about the crumbling cement on the front steps, the rotting wood on the support to the porch roof. "There's going to be an accident here," she tells the landlord, "and then it's really going to cost you money." As the man moves across the lawn toward his car, Kaydawn hugs Karen's legs and yells from the porch, "This is my mommy. You don't have a mommy, 'cause this is my mommy."

Kevin has finished his training but simply can't find any position that employs computer troubleshooters. He says he has friend in Nyack, a town close to New York City, who promised he would hire him at $20 an hour, but that would require him to move away from Karen and Kaydawn. He has also heard that Jim Rieker, the human resources manager at Rynone, would hire him back "in a minute," even promote him to the position of sprayer, a level-three skill category at the plant, at $12 an hour. But Kevin almost gags when he recalls the smell in the Rynone factory, that chemical odor and the marble dust. If you don't get your hand caught in one of the curing machines, he reckons, the dust and the chemicals will get you. It is like being caught in a crossfire. The factory has a good safety record, Kevin contends, because people don't get sick and die until years later. Despite all his talk about Kennedy Valve, Kevin would rather get shot or locked up than get sick. Just about all he has is his health and he isn't about to sacrifice it even for $12 an hour.

Then there is Joy. Kevin isn't kidding himself; he knows that Karen has heard the rumors that Joy has borne him a son, a burly ocher-skinned boy, strong and jolly, a little boxer. Kevin congratulates himself. He can sure make some beautiful kids with these Elmira women. But in his heart Kevin knows that the baby by Joy will be too much for Karen. There is an air of mourning over the family proceedings now. It was bad enough when Kevin was an inconsistent contributor to the household expenses, not a husband but a boyfriend who didn't come home every night. Now he is an illegal presence in the house. If Karen's parole officer finds out he is spending the night, she can be found in violation, sent back to Bedford Hills for six months to finish her sentence.

Karen has heard Kevin's denials about Joy many times, listened to him scoff at her fears. Kevin was "real" on the streets and in prison. He could be trusted to stand up on principle or hold money for someone. He is known to tell the truth and stand by it. So what? Karen thinks. He sure can't tell the truth to the woman he loves. The obvious facts are that he has run a common scam right in her face for years and Kaydawn is going to grow up with siblings all over town.

Julia is in her room on the phone when she hears a thud and a scream. Karen is crouched in the corner of the living room by the front doorway, holding her head and moaning, and Betsy is moving toward her. There is a cell phone in pieces on the floor. Kevin had borrowed Karen's phone and spotted some sexually suggestive text-message gossip. When the police arrive, Karen blurts that Kevin beat her with the phone, held her down and pounded her with it. Kevin insists over and over again that he merely threw the phone, and that Karen hit her head as she ducked. He explains that Karen had concocted the story because she wants him out of the house, because she doesn't want her parole violated.

Kevin is arrested, held on $10,000 bail on a charge of felony assault and unlawful imprisonment. The case comes before Judge Ramich, who is saddened by the spectacle. He had harbored hopes for Kevin Davis as a role model for youth and a leader. There is no hospital report, no serious injuries. But on the witness stand at the grand jury, Betsy supports Karen's version of events. "A perjurer and a schizophrenic," Kevin growls, and is led back to the county jail, trying to figure out ways to raise bail.

Karen knows about Amboy Street and is frightened of Kevin, afraid that loss of his woman, his home, and his daughter, along with his incarceration, will launch him into a homicidal rage.

From jail, Kevin scoffs at such fears. He hadn't really injured Karen, hadn't even retaliated when he was hit in the face with a hammer by Shiloh in Ramsey's Place. Sure, he had used that killer image to gain advantage over the years, but he hadn't really hurt anyone since he got out of prison, and that was eight years ago. The man who had stormed onto Amboy Street fifteen years before no longer exists.

Yes, she will press charges, testify, and remain available to the court, Karen promises prosecutors. When she speaks to the prosecutors, to the judge, to the grand jury, it sounds as if the love has been scoured from her heart. It is not about Kevin anymore. He has made a fool out of her and a victim, made a joke out of their whispered devotions. All that is left in place of their desiccated vows is bald accusation.

From jail, Kevin's anger heats to lava as he regales Joy, his mother, anyone who will listen. "They lied. Karen lied, Betsy lied. Put their hands on the Bible and lied, used the fuckin' police to get back at me 'cause she didn't want to go back to prison. Police probably threatened her with parole violation. She's nothing but a snitch," he says, "and I have no more feelings for her."

Any idea that prison was the right place for him to regroup and think is quickly dispelled by the reality of incarceration. Kevin had often used bursts of anger as a tool to achieve specific ends. This time his fury at the perceived betrayal leaps over itself, mounting, expanding, forming its own logic. "A fuckin' snitch! Karen could never be my woman again after this," he proclaims. The obvious truth is that the future of the relationship is out of his hands.

Meanwhile, Kevin steams and waits. Another court appearance. "Ask them where the hospital records are," Kevin orders his lawyer. "The only witness is a schizophrenic who can't even get her story straight. Tell that to Ramich."

The lawyer nods, and when he is told, Judge Ramich purses his lips. Kevin may win the case but he has lost his family. And he is still in jail.

As he waits behind bars, Kevin's thoughts are about Karen and betrayal. There is scant attention paid to who he is and how he became that way.

After a few weeks, Joy's grandmother, a spry eighty-three-year-old former Broadway singer and dancer, fronts the $2,000 bond, throws her house up for collateral, and springs Kevin from the county jail.

"Relax, forget Karen, and let the situation cool. You'll get visitation and everything will be fine. Just be easy." Kevin hears the words from his mother and the same message from Joy and her grandmother, from everyone around him. But he is a man who follows his own counsel. He will not take this lying down. Sure, he had managed to control himself after the attack by Shiloh, but as bloody as that assault was, it was not betrayal. The moment he is released, Kevin wriggles free from his supporters, his advisors, and charges straight to Livingston Street. Karen has an order of protection against him but that means little to Kevin. What are the stakes in violating an order of protection? A few months in jail? Karen is threatening his entire life, trying to take away his child and send him to prison for years, and she is doing it in collusion with the police.

As Kevin moves into the center of the darkened backyard behind Livingston Street, the motion sensor springs to life: lights flash, flooding the yard. Kevin measures the distance to the edge of the light, considers bounding into the dark bushes. Instead, he stands statue-still in the brightness, waiting, watching. After a moment, Karen appears behind the blinds of the kitchen window. Carefully, she separates the slats and peers out to see what has set the lights on. In her heart she knows Kevin is out there. Karen even calls his mother a few minutes later to ask if Kevin is out of jail. But for the moment, because of the glare she looks directly at the spot where Kevin stands and sees nothing.

Through the spaces between the slats, Kevin can see Karen's shape as she moves away. It would be nothing to kick through that back door and show Karen what her police and her flimsy orders of protection are worth against his anger, his resolve, his manhood. Then Karen appears once more, pauses in the window, her head tilted down. She is surely speaking to Kaydawn, explaining something, answering some kind of question.

Kevin releases a sigh that ends in a shudder. Suddenly he cannot watch the woman in the window any longer, cannot move toward the house or leave. Finally, slowly, he turns away.

In Joy's apartment on Grove Street, Kevin keeps his personal items tied in a plastic bundle, the same way he did when he was in jail. He is changing diapers again, spending long days trailing another toddler, talking with his lawyer about visitation rights, about ways to beat the assault and unlawful imprisonment charges. Once visitation is approved, he argues bitterly with his mother, who, concerned about Kevin's anger toward Karen, is reluctant to pick up Kaydawn and bring her to Kevin.

There is another problem. Three years before, when Joy's father, a youthful fiftysomething waste-management contractor, discovered that his daughter was seeing a black man, he had approached Main from behind and leveled a gun at his head. Kevin had not witnessed the incident but had heard about it, chuckled over it many times.

He doesn't laugh when he hears pounding on the front door of Joy's apartment. Kevin is off the couch and down the stairs in a bound. In the basement, he crosses over to the stairs leading to Joy's brother's apartment, bolts up two flights, and mounts a step to the roof. He moves carefully across a ledge to the balcony over Joy's apartment and looks down on the six-foot-three white man, Joy's father, as Joy herself opens the door.

Joy has no idea where Kevin has gone; for all she knows, he is still in the apartment. Mindful of her father's reaction to Main, she steps outside and closes the door tight behind her.

From above, Kevin listens. This is going to be interesting, he thinks. I'm finally going to hear what these rednecks think about their daughters being with blacks, finally gonna hear the other side of the story in Zebratown.

"You pregnant again?" Joy's father begins evenly.

"Yes, I am."

"So you are?"

"Yeah, just found out."

"I couldn't tell. I heard, so I wanted to check it out."

"Well?"

"You are my daughter."

Joy stays quiet and prepares for the explosion.

"Just wanted to tell you that it's gonna be hard," Joy's father says gently.

Joy wets her lips and runs her hand through her hair but doesn't speak.

"It's gonna be real hard. I wanted to tell you that, and that I love you. You know that."

"Thanks, Daddy."

"Who's the father?"

Joy stiffens. "Kevin."

"Hmm."

Joy's father steps forward and wraps his arms around his daughter, holds her close as he moves his hand to the back of her head, leans slightly and kisses her on the cheek.

"Whatever you need, baby. You call."

A few feet above, Kevin is amazed. No curses or threats, no damnation, no mention, even, of blackness.

That doesn't mean Joy's father doesn't believe in intimidation. A few days later Kevin sits quietly in the man's narrow living room, as Joy's stepmother taps away at a computer in the corner. The older man goes on about thirty-aught shotgun shells and rifles with scopes, about hunting squirrels and deer and even bear, about blasting animals from close range and far afield. Kevin nods politely, even responds with appropriate enthusiasm at the reenactments of manly exploits in the woods. Kevin even manages to remain quiet when the man curses assorted "jailbirds" he has known and promises that he will never hesitate to pull the trigger if called upon. "I'll shoot anything, anytime," he says, tousling the hair of his younger daughter, a prim straight-A student at Elmira Free Academy.

This is a game Kevin knows. He plays the perfect gentleman, is on particularly good terms with Joy's grandmother. The boxer and the former hoofer chat about workout regimens and the grandmother pulls out her scrapbook, tells stories of sharing the stage with Sammy Davis Jr. She produces a card Sammy gave her when she retired from the New York stage.

As accustomed as he is to such shifts in fortune, the exchange of households is disorienting to Kevin. Joy's family members are jolly, supportive, and, despite the Main incident, seem devoid of racism. They are delighted with Kevin's pleasant demeanor, though there are questions about why he isn't working. "I had to give up my career to raise a family," the grandmother explains. "Sometimes you just have to give things up and accept responsibility."

Kevin nods understandingly but offers few explanations for his joblessness. The less said, he believes, the better. He sure as hell isn't going to take a job working in waste management with Joy's father, if that's what they have in mind.

The baby boy is delightful, waddling from one end of the crowded living room to the other, absorbing the love, smiling, tumbling over, and listening to the adults call his name.

There are smiles all around. Then comes a yelp from the corner, where Joy's stepmother is seated at the computer. In her Internet explorations, she has come across an article that describes Kevin Davis's criminal background. The truth shimmers on the blue screen and the woman cannot stifle an exclamation.

"Kevin, is this you?"

Kevin grimaces.

"Did you kill somebody? For God's sake, did you shoot somebody?"

"That's what they say."

Joy stands to Kevin's defense. "That man was beatin' on an eight-year-old child. He done it more than once *and* he was beatin' Kevin's girlfriend. He was a child abuser."

"Well, then," the stepmother decides quickly, "he deserved what he got. Didn't he, Kev?"

"Nobody deserves to die," Kevin answers slowly. "Was somethin' that shouldn't a happened." Kevin's sad wisdom wins over everyone in the room. Only the hunter remains concerned, only Joy's father has another question about Amboy Street.

Tellingly, he addresses the inquiry to his wife. "Does it say if he had time to think before he shot?" Slowly, he turns to Kevin and asks him directly. "Was there time to think before the shot?"

Kevin's anger rustles in his chest and he breathes slowly to quell it. He wants to ask the man if he had time to think before he pointed a pistol at Main's head, before he threatened to blow the boy's head off, presumably just because of the color of his skin. Instead Kevin shakes his head.

"No time at all," he avows.

There is no more talk of gunplay around the dinner table, there are no tales of shotgun blasts or killing animals large or small.

Back in their apartment on Grove Street Joy's shrill voice pierces Kevin's skull; he cannot stay in Joy's apartment, just as he could not tolerate the noise and the confusion with Karen. Kevin is driven out into the night.

It is past midnight, late April 2009, and Kevin is trudging over the Main Street Bridge. Out of circulation and out of touch, he has no money in his pocket, not one dollar, and zero minutes on his cell phone. In the last two years he has lost twenty pounds on his five-foot-four frame, so that now he no longer looks like the strapping athlete, the roughneck. He feels as if he is slowly fading away. Curiously, the sensation of drifting into nothingness is vaguely pleasant. Since his days as a boy in Brownsville, Kevin has savored the effect of exit, the wonder of disappearance.

Broad-backed gulls are skimming low over the swollen Chemung, tilting their white wings, searching the shadows. Some lunatic has blasted twelve people in Binghamton at a community center, backed his truck to the back door so nobody could escape and killed a bunch of people not far from Randolph's barbershop. A black Jeep Cherokee slides now to a stop in front of Kevin and the window rolls down. It's Bloody Rah, a local drug dealer, originally from somewhere in south Queens. Despite his New York pedigree, the man is young and inexperienced. He is making a success here in Elmira because Weed and Griffin don't know who he is yet, because the locals don't really understand the difference between real and fake. But Kevin knows and so does Rah.

Kevin approaches, eyes the glittering rims, leans in the window, smells the new leather, and studies the dog-faced Rah.

"Yo, Kev, you wanna ride?"

"Nah, need the exercise."

"No doubt, Kev. You da man."

"Yeah," Kevin answers, his voice sour.

Uneasy with the silence, Rah chants, "Yeah, yeah."

Kevin sniffs at the inanities. "Bloody Rah, if I'm the man, break me off two hundred." He stares across at Rah, who reaches in his pocket and peels off the tribute. Kevin stretches his arm across and snatches the wad of bills with a downward motion before it is fully offered. "Yeah, yeah," Kevin repeats, as he backs off.

POSTSCRIPT

||||||||||||||||||||||||||||||||||||||||||||||||||||||||||||||||||||||||||||||||||||||||||||||||||||

Over the following months, Karen Tanski kept at her job with the dry cleaning company, caring for Julia and Kaydawn, while Kevin Davis wrestled with the realization that his estrangement from the family was probably permanent. News that the prosecutor was offering a reduction of charges for the cell phone attack to a misdemeanor seemed to soften the loss and cool his anger. But one night, when he spotted Karen coming out of a club in the company of a male companion, Kevin snapped, attempting to drag her out of her car.

A few days later police arrested Kevin for felony assault. Prosecutors, fearful he was capable of further violence against Karen, set high bail.

As had been his habit, Kevin put the following month in prison to the best use, counseling his demons, resolving himself to the loss of control over Karen and the lengthy absence of Kaydawn from his life. He ate heartily, did thousands of push-ups, and sought to regain his composure. When released, in much better physical and mental condition, he returned to work at Rynone. The only days he took off from work were for court appearances.

As months passed, it seemed apparent that, if only for his own survival, Kevin had finally resigned himself to the loss of Karen and Kaydawn. But as Kevin Davis ratcheted down his anger and his expectations, accepted the commonplace life of a factory worker and father to Joy's son and coming baby, prosecutors were turning up the heat.

On October 26, 2009, Kevin Davis appeared in Judge James Hayden's court. Davis was not in the spectator section jawing at Hayden as he had been when Karen Tanski was sentenced. He was in the dock, and the best the state was offering was one and three-quarters to four years. Following a two-day trial, Kevin Davis was convicted of criminal contempt in the second degree for violating an order of protection and assault in the third degree. He was acquitted of assault in the first degree.

Six weeks later, when Kevin Davis was sentenced to one year in county jail, handcuffed, and led away, Karen Tanski was not in the courtroom.

ACKNOWLEDGMENTS

IIIIIIIIIIIIIIIIIIIIIIIIIIIIIIIIIIIIIIIIIIIIIIIIIIIIIIIIIIIIIIIIIIIIIIIIIIIIIIIIIIIIIIIIIIIIIIIIIIIIIIIIIIIIIII

I would like to thank my father, Jack Donaldson, for his poetry and counsel. Among those who encouraged me to follow my instincts and write this book and who helped guide me through the difficult times, Bill Reynolds stands first. For many years a generous friend, he was enthusiastic about this project from the beginning and a source of valuable professional advice throughout.

John Capouya and Bonnie August read early drafts and helped focus the manuscript, as did Amy Green, a colleague at John Jay College of Criminal Justice. Also at John Jay College, Lorraine Moller, Martin Wallenstein and Dara Byrne provided support, while Ric Curtis gave me access to his research on upstate drug markets. John Mogulescu and Sandye Wilson have always given sage advice. Sam Freedman at the Columbia School of Journalism directed me to read John Edgar Wideman's *Brothers and Keepers*, which helped me make some important choices for the book. Suzanne Farwell offered early and continuing support and Jamille Weaver kept me up to date on hip-hop. David Young made valuable comments on the final draft.

Thanks to Alana Phillips for her technical help, Dan Khan for research assistance, and Michelle Hershkowitz for fact-checking.

Delores Jones Brown of the Center for Race Crime and Justice at John Jay College offered encouragement and a public forum to discuss the intersection of journalism and ethnography. Judge Bill Mogulescu helped me understand the nuances of the law. Mike Botinni was, as always, a good friend and valuable truth-teller. Thanks to my sister, Christa, for her courage and confidence in me, and to my brother Pete for his example.

Rick Mayo and Greg Jackson of the Brownsville Recreation Center enriched my understanding of the world Kevin Davis came from.

Thanks to my students over the years, who lifted my spirits with their unflagging interest in *Zebratown*.

I would also like to express my appreciation to Chief Scott Drake of the Elmira Police for his time; Gary Lemite for helping me with police procedure; Mike Marino, Mark Asnin, and John Minovich for their interest. Thanks to Linda Foglia of the New York State Department of Corrections for facilitating my access to the Elmira Correctional Facility. Jim Pfiffer of the *Star-Gazette* and Naphtali Coleman and Lois Wilson of Elmira College provided valuable assistance. The Chemung Historical Society was an important resource, as were Jim Barstow's *New York Times* articles about McWane Industries. *Chemung County 1890–1975* by Thomas E. Byrne, *Elmira: Death Camp of the North* by Michael Horigan, and *Underground Railroad Tales* by Emerson Klees helped me trace the history of the region. Thanks also to the New York State Department of Corrections for supplying Kevin Davis's prison records.

Thanks to Judy Clark for her trademark wisdom and generosity, Margaret Davis for her time and trust, and, of course, Kevin Davis and the woman I named Karen Tanski in this book for opening their lives to me.

Over the long duration of this project, my partner, Ingrid Griffith, graciously allowed me to give the book priority over all but the most basic obligations and helped me rediscover my voice when I faltered.

My agent, David Larabell, of the David Black Agency, managed to hit all the right notes and helped guide the project to publication with a steady hand. Finally, Colin Harrison of Scribner was simply a gift. Years ago, when he was an editor at *Harper's*, he read a piece I had submitted and referred to the material as "culturally privileged information." Colin's deep respect for the similarly sensitive material of this book, his ear for language, and his dogged attention to detail enabled me to write the best book I could.

About the Author

Greg Donaldson was born in New York City to a novel-writing letter carrier and a University of Pennsylvania–educated medical secretary. He is now an associate professor at John Jay College of Criminal Justice. Greg Donaldson is the author of *The Ville: Cops and Kids in Urban America*. He lives in New York City.